POSTCARD HISTORY SERIES

Around Hughesville

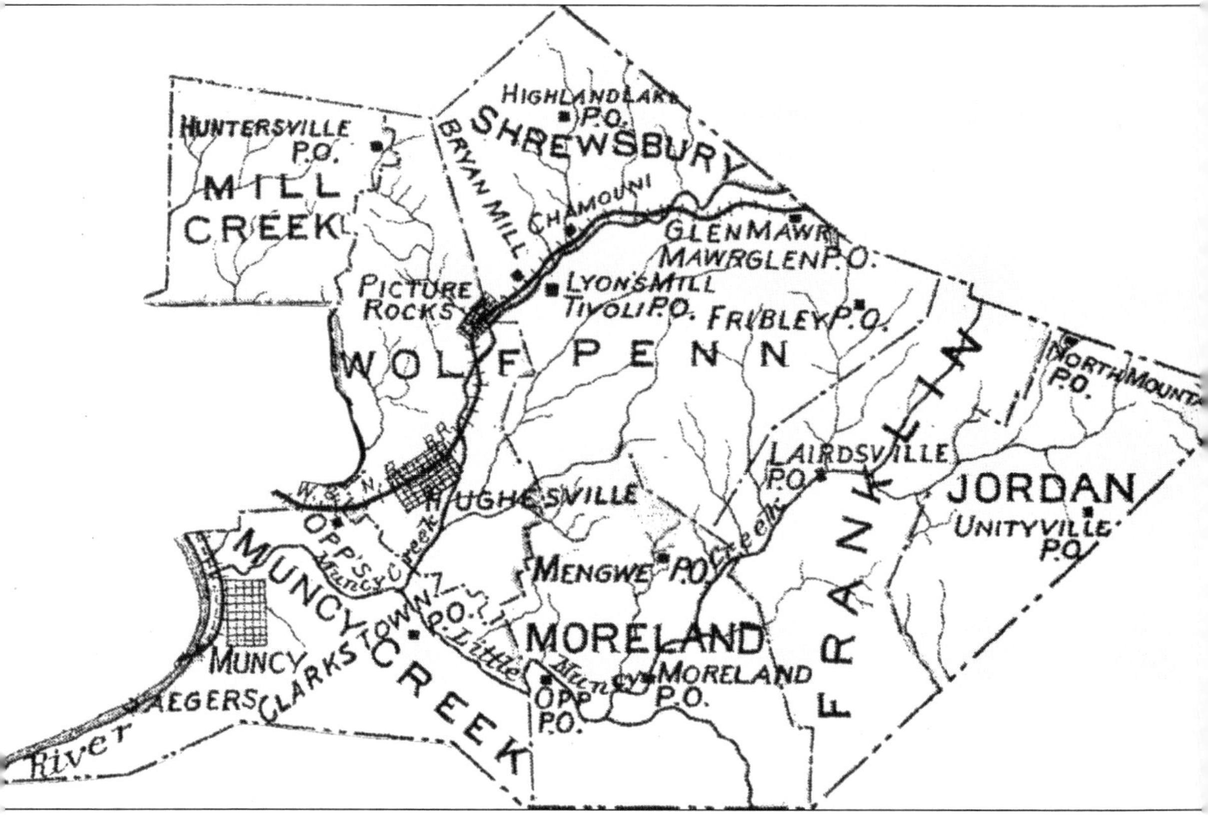

Much of what is known about Hughesville and its early settlers is found in John Franklin Meginness's *History of Lycoming County, Pennsylvania.* Meginness was a journalist and newspaper editor who understood the importance of recording and preserving local history. The map detail (above) is from the 1990 reprint of this local historian's 1,200-plus page reference book, which was originally published in 1892.

On the front cover: Next stop, the 1908 Hughesville Fair. Riding in the back of this ox-drawn wagon are (from left to right) John Flick and Brady Chestnut, and in front is an unidentified friend with Herb and George Arthur Chestnut. (Courtesy of Harold Hill.)

On the back cover: The Williamsport and North Branch Railroad depot in Hughesville was the major point for deliveries and travel between the 1880s and the 1930s. (Courtesy of the East Lycoming Historical Society.)

POSTCARD HISTORY SERIES

Around Hughesville

Joan Wheal Blank

ARCADIA PUBLISHING

ISBN 978-0-7385-5457-0

Published by Arcadia Publishing
Charleston, South Carolina

Printed in the United States of America

Library of Congress Catalog Card Number: 2007923972

For all general information contact Arcadia Publishing at:
Telephone 843-853-2070
Fax 843-853-0044
E-mail sales@arcadiapublishing.com
For customer service and orders:
Toll-Free 1-888-313-2665

Visit us on the Internet at www.arcadiapublishing.com

Dedicated to the memory of my ancestors—those who left behind the clues so that their stories can be told; but most especially to the memory of my father, Clarence Woodruff Joseph Wheal (1910–1999).

Contents

Acknowledgments

I want to first acknowledge and give credit to the pioneering men and women who settled the area that we now know as Hughesville. They left behind little mementos, faded photographs, and albums filled with picture postcards. More than 100 years later, these items have been saved by family members who now share them with us. To the following, thank you for your help in so many ways: Joe Barlett, Tom Crawley, Randi Doebler, Jerry Fought, Chris Foresman, Polly Hess, Harold "Mick" Hill, Stewart and Sandra Hill, Nancy Hodge, Aaron Houseknecht, Charlie Hughes, Don Hughes, Janet Kohler, Elizabeth "Sis" Rogers Knyrim, H. Scott Knyrim, Nancy Messinger, Bill Odell, Mary Fox Odell, Kenneth D. Poust, Dave Richards, Sue Shaner, Lois Sites, Cynthia Hughes Smith, Edward Smits, Beth Spotts, Dora VanDine, Lynn VanDine, Dale Wagner, and Diann and Max Walters.

I would also like to thank Phyllis Stevens and Carol Shetler at the East Lycoming Historical Society; the staff at the Sullivan County Historical Society and Museum and the Lycoming County Genealogical Society; my editor, Erin Vosgien; and Samantha Bouffard, Heather Carreiro, Jan Cronan, Gia Manalio, and Jennifer Renk, for their impeccable editorial advice. To my mother, Clara Wheal, and my aunt and uncle Ruth and Lewis Jones, who researched the Houseknecht family, and to my aunt and uncle Helen and Joe Wheal, who carry on the English traditions, thank you for leaving us such a wonderful legacy; and to my brother, Alan, thank you for your help during the past year.

Finally, and most importantly, I appreciate my family's understanding when this project occupied my time and thoughts. A special thanks to my children, Dave, Stacey, Jacquie and her husband, Dan, for their long-distance encouragement, Rachael, for allowing me to clutter your space with boxes of faded photographs, and Caleb, for your technical expertise and lending me your laptop, and to my wonderful husband, Steve, for encouraging me to accept this project—the first of many stories I want to write.

One last thing; label your photographs and write down those family anecdotes, even if your kids are not interested in them now. In 50 years, they will be—and they will thank you.

INTRODUCTION

For over 200 years, many tales of the first Hughesville-area settlers have been told. There is the story of David Aspen who built his solitary cabin northeast of Fort Muncy, near the southern boundary of present-day Hughesville. The year was 1775 when surprise Native American attacks made it a dangerous time to settle in the forests along Muncy Creek. Unfortunately, after he had been alerted of impending raids and sought shelter at Fort Muncy, Aspen returned to his cabin only to be killed and scalped by Native Americans in 1778.

Townships formed slowly as areas east and north of Fort Muncy were populated and communities took root. Muncy Creek Township was created in 1797, Shrewsbury Township in 1804, and Moreland Township in 1813. It was around this time that a young pioneer named Jeptha Hughes, a native of Danville, ventured north up the Muncy Creek with his brothers Isaac, Jesse, and Jonathon, and settled in what was then still considered Muncy Township. In 1816, 25-year-old Hughes purchased land from John Harrold and laid out a community he called Hughesburg. That year, he also married Elizabeth (Betsy) Hill from Lock Haven and fathered three children with her before 1820, the year he sold the property and relocated his family north to Tioga County, where he and Betsy settled and raised a total of eight children.

To the east of Hughesburg, the settlements of Fribley, Strawbridge, and North Mountain grew, and Penn Township was created in 1828. In the meantime, Hughesburg had established a school in 1818, and a number of religious societies began meeting regularly. A gristmill and a blacksmith shop were founded, as well as a chair-making shop in 1829. As a result of this growth, Wolf Township was formed in 1834 with the settlements of Hughesburg and Picture Rocks, its neighbor to the north, within its boundaries.

In 1852, Hughesville was incorporated as a borough, the same year that the Pennsylvania Railroad completed its line between Philadelphia and Pittsburgh. In the extreme eastern part of the county, the township of Jordan was formed in 1854, with Unityville as its only village, and the boundaries of Franklin Township were set in 1882. The Franklin Tannery, located near Lairdsville, was considered one of the largest in the state at the time. In 1879, the last township formed in eastern Lycoming County was Mill Creek, which included the village of Huntersville.

As one of only a few larger boroughs in the area, Hughesville became the center of commerce and activity for the communities lying to its north, east, and south. During the 1850s, the lumbering boom spread from Williamsport, where sawmills and wood manufacturing facilities capitalized on the vast stands of timber found throughout the county. Events such as major flooding along the Susquehanna River and the Civil War caused local and national anguish during the early 1860s, but when the railroad came to Hughesville in 1872, things started looking up. Industrial growth began to occur, especially in the communities located along the tracks of the Williamsport and North Branch Railroad, which ran from Pennsdale, through Hughesville, and north through Picture Rocks, Tivoli, Glen Mawr, and the Sullivan County towns of Muncy Valley and Eagles Mere. The railroad shipped logs and hemlock bark out of the lumber camps to the north and provided a convenient mode of transport for vacationing residents on their way to the summer resorts built around Shrewsbury Township's Highland Lake and Muncy Valley's Lake Mokoma.

Some marvelous innovations were being introduced; in 1876, Alexander Graham Bell patented the telephone, and in 1879, F. W. Woolworth opened his "Five and Ten Cent Store" in Utica, New York, the same year that Thomas Edison applied for a patent for the light bulb. The Wright brothers took to the air, and in 1908, Henry Ford started producing the Model T car. About that time, Kodak introduced an inexpensive and easy-to-operate pocket camera. This compact device provided the means for anyone to capture an image on film, transfer it onto a pre-printed postcard, and then mail it for a penny to family and friends in the next town or across the country.

In 1901, the United States government permitted an envelope-free postcard to be mailed if the name and address of the recipient was written on what is now commonly referred to as the undivided back. The front side was reserved for an image or design, with the sender's message squeezed into its margins. Around 1907, a divided-back postcard was introduced, which allowed the message to be written on the back, next to the address. Saving penny postcards in albums became a national phenomenon. By 1910, postcards were the primary means of communication for those living more than a horse or carriage ride away, especially since telephones were not commonly used in rural homes for at least another 10–15 years. Picture postcards also served as a way to document generations of families, buildings and homes, city streets and country roads, fires, floods, parades, and other important and less important, but interesting, events and groups of people.

In *Around Hughesville*, you will find a variety of images, the majority taken from real-photo postcards. First you will see and read about the town itself—the spacious streets, the homes that were built with care and pride, and some of the people who lived, worked, and played there. Then you will find the hotels, the banks, the factories, and the family-run stores that made Hughesville hum between the 1880s and the 1930s. Next is a look at the surrounding communities—the residents of Mill Creek, Shrewsbury, Penn, Jordan, Franklin, Moreland, Muncy Creek, and Wolf townships. These people were the farmers, the loggers, the millers, and the tanners; the resourceful men and women who not only survived the harshness of rural living but thrived in this environment. They were also the founders of the Muncy Valley Farmers' Club, the group that brought the annual tradition of the fair to Hughesville in the 1870s.

Next is a chapter devoted to the churches and the schools in and near Hughesville, beginning with the mother church, Immanuel Lutheran Church, organized in 1791. The log school that was erected on Hughesville's Main Street in 1818 was the beginning of formal education for the town's children. Groups of students and some of the school buildings are pictured, in addition to a map that locates the 57 schools in the area. Finally, scenes of Muncy Creek and its tributaries, modes of transportation (including the horse and horseless variety), and the roads on which they traveled are illustrated. The final pages of *Around Hughesville* document the Williamsport and North Branch Railroad in the early 20th century, and its eventual demise in the mid-1930s.

The images on the following pages are from collections that have been passed down to family members or rescued from an occasional auction or yard sale. These are the postcards that help tell the stories of our ancestors and have become the foundation of the stories that will be told to future generations.

One

The Town and Its People

In August 1907, a postcard was delivered to a home in Illinois that read, "Dear Hannah, We are moved into our new house here in Hughesville and we are all fine. There are hills all around us and the people seem to be very kind. Two of our neighbors came by last night with food. A peck of apples was found on the porch this morning. I hope you can come visit us soon. Your cousin, Sadie"

That may have happened a hundred years ago but new home owners in Hughesville today, should not be surprised if a neighbor stops in with a casserole or if a basket of fruit is left by the front door. The people of Hughesville have always cared for one another, beginning with the infamous Rachel Silverthorn, the courageous woman who volunteered to warn David Aspen and others living along Muncy Creek of probable Native American attacks in 1778.

Selfless concern and care for family and neighbors have always been a part of Hughesville's early history. Census takers in the 1800s and early 1900s recorded many households that included brothers- and sisters-in-law, cousins, and elderly parents. If a neighbor girl needed a place to stay until conditions in her own home improved, there was always someone nearby who was willing to take care of her. Family came first and everyone considered the neighbors to be part of the family, and in many cases, they were. Extended families gathered for reunions and Sunday school picnics. Coming to town to see friends was a weekly diversion. This chapter takes a look at Hughesville when its Main Street was the place to be on Saturday night.

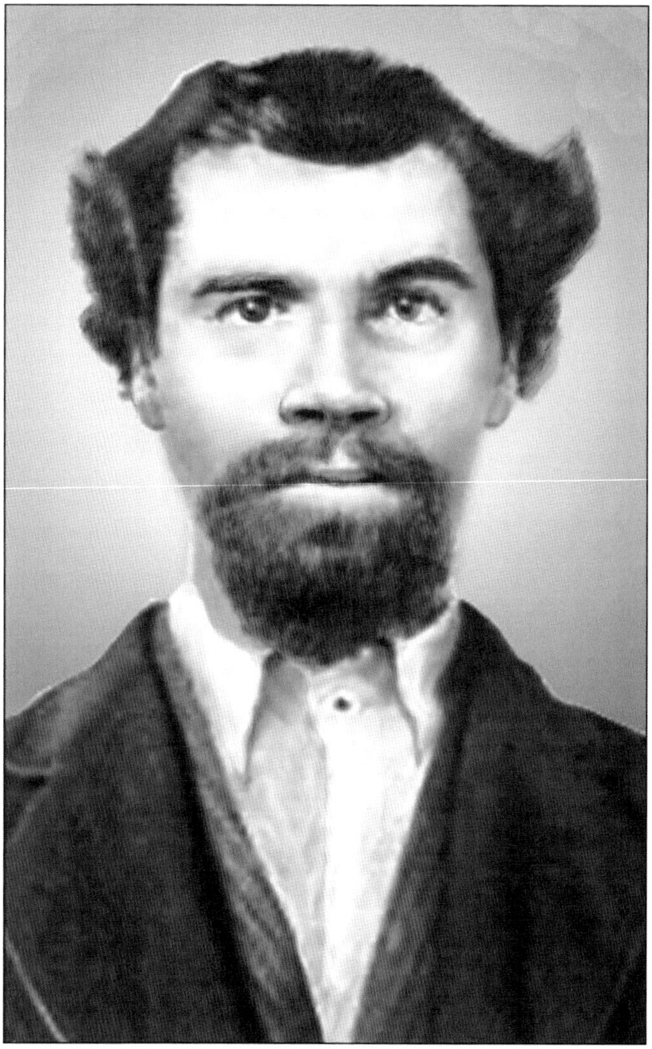

When this photograph was taken, Jeptha Hughes was almost 70 years old. More than 40 years earlier, he had left his legacy behind in Hughesville, when he named a plot of land near Muncy Creek after himself. One of the true pioneers of the valley, Hughes and his family spent only four years in the Hughesville area and then moved north in search of new opportunities. (Courtesy of the Hughes family.)

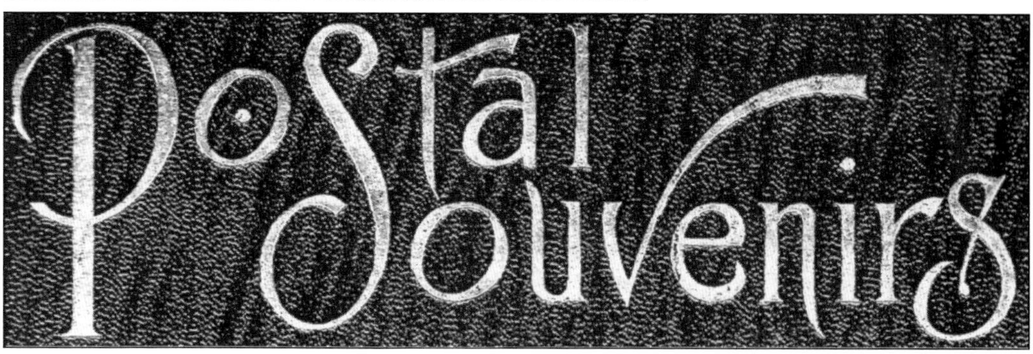

Between 1905 and 1915, the years referred to as the golden age of the postcard in America, millions of cards were mailed or saved in albums; almost every home had one that displayed the family collection. Postcard designs included reproduced artwork, while some of the most popular ones, the real-photo postcards, captured the essence of small-town life, as will be seen on the following pages. (Courtesy of Mary Fox Odell.)

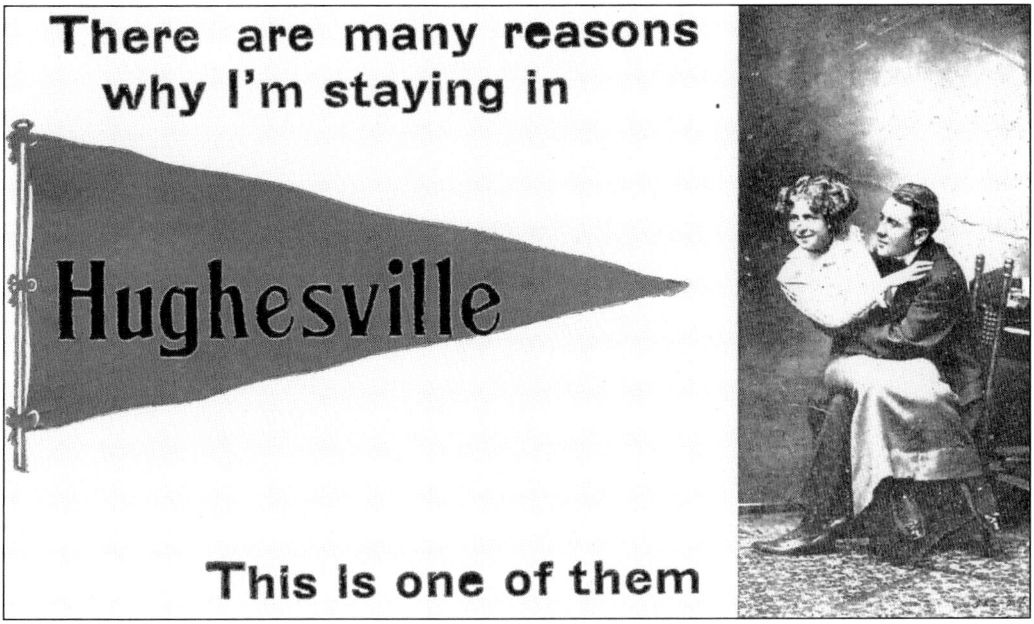

Postcards were used to share news, to send an invitation, to make plans to meet at a church festival ("if it don't rain"), or to just say, "How are you by this time. I am fine so far." Mail delivery was fast—a postcard could be sent in the morning with the assurance that the recipient would receive the card within the next 24 hours. (Courtesy of Stewart Hill.)

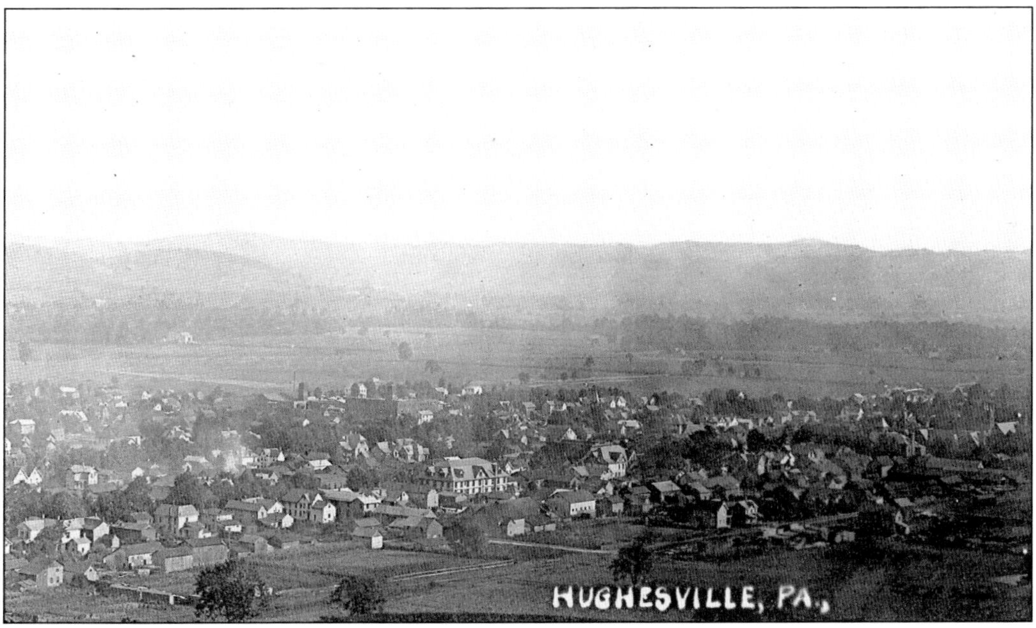

Surrounded by the rolling hills common to central Pennsylvania, Hughesville was a rural community that adapted to change. Prominent in the center of the photograph is the rear of the Rohrhirsch Hotel, which was sold in 1923 and became known as the Cadman Building. It was converted into street-front stores and eight apartments, which were located on the upper floors. (Courtesy of the East Lycoming Historical Society.)

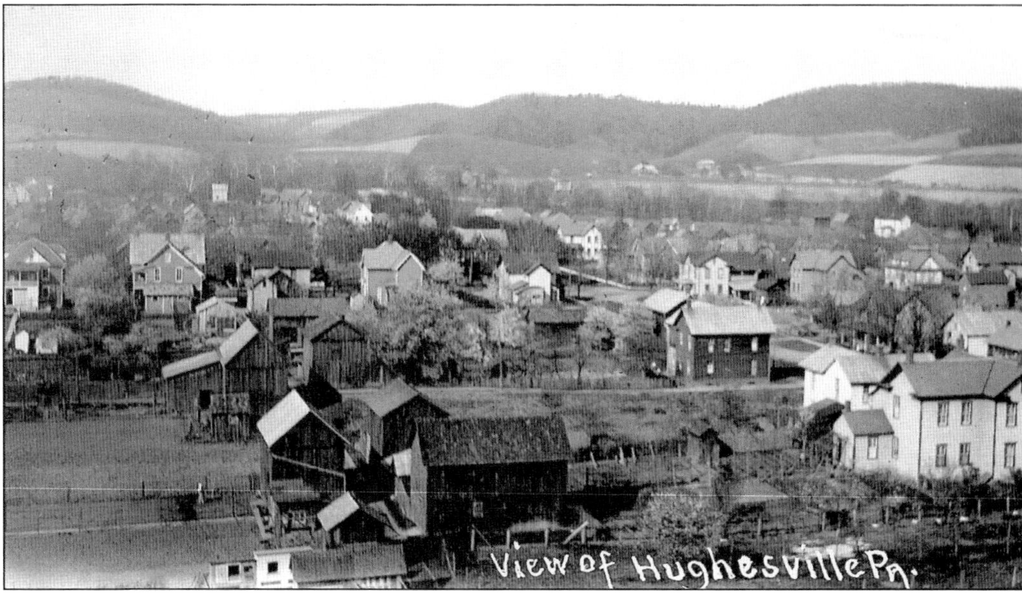

In this image, cultivated fields appear as light-colored rectangles against the hillsides. Behind the houses, between the sheds and an occasional outhouse, gardens are seen in the foreground, located wherever a plot of land can be tilled and a handful of seeds can be thrown. These kitchen gardens provided an inexpensive source of vegetables and were a common sight in town until the end of World War II. (Courtesy of Mary Fox Odell.)

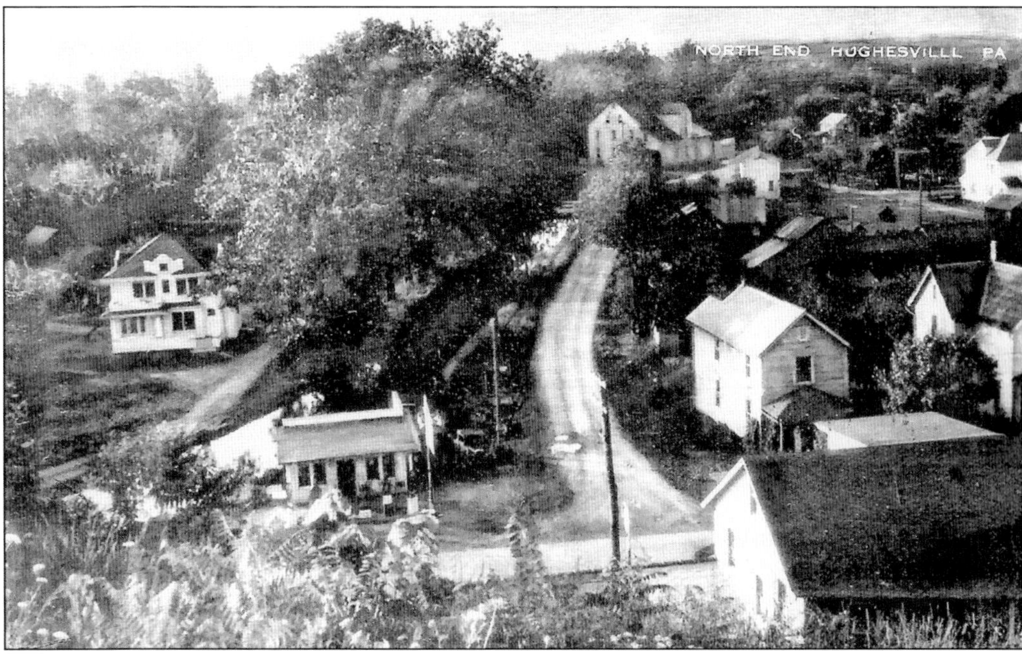

Between 1908 and 1940, Sears, Roebuck and Company sold more than 100,000 homes through their mail-order Modern Homes program. As one approaches Hughesville from the north end of town, one of Hughesville's Sears houses is seen at left. Supplies to construct entire homes would arrive by railroad and included precut lumber, windows, nails, and varnish. Prices ranged from $650 to $2,500 in 1908. (Courtesy of Stewart Hill.)

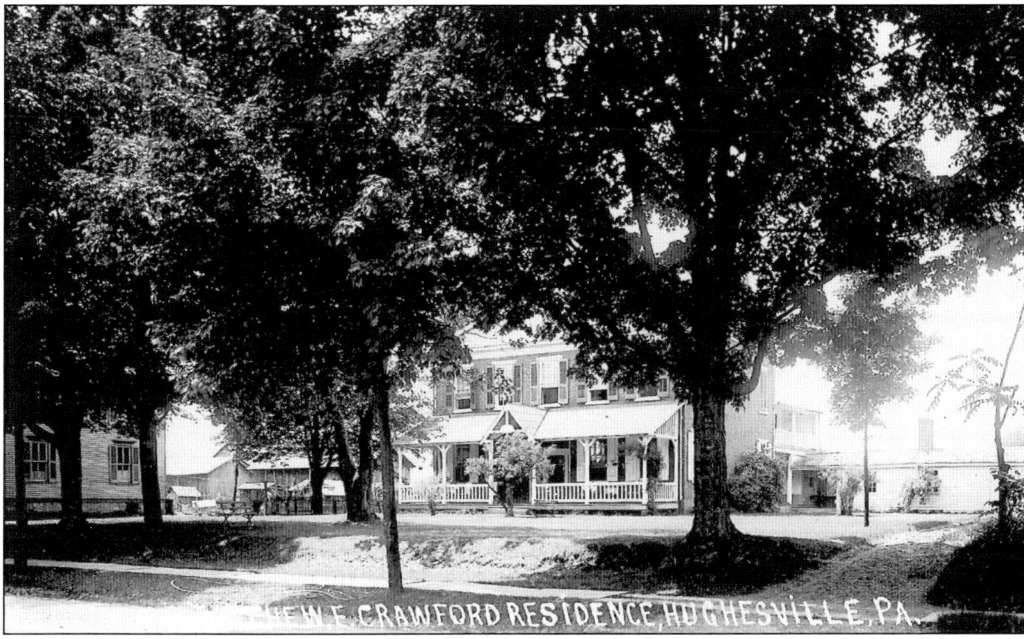

Located on the west side of North Main Street, this Colonial brick home was purchased by Hughesville's first resident lawyer, William E. Crawford. Admitted to the bar in Lycoming County in 1873, he practiced law in Williamsport for a few years before relocating to Hughesville. Built in 1846, the home is one of the oldest remaining original structures on Main Street. (Courtesy of Mary Fox Odell.)

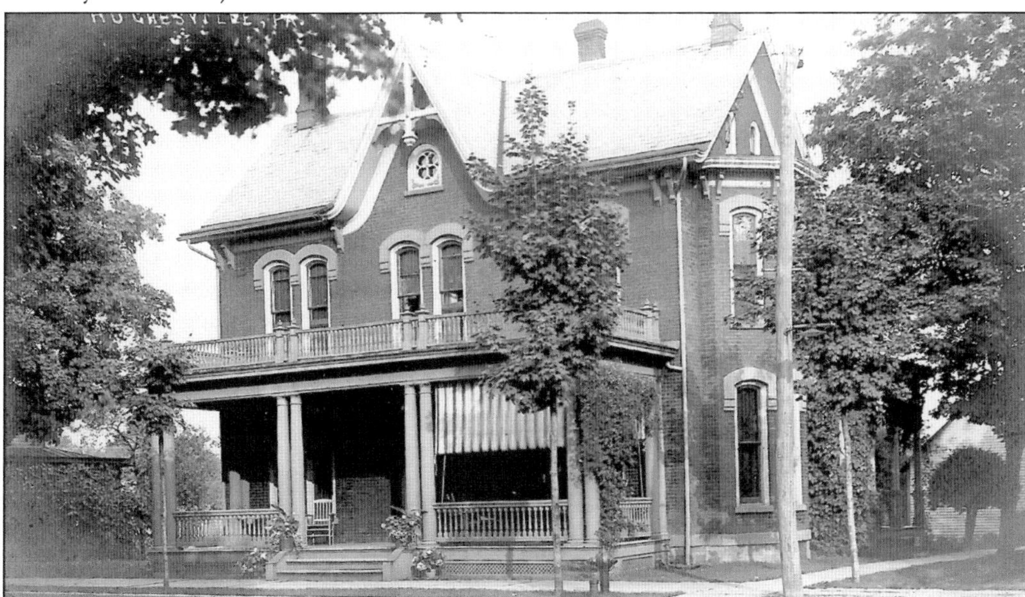

At the corner of North Main and Walnut Streets, a short distance from the Crawford house, is this home owned first by William Frontz and then his son, Walter. The younger Frontz was a cashier at the First National Bank from 1889 until 1910, when he was elected bank president. The original structure of the house is still evident today, even after several renovations. (Courtesy of Mary Fox Odell.)

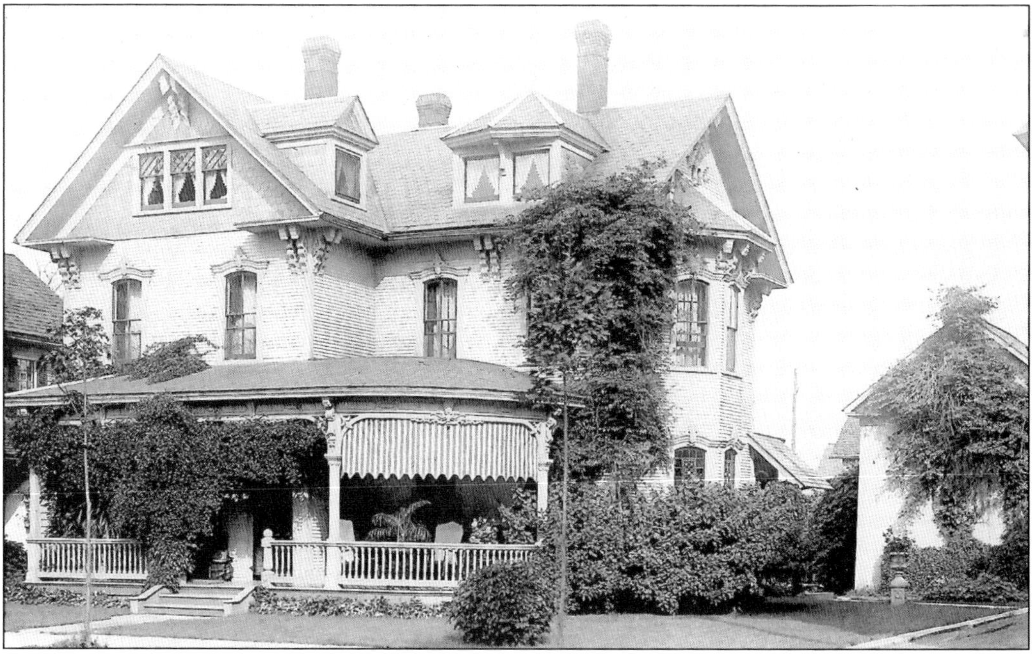

Also located on North Main Street, this home was owned by lumber dealer and banker DeWitt Bodine. He enlisted in the 14th Pennsylvania Emergency Regiment after his graduation from Williamsport's Dickinson Seminary. Upon his return from service, he began a lumber business with his uncle George Bodine and eventually became sole proprietor. DeWitt donated land to the borough in 1916 to establish Bodine Park. (Courtesy of Mary Fox Odell.)

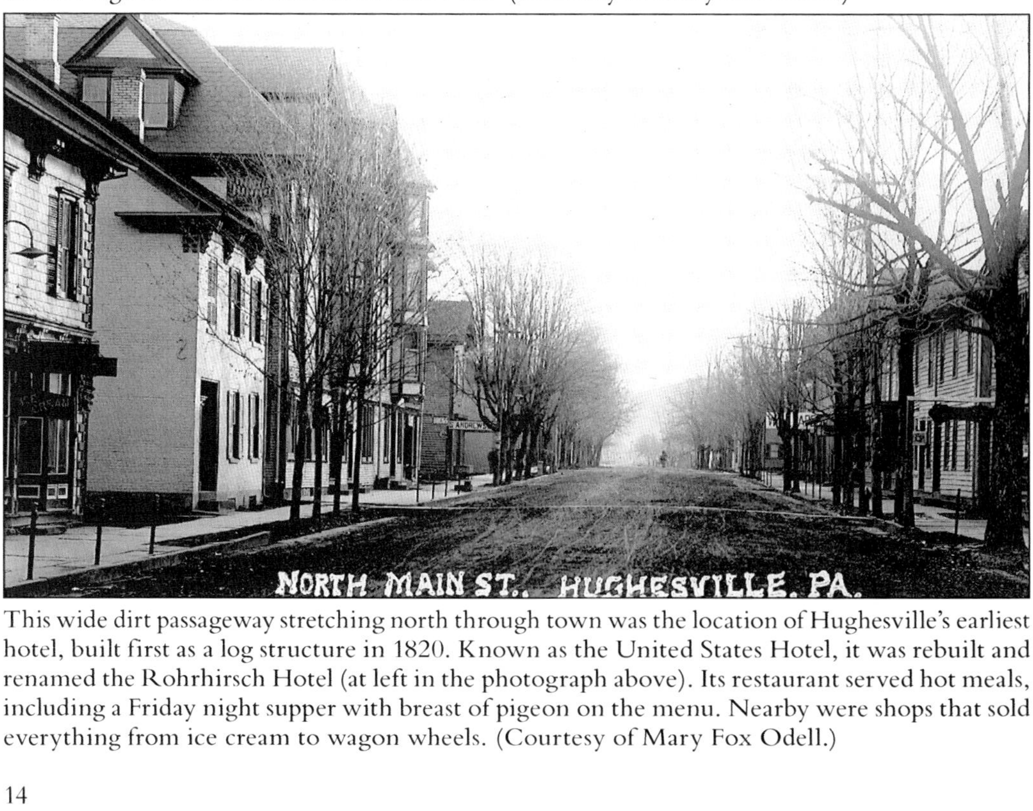

This wide dirt passageway stretching north through town was the location of Hughesville's earliest hotel, built first as a log structure in 1820. Known as the United States Hotel, it was rebuilt and renamed the Rohrhirsch Hotel (at left in the photograph above). Its restaurant served hot meals, including a Friday night supper with breast of pigeon on the menu. Nearby were shops that sold everything from ice cream to wagon wheels. (Courtesy of Mary Fox Odell.)

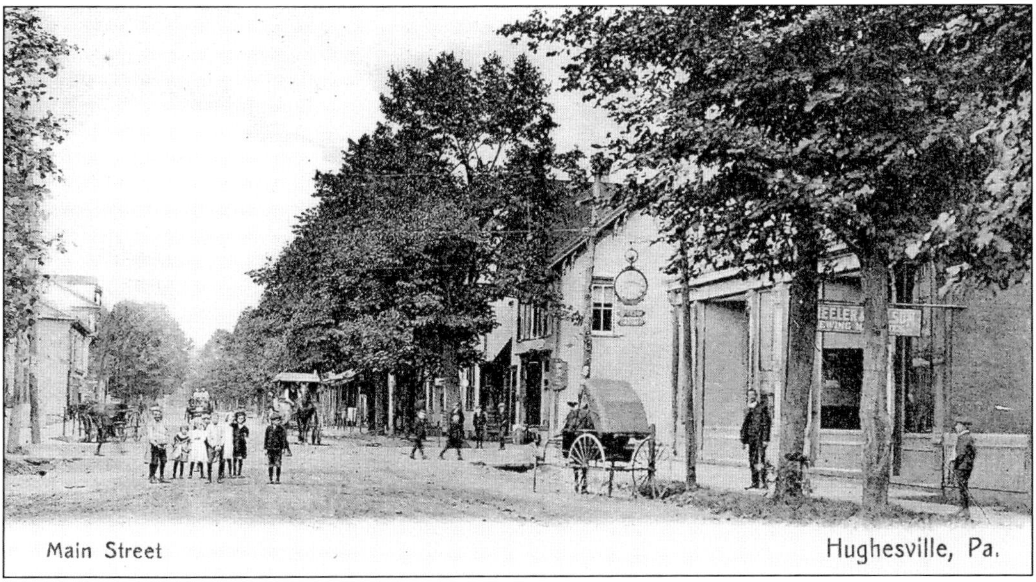

In this early scene at Main and Water Streets, one of the children, the girl in the dark coat on the left, is identified as Caroline Hill Kohler. When she was a young girl, Kohler thought that the spelling of her name was old-fashioned (she was named for her grandmother) so she changed it to the more modern version, Carolyn. (Courtesy of Elizabeth Rogers Knyrim.)

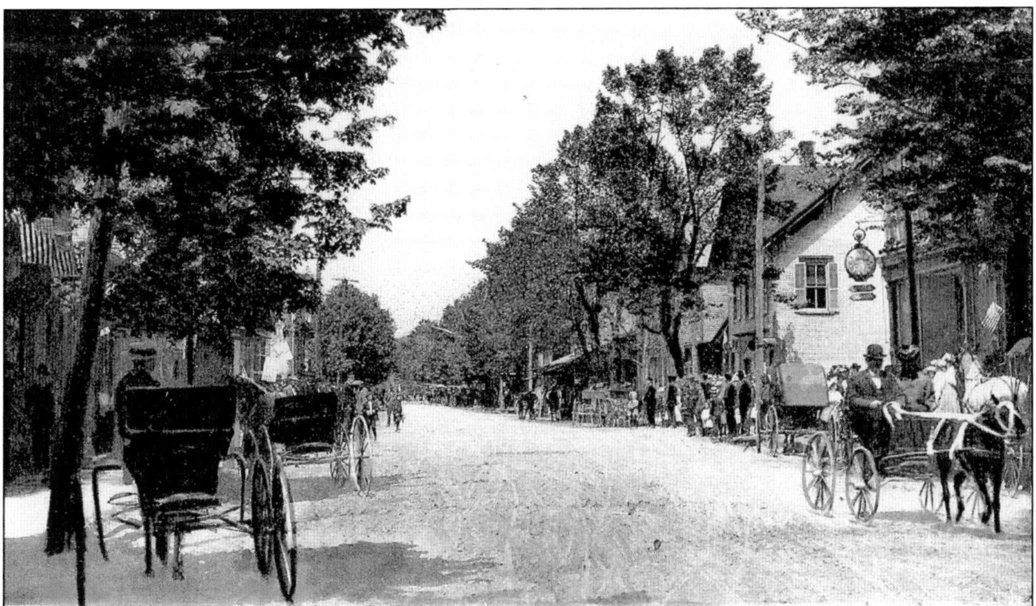

In another view of Main and Water Streets, Hughesville's main crossroad comes alive as those living out of town traveled in by horse and carriage to do their banking, visit with friends, and shop for necessities. The clock hanging from the building (on the right in both photographs above) advertised Charles F. Johnson's business in the Laird Building where he sold eyeglasses, watches, and jewelry. (Courtesy of Polly Hess.)

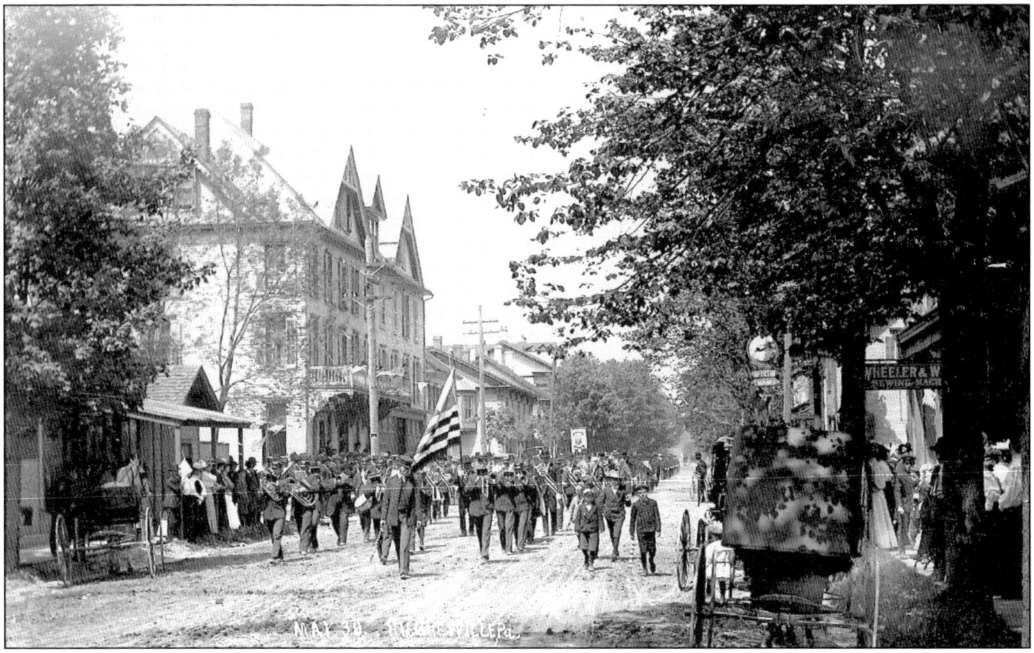

The marchers seen above in this Memorial Day parade were members of the Hughesville Fireman's Band, who are also pictured on page 31. The photograph above was taken before 1907, because the building pictured on the left is the one-chair barbershop where Billie Weel sold penny candy and roasted peanuts. In the photograph below, the First National Bank, which was built in 1907, is now seen where Weel's shop once stood, across from the American House Hotel, at the corner of Main and Water Streets. (Above, courtesy of the East Lycoming Historical Society; below, courtesy of Nancy Hodge.)

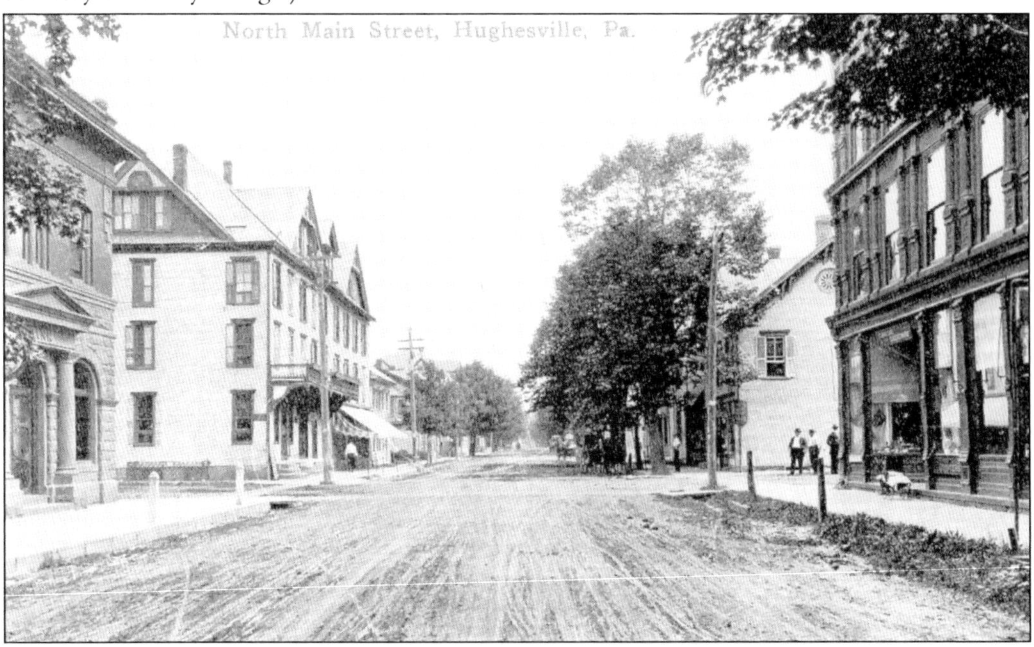

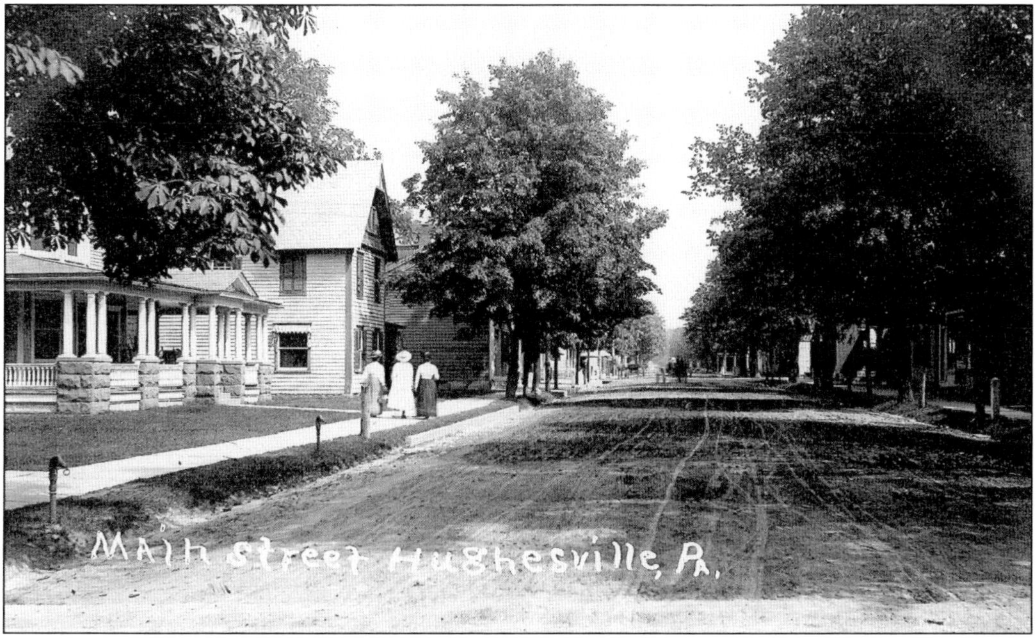

A variety of shopping and eating establishments await these three ladies (above) as they walk up Main Street toward the center of town. It could be that they are heading for the tailor's shop, the photography studio, the grocery, the bake shop, or the ice-cream store. As this photograph was taken, they were passing the home of Howard Reed (see close-up below), who was the proprietor of a general store located further up Main Street between the Rohrhirsch and the American House Hotels. (Courtesy of Mary Fox Odell.)

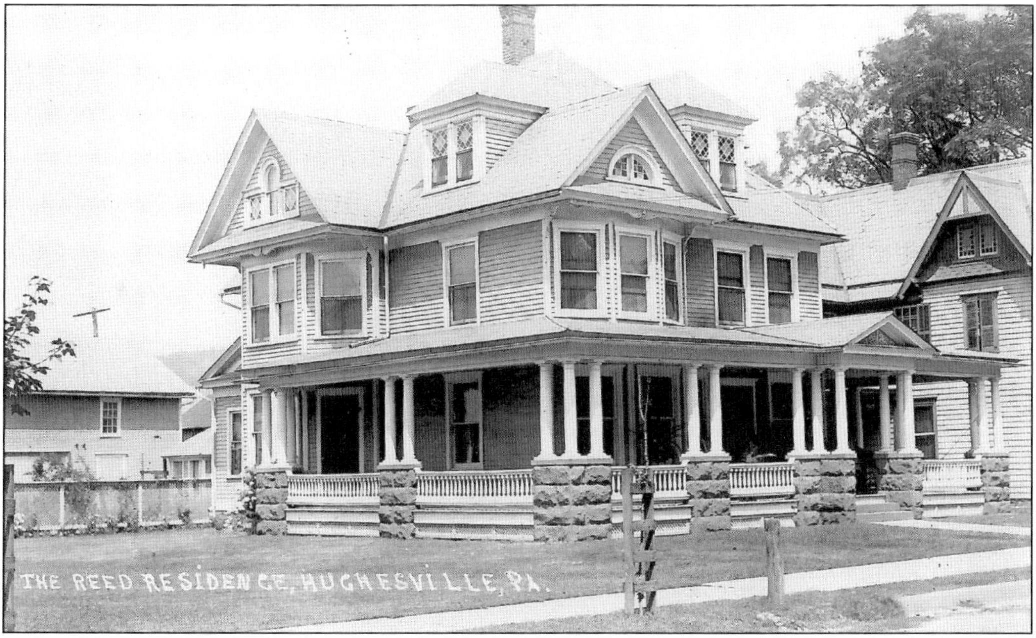

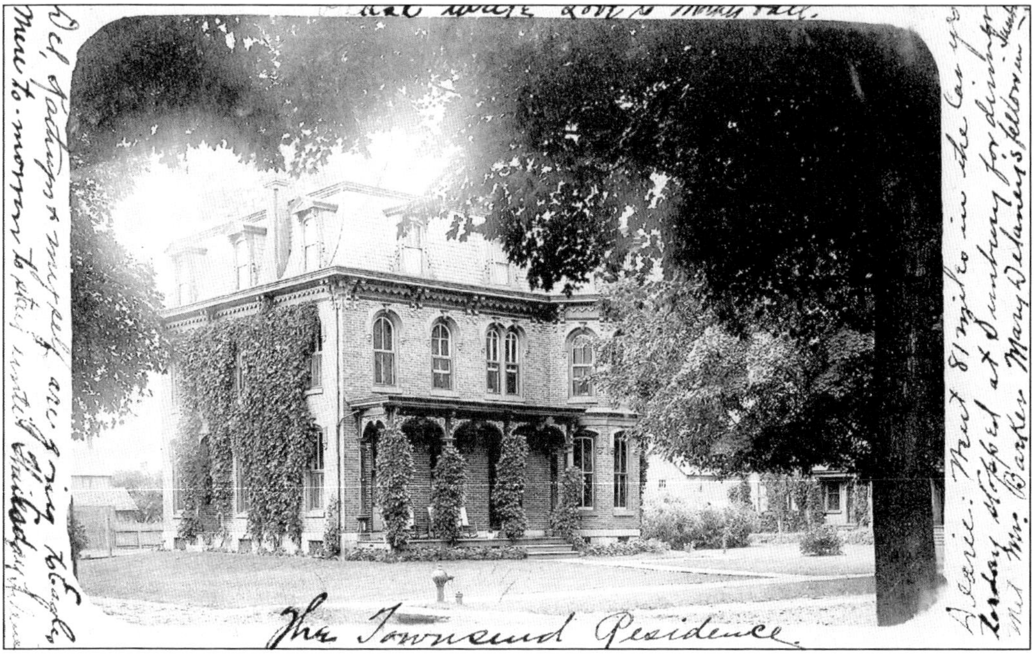

A native of Philadelphia, Samuel D. Townsend became auditor for the Williamsport and North Branch Railroad Company in 1891. He lived in this house with his wife, Mary, and their daughters, Linda and Jeanie, and Delmar, Samuel's son from a previous marriage. In 1898, Samuel became part owner and general manager of the railroad, a position that Delmar assumed in 1917 when Samuel died. (Courtesy of Elizabeth Rogers Knyrim.)

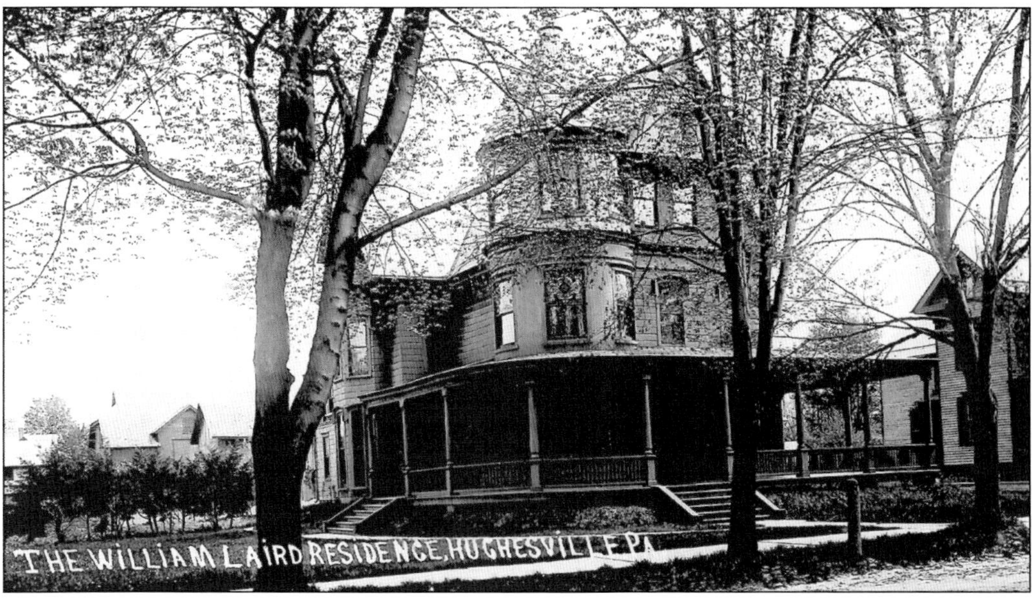

William Lamon Laird lived in this home on South Main Street at the beginning of the 20th century with his wife, Annie, and their son, Raymond. The elder Laird built the Raymond Hotel in Eagles Mere, which he named after his son, and was the owner and proprietor of the hotel until his death in 1919. In 1942, the expansive resort hotel was destroyed by fire and never rebuilt. (Courtesy of Mary Fox Odell.)

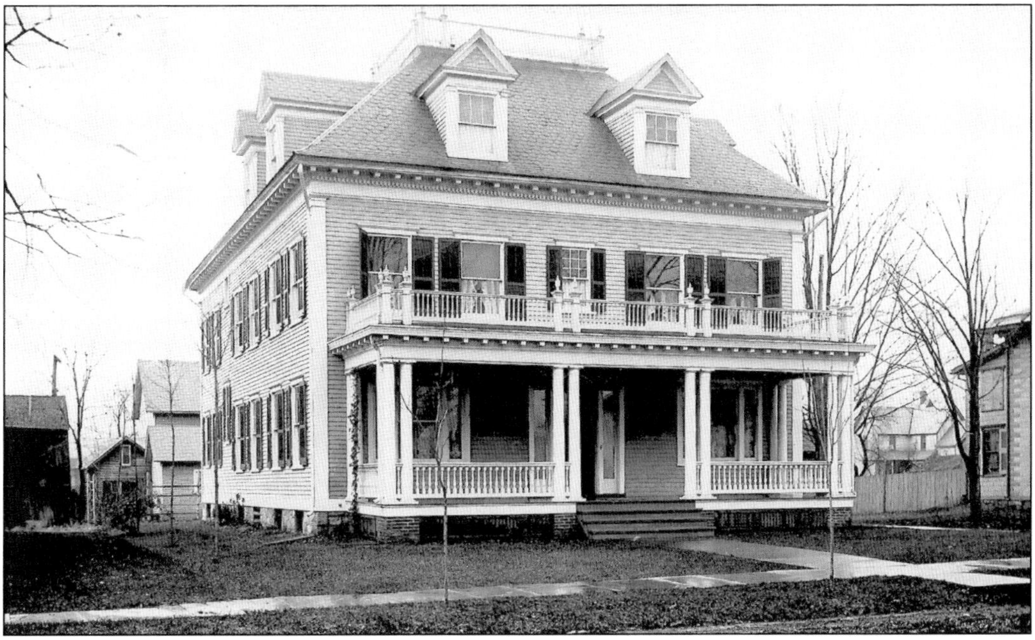

This house (above), known as the Townsend House, was built in 1903 as a Victorian-style boardinghouse. It had 19 rooms with 9 bedrooms and 3.5 bathrooms and approximately 5,680 square feet of living space. While the Samuel Townsend family lived across the street in an apartment, they rented out this house to tenants for more than 20 years, beginning the winter of 1903. In 1923, Samuel's son, Delmar, and his wife, Catherine, purchased the house. After they divorced in 1925, Delmar remarried, and he and his new wife, Louise, raised two children. The house next door (below) was built in 1905 as the residence of Howard and Anna Lyon. Lyon served as Hughesville's burgess during World War I and through the early 1920s. (Above, courtesy of Stewart Hill; below, courtesy of Mary Fox Odell.)

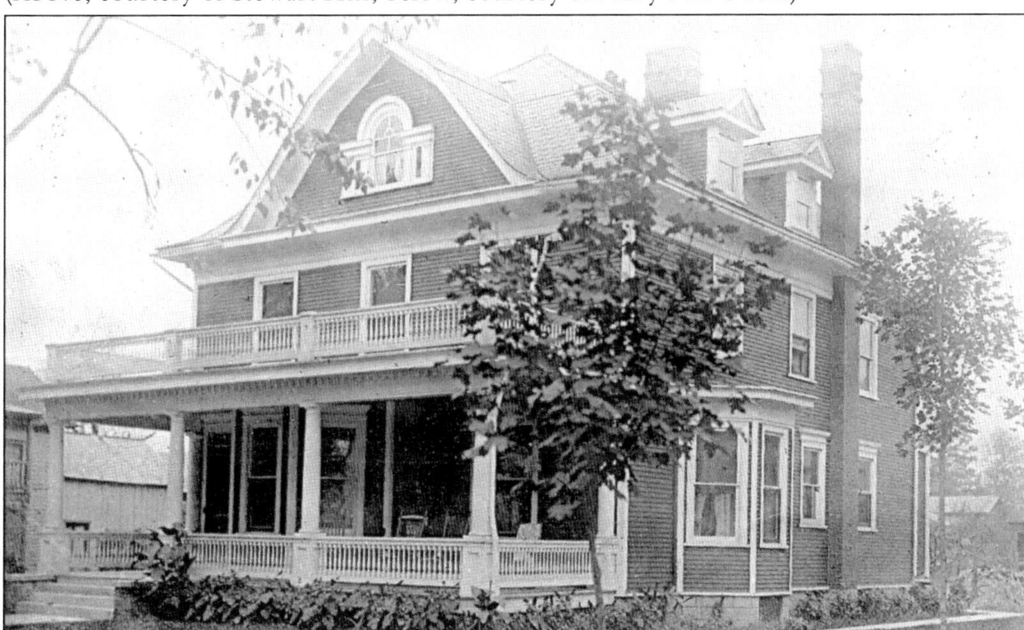

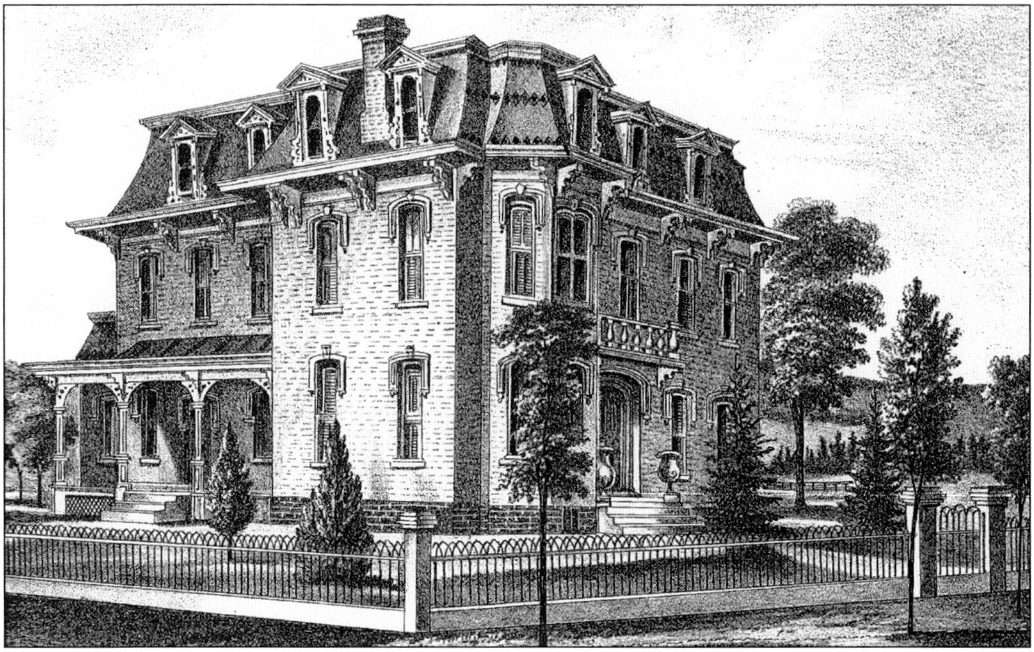

Hughesville native Michael Steck's first child, a daughter, was born in the territory of New Mexico when he was the superintendent of Indian Affairs. His sons were born in Hughesville after he and his wife, Elizabeth, moved into this home on the corner of Main and Academy Streets in the early 1870s. By 1880, however, Steck's lost investments in the bankrupt railroad forced him to sell it. (Courtesy of *History of Lycoming County Illustrated*, 1876.)

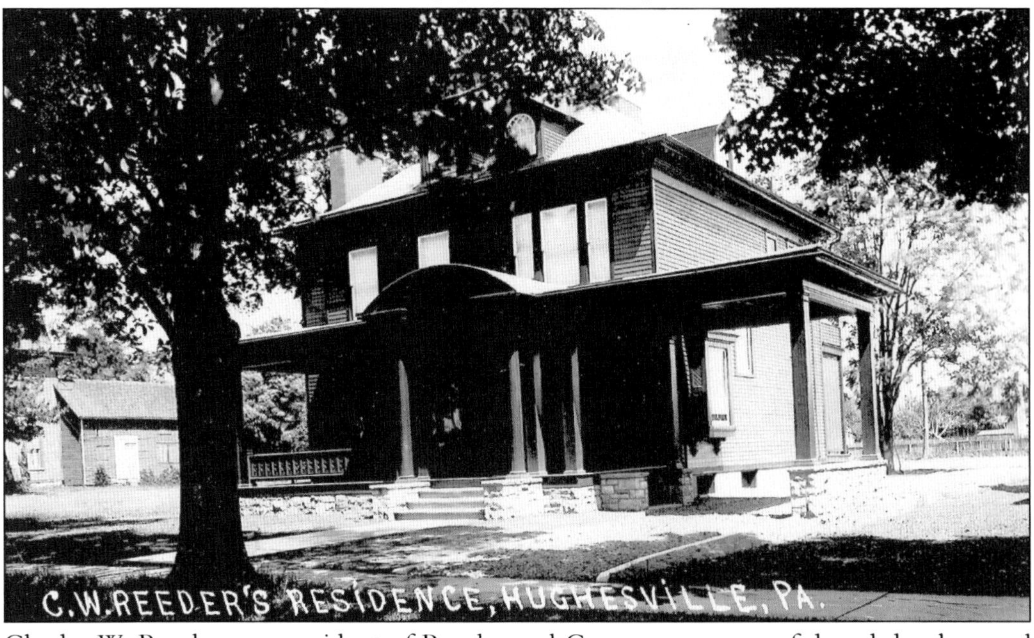

Charles W. Reeder was president of Reeder and Company, a successful coal, lumber, and building supply business located at the corner of Water and Railroad Streets. He and his wife, Arielle, raised their family in this home on South Main Street during the early 1900s. (Courtesy of Mary Fox Odell.)

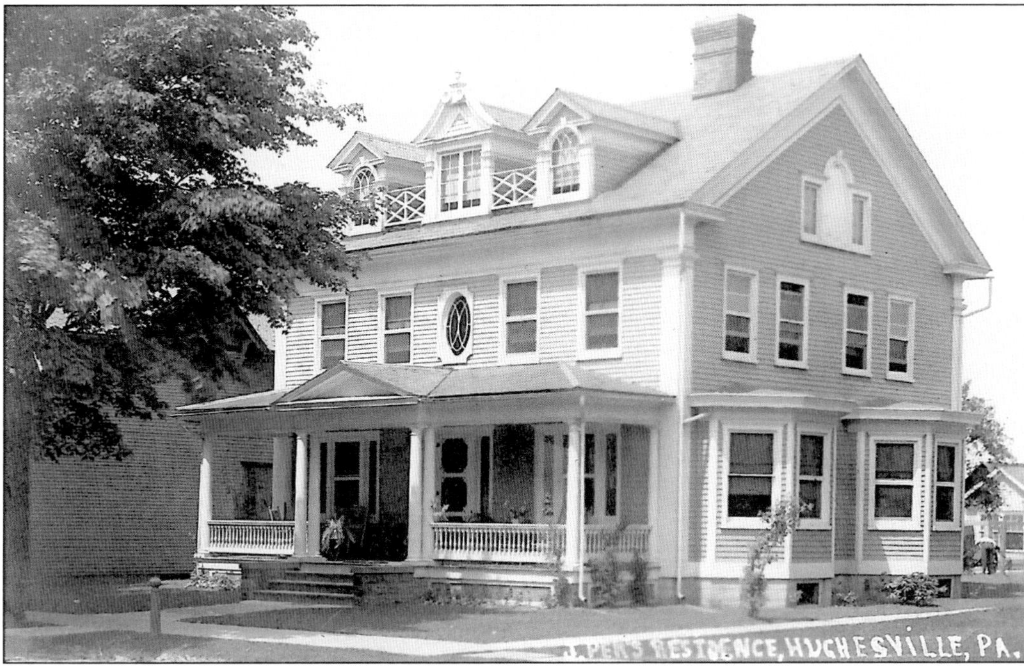

Jacob Per came to America from Russia in 1885, settled in Lock Haven, and opened a clothing store. He opened another store in Hughesville's American House Hotel and another one in Lopez. Consequently he is considered one of the first men in the area to operate a chain of stores. Per and his Russian-born wife, Katherine, lived in this home on South Main Street. (Courtesy of Mary Fox Odell.)

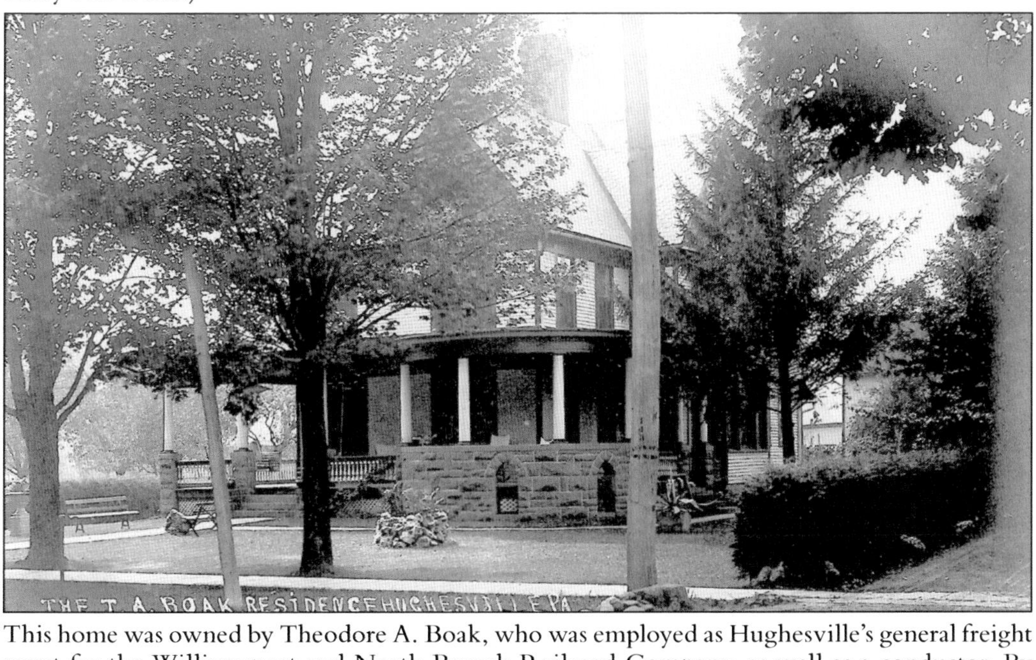

This home was owned by Theodore A. Boak, who was employed as Hughesville's general freight agent for the Williamsport and North Branch Railroad Company, as well as a conductor. By 1891, he and his brother James had purchased controlling interest in the furniture factory on Railroad Street. (Courtesy of Mary Fox Odell.)

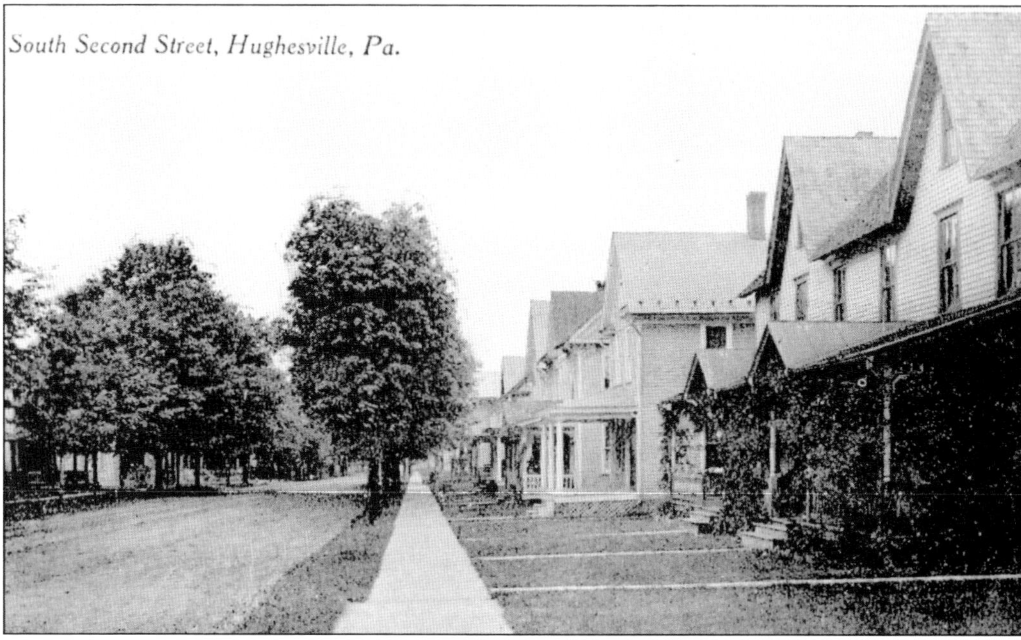

Neat rows of houses, carefully manicured lawns, and mature trees were a common sight in Hughesville, as seen here on South Second Street. While poles brought electricity to the businesses and residences on Main, Water, and Railroad Streets, the residents living on the remainder of the streets lit their oil lamps as evening fell and the streets grew dark. (Courtesy of Harold Hill.)

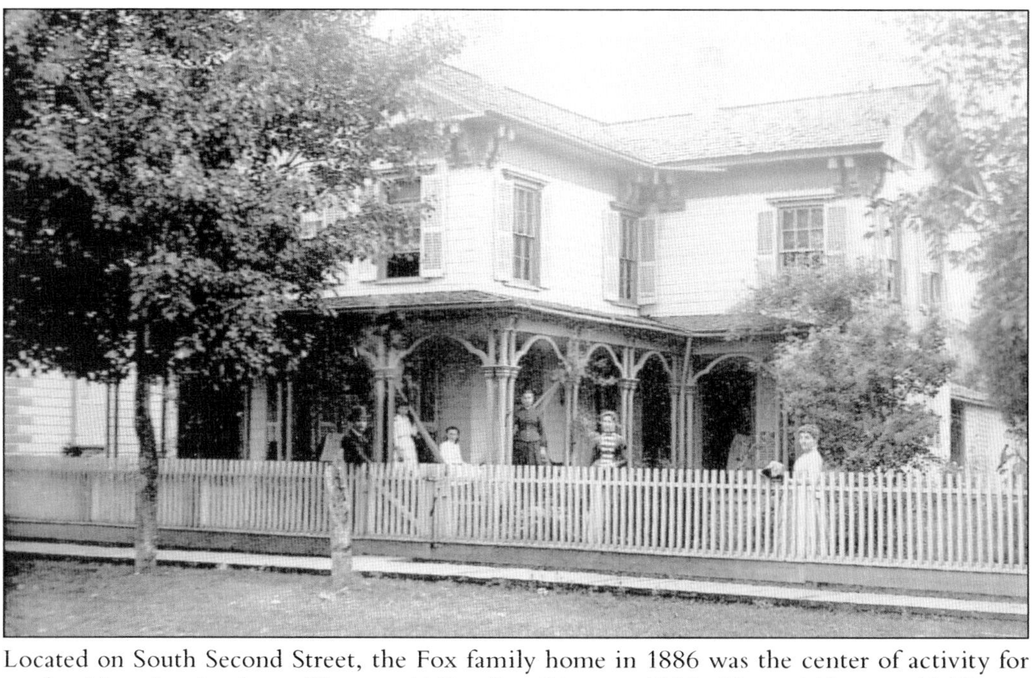

Located on South Second Street, the Fox family home in 1886 was the center of activity for mother Mary, her daughters, 28-year-old Caroline, 26-year-old Matilda, and 12-year-old Alberta, and son John, who was 24 at the time. Widowed at a young age, Mary provided a home for her unmarried children for more than 30 years. (Courtesy of Mary Fox Odell.)

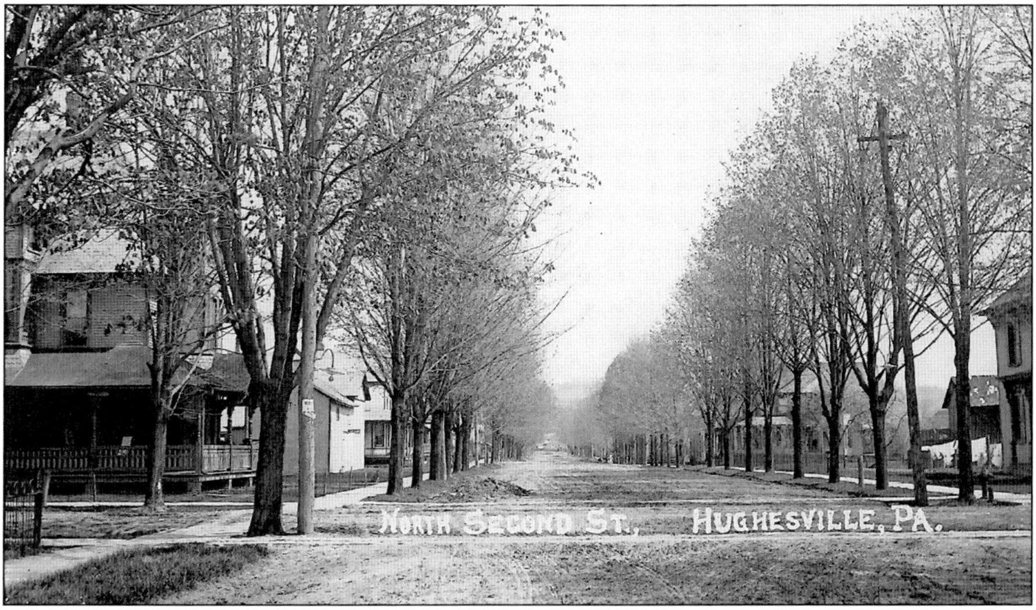

Homes in Hughesville did not have access to electricity until the 1930s, and even then, it was unreliable and could only handle small appliances such as fans and radios. Streets such as North Second Street remained unpaved until around 1920. Planks and boards were laid down to provide relatively mud-free footpaths. (Courtesy of Elizabeth Rogers Knyrim.)

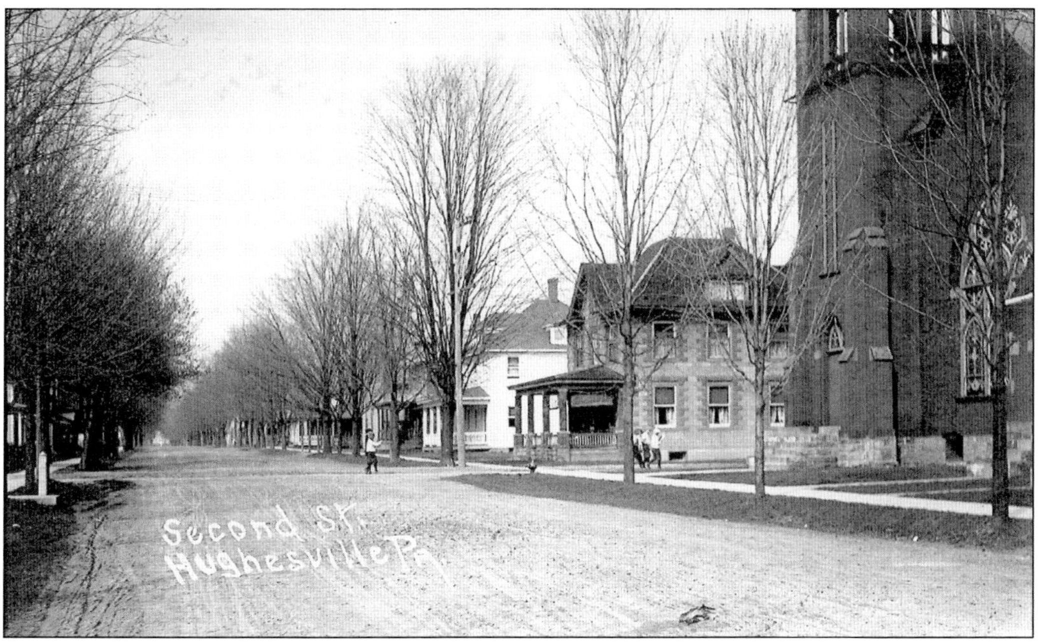

This view of Second and Academy Streets shows the front steps and stained-glass window of what was known as the "E.V. Church." This structure was completed in 1897 at a cost of $5,850, not including the stained-glass windows, which cost an additional $600. To replace just one of the windows today would cost more than the entire building did 110 years ago. (Courtesy of Mary Fox Odell.)

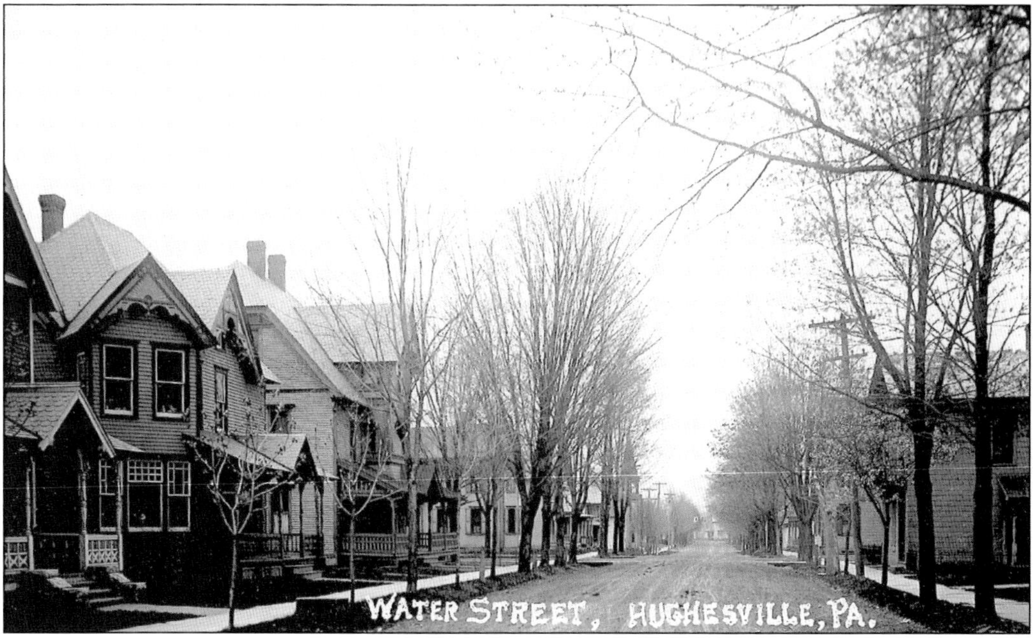

The only way to get into town from the east was to cross the Muncy Creek at the end of Water Street. Before 1923, one would travel over the covered bridge known as the Biddle Bridge, but a cement bridge replaced it when Water Street was paved. Halfway between the bridge and the center of town is the Baptist church (below), which was built in 1891 at the corner of Water and Third Streets. A very determined and dedicated group of only 21 members erected the building with minimal outstanding debt. (Courtesy of Mary Fox Odell.)

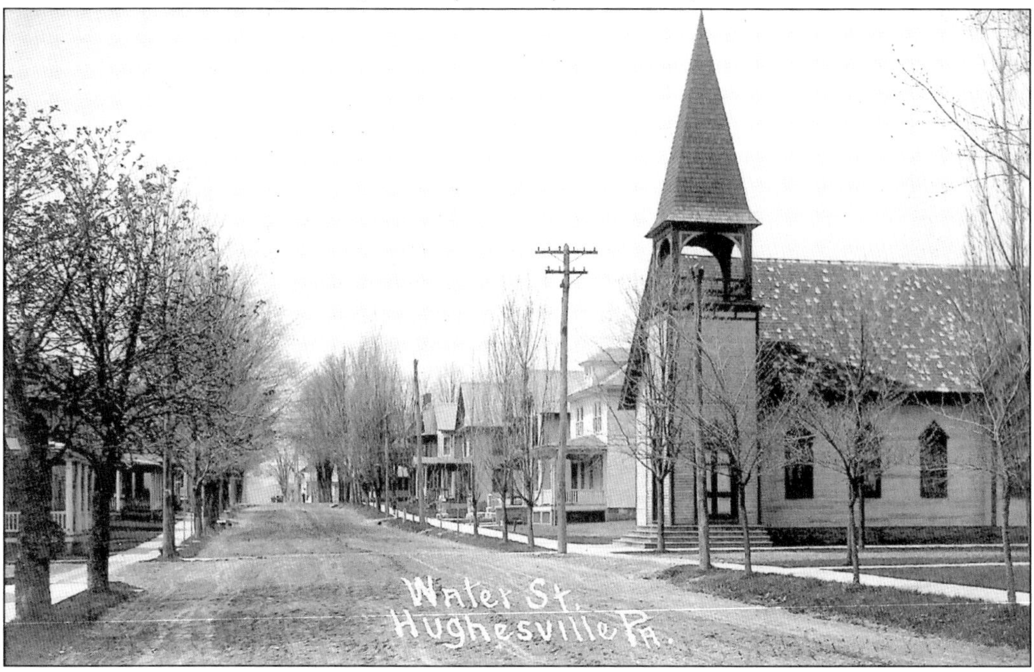

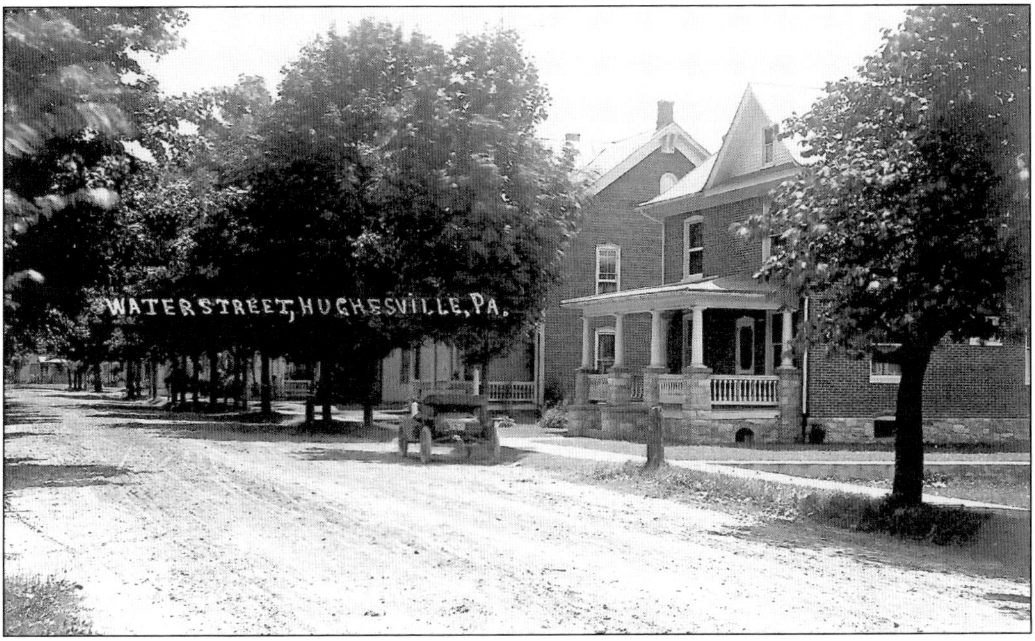

The first houses built in Hughesville were made of rough-hewn logs. Later ones were also constructed of wood and covered with locally-made wooden shingles. Building brick houses became popular, and the two-story, square shape of the foursquare style also became a standard. This brick house on Water Street (above, with close-up below) is a variation on the foursquare style, with a porch spanning the entire front of the house, boxy columns supporting the porch roof, quadrant window placement, and symmetrical, clean lines. Built between 1910 and 1920, this was the home of Brady and Almeda Poust. (Courtesy of Mary Fox Odell.)

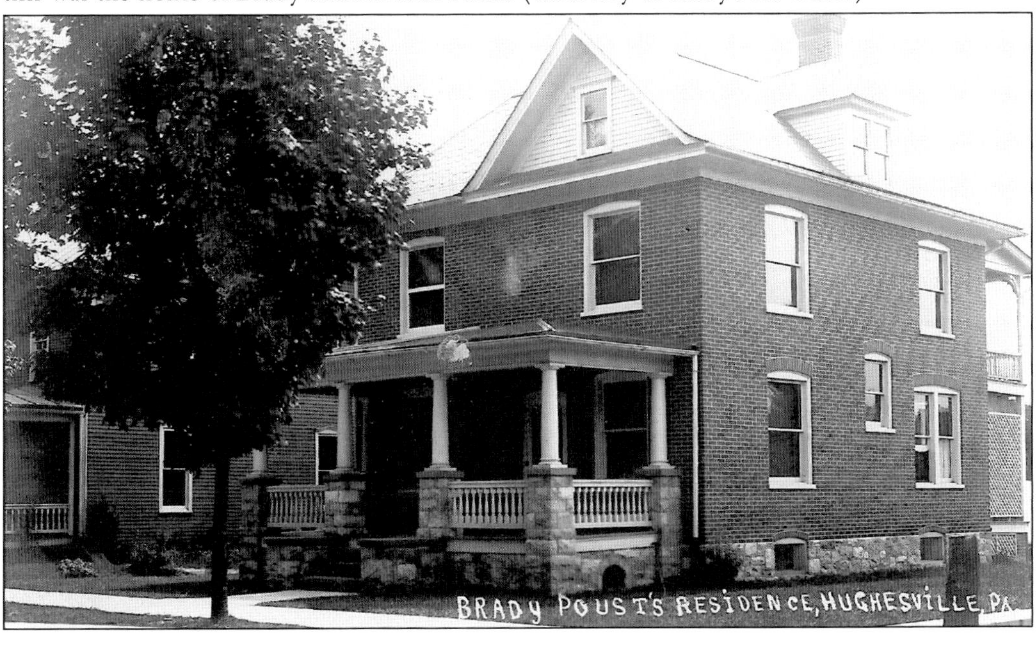

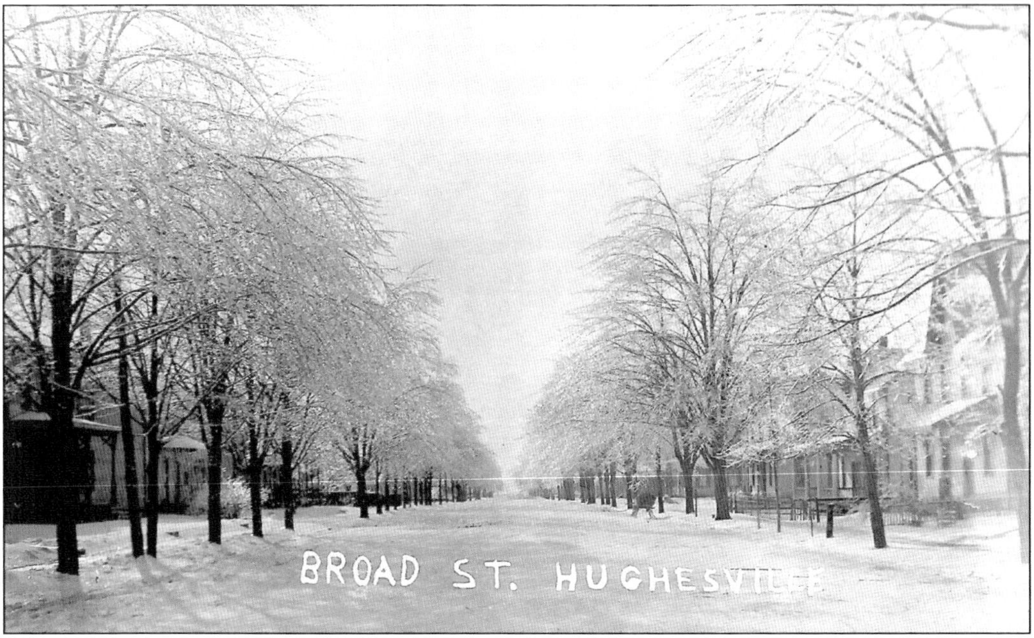

Many have heard, "When I was a kid, the snowdrifts would reach the top of our front door" or other tales just as dramatic. Were snowstorms really worse 100 years ago? In March 1888, a major storm paralyzed the Northeast when it dumped between two to four feet of snow with drifting reported at over six feet. At the end of the 19th century and the beginning of the 20th century, winter ice and snowstorms halted most travel until the train tracks could be cleared or horse-drawn sleighs could find a way to maneuver the slippery streets, since motorized plows and dump trucks were not available until the 1920s. Here on Broad Street (above) and at the corner of Broad and Academy Streets (below), ice and snowstorms are keeping everyone at home and off the streets. (Courtesy of Mary Fox Odell.)

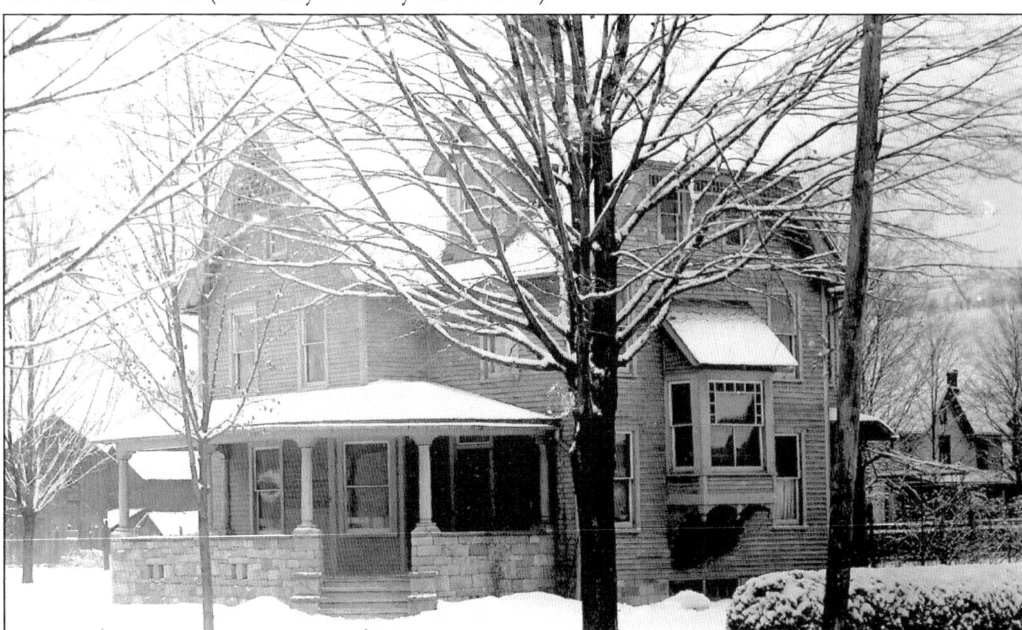

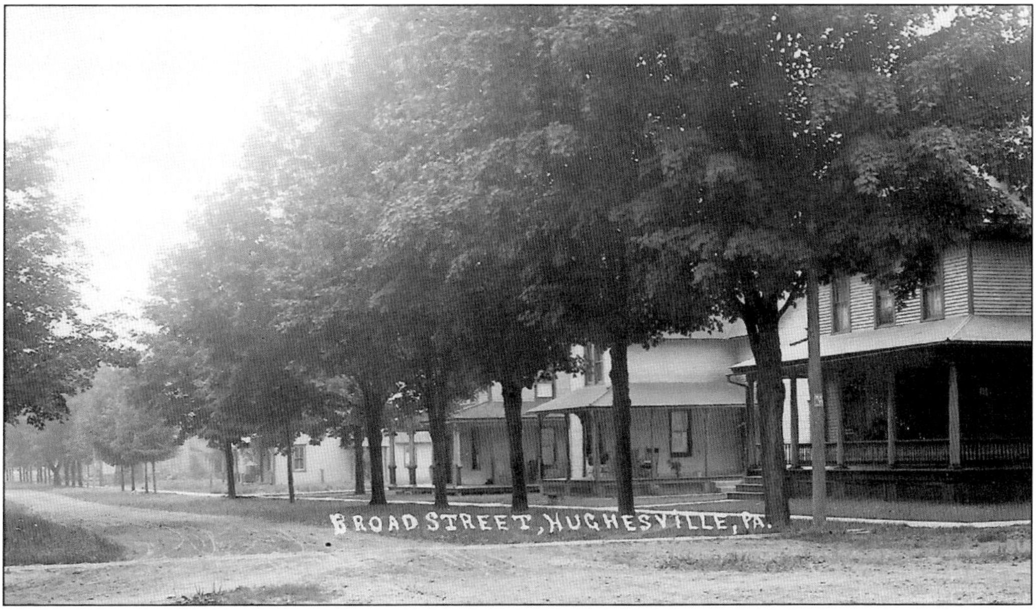

Situated one block west of Railroad Street and two blocks from Main Street, Broad Street (above) has always been residential. Those living here were near many of the businesses, such as the Snowden Brothers Foundry and Machine Shop, the Swartz Planing Mill (around 1900), the Shindel Silk Factory, and the furniture factory that has been called Boak's, Lycoming, and Mellen's over the years. On the east side of town, Third Street (below) was also residential but had the Rishel Furniture Factory at the south end and the Keystone Mill at the north end. (Courtesy of Mary Fox Odell.)

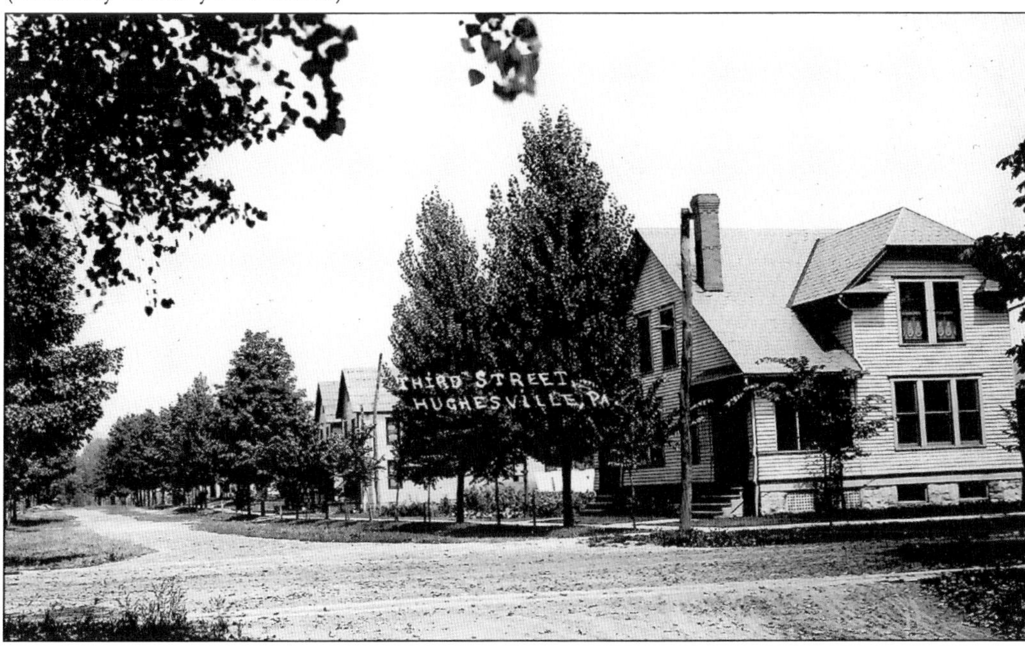

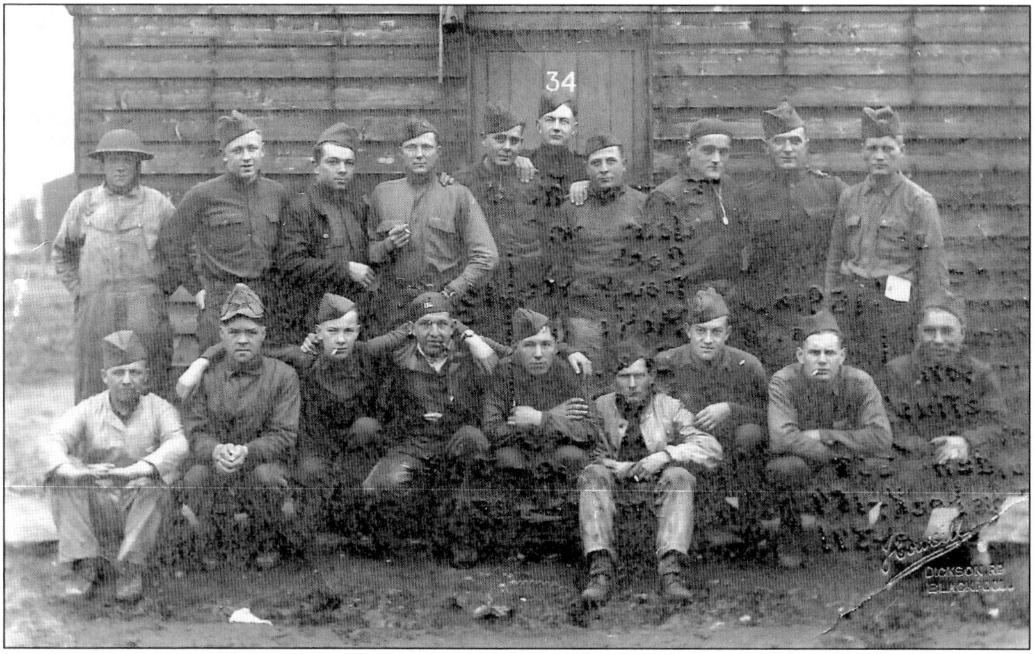

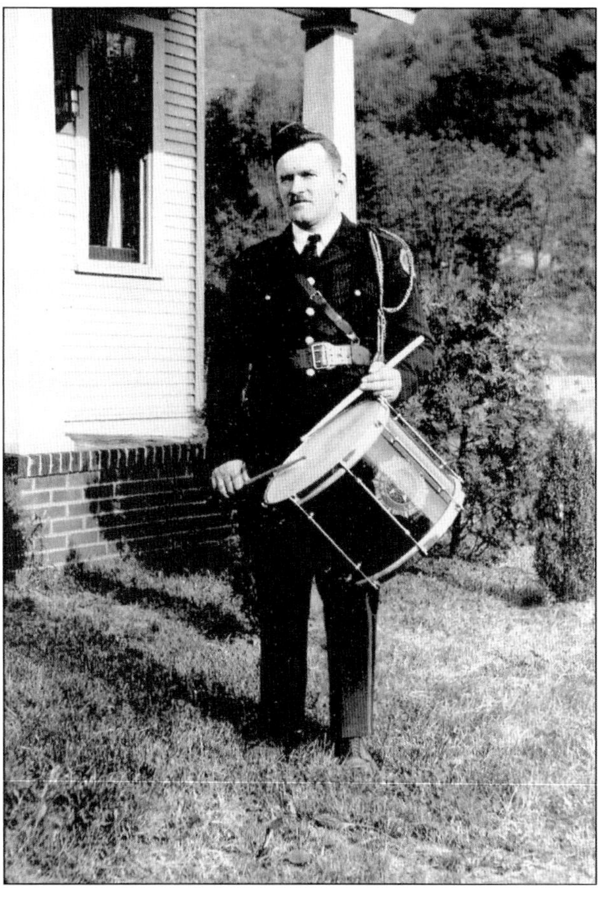

This postcard image shows a group of World War I–era soldiers (above) mostly identified only by their last names and squadron numbers. They are, from left to right, (first row) Johnson, Cook, Daugherty, Pickard, Era, King, Ramer (159th Squadron), Kunkle (308th Squadron), and Smith (159th Squadron); (second row) Snyder (wearing the distinctive "Doughboy" or "Brodie" helmet), Sikes, John Kenneth Fox (a Hughesville native), Rhodes, Johnson, Rosetius, Jones (159th Squadron), Golden (308th Squadron), Revsbeck (159th Squadron), and Satterlee (371st Squadron). Hughesville's only World War I casualty was Glenn Sharrow, who died in France on October 3, 1918, and was buried in Pleasant Hill Cemetery in 1921. The Glenn Sharrow American Legion Post 35 was named in his memory in 1920. At left is Earl Kohler, legion commander in 1922. (Above, courtesy of Mary Fox Odell; left, courtesy of the Glenn Sharrow American Legion Post 35.)

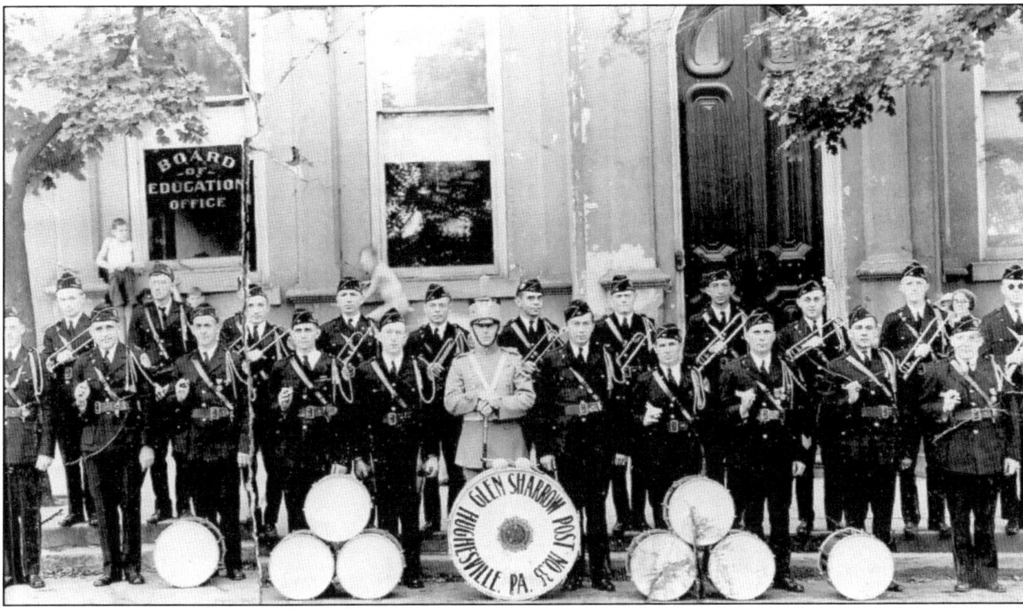

Members of the Glenn Sharrow Band in 1934 are seen above, from left to right, (first row) C. Kisner, R. Smith, H. Weaver, P. Schneider, L. Kohler, A. Wilkins, M. Shaffer, A. Springer, H. Rogers, C. Shipman, and R. Hill; (second row) ? Minier, W. Harriman, P. Barner, J. Siegfried, Reverend Stock, W. Bubb, R. Fought, G. Poust, E. Houseknecht, ? Fiester, and A. Hendershott. In September 1938, a group from Hughesville (below) attended the American Legion Convention in New York City. Standing on the top of the Empire State Building, which was completed in 1931, with the Chrysler Building in the background are, from left to right, Arthur "Jack" Springer, Edna McClain, Jack McClain, Arthur Hendershott, "Babe" Fought, Earl Kohler, Blanche Fought, Valle Fought, and Frank "Granny" Fought. (Above, courtesy of the Glenn Sharrow American Legion Post 35; below, courtesy of Janet Kohler.)

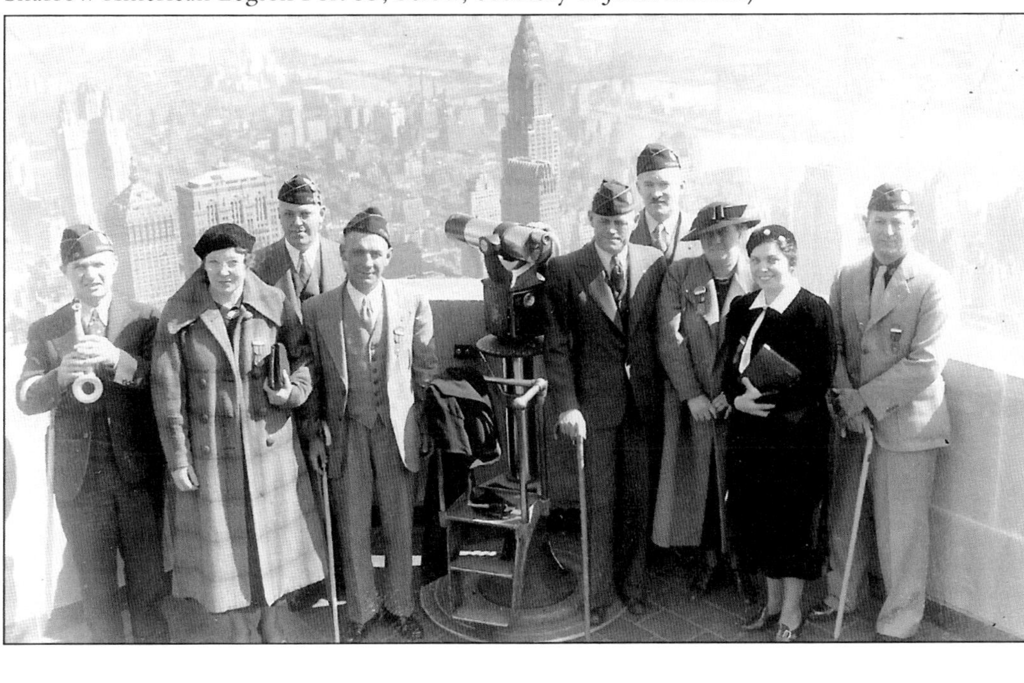

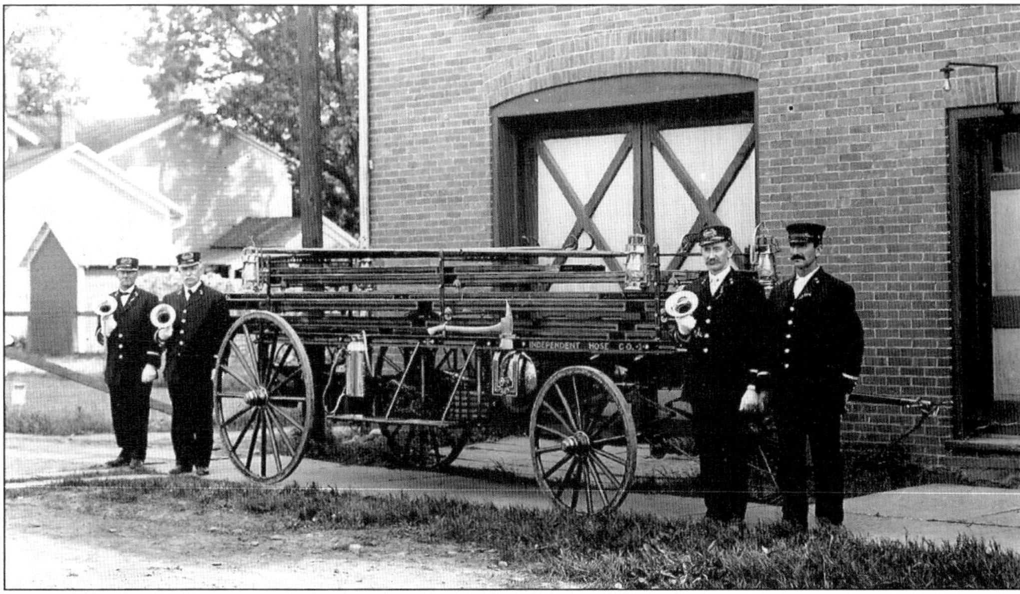

Hughesville's Independent Hose Company No. 1 organized in 1892. Pictured above with the new four-wheeled ladder truck in 1901 are, from left to right, George Koons, John Hauke, Chief Jim Winters, and William Barto. In 1909, the company (seen below) included, from left to right, (first row) unidentified, Brady Bartlow, Willis Miller, Charles Bugh, ? Smith, ? Barto, ? Snyder, unidentified, Charles Hughes, and Jappy Houck; (second row, sitting) Milton McCarty, Emory Boyer, George DeWald, Clyde Shipman, Bill Kahler, unidentified, ? Hoffman, and Charles Houck; (third row) ? Winters, Frank Gordner, unidentified, unidentified, unidentified, Clyde Weaver, unidentified, Clyde Taylor, Alvin Houseknecht, ? Springer, Pete Shaffer, Ellery Swank, John Buck, Charles McCarty, and ? Barto; (fourth row) Delay Buck, George Kuntz, Henry Stiger, Ollie Herman, Bunt Springer, Bob Croman, ? Confer, Milt Springer, Lew Corson, unidentified, ? Hoffman, unidentified, Bill Bubb, and unidentified. (Above, courtesy of Mary Fox Odell; below, courtesy of the East Lycoming Historical Society.)

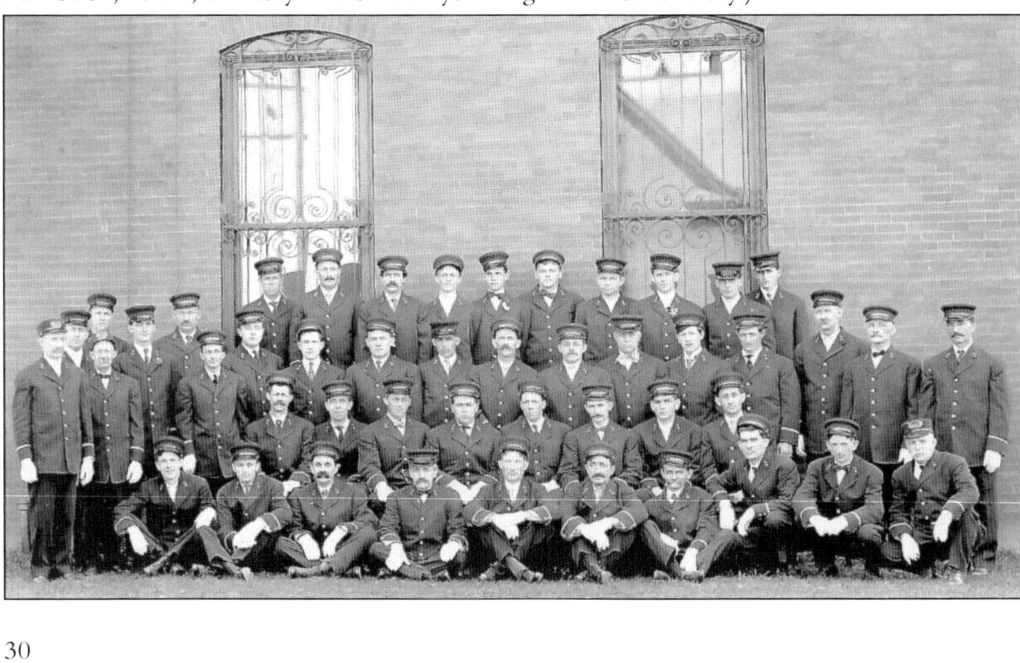

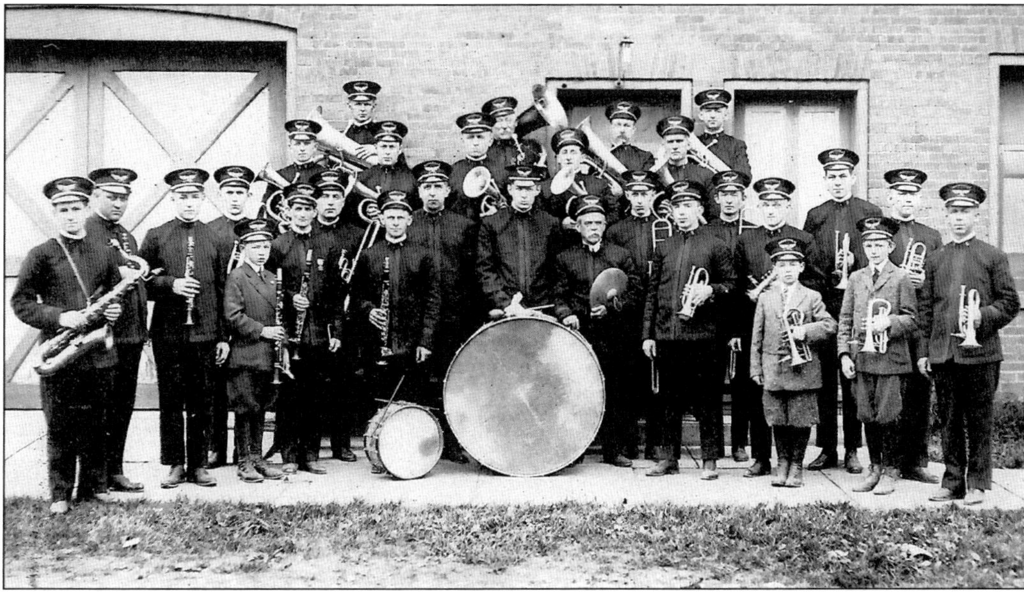

The Hughesville firemen formed a band that is pictured here around 1918. Band members are, from left to right are (first row, starting with small boy) Arthur Wilkins, William Hughes, Emory Boyer, Ward Smith, Cameron Boak (drum), Harvey Simmons (cymbals), Joseph Siegfried, Kenneth Boyer (in knickers), Benton Sevison (in knickers), and George Robinson; (second row) Clyde McCarty, George Dewald, Clinton Beeber, Grant Hughes, Irvin Palmer, Louis Kahler, William McClintock, Emerson Nixon, Raymond Faus, William Shuler, Stephen Lutz, Raymond Smith, Dan Belick, Brady Bower, Harold Higgins, Harry Travelet, Clarence Birdsell, Luke Shires, and Luray Swartz. According to company records, the building pictured below was built before 1900 to house their pumper and two-wheeled hose cart. (Above, courtesy of the East Lycoming Historical Society; below, courtesy of Kenneth D. Poust.)

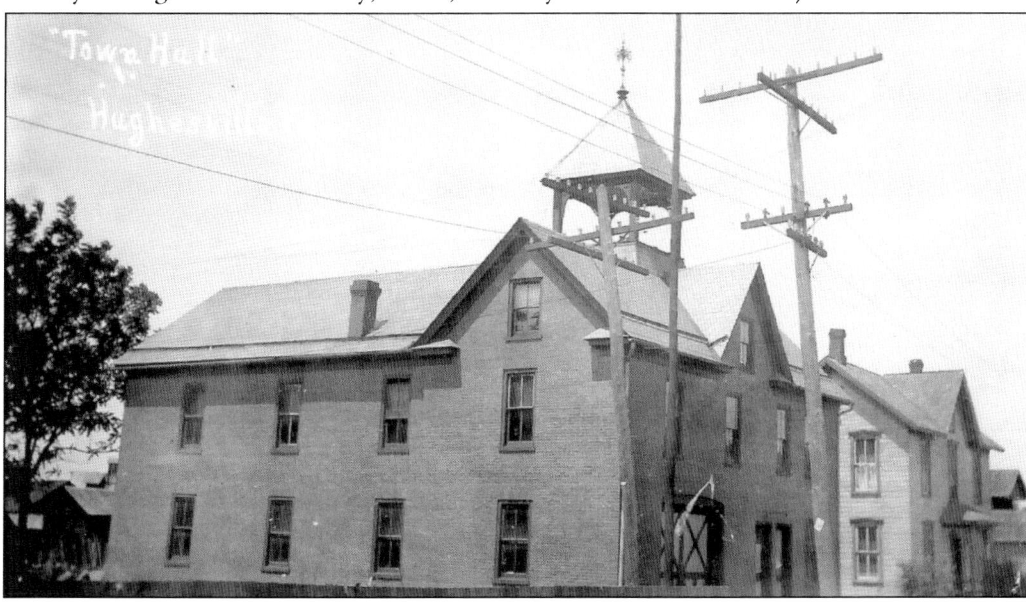

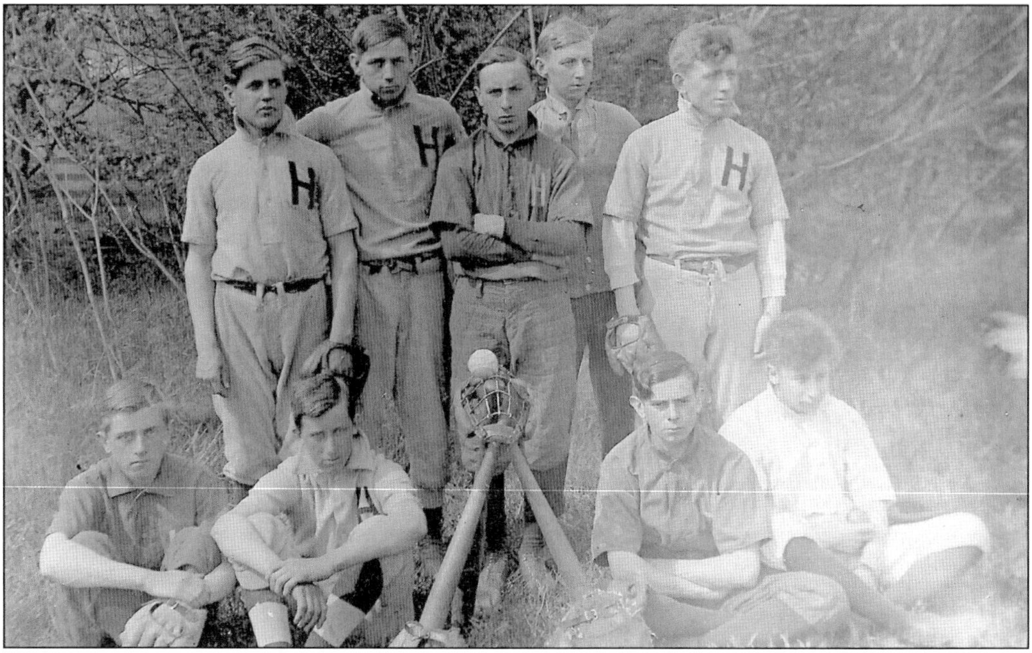

Hughesville was the home of several baseball teams including the 1905 "Soda Water" team pictured above. From left to right are (first row) Louie Gansell, Steck Hill, Bill Bubb, and Rud Morgan; (second row) ? Springer, Ralph Swartz, Charlie Wetherall, unidentified, and Ward Smith. Below is the town baseball team that was runner up for the county league pennant in 1908. They are, from left to right, (first row) Lawrence Swartz (pitcher), George Poust (mascot and bat boy), and Pete Ritter (coach and catcher); (second row) Robert (Bobbie) Roberts (third base), William Byrnes (second base), Claude Wyckoff (right field), Burrus Woodley (pitcher), Pierce Travelet (first base), and Danny Fisher (catcher); (third row) Judson Coleman (manager and town undertaker), William (Billie) Hughes (left field), Ellery Swank (center field), Ralph Croman (shortstop), and Charles Hauck (manager). (Courtesy of Mary Fox Odell.)

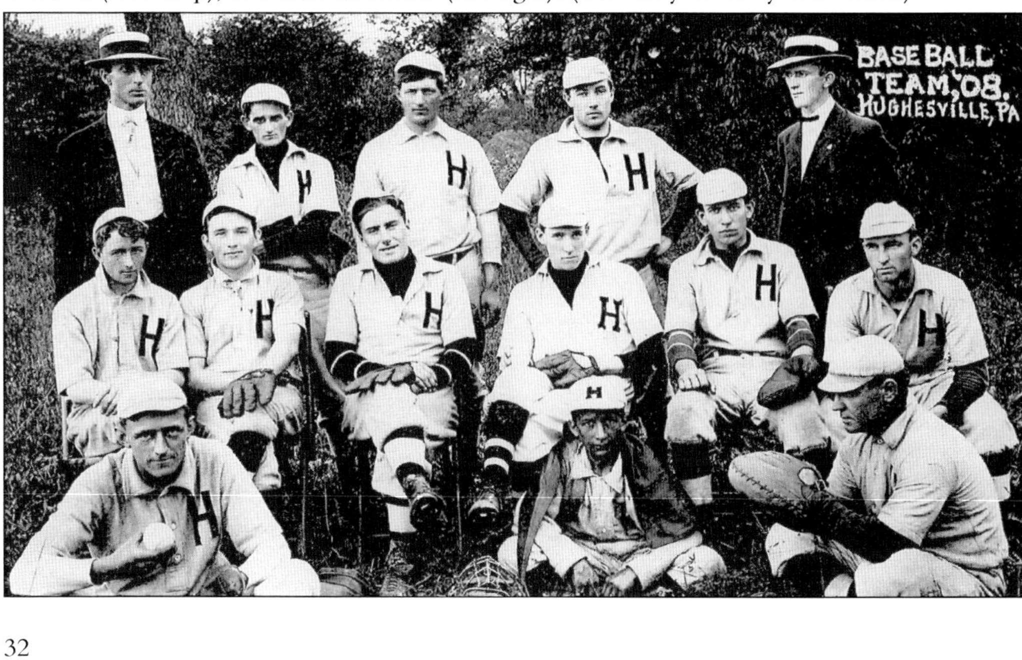

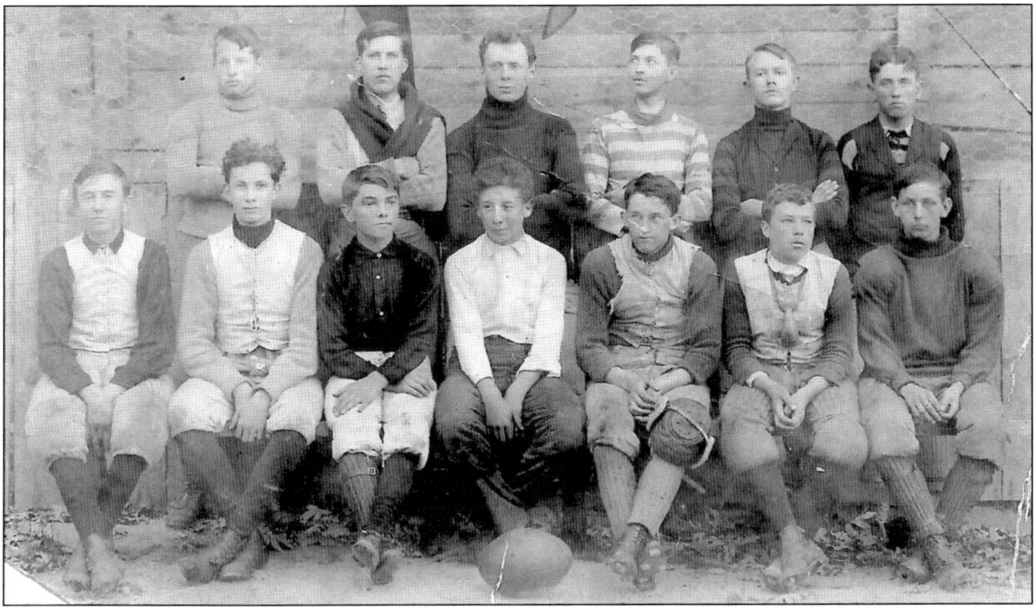

These boys who played on the high school football team in 1909 did so wearing leather helmets (see Clarence Birdsell's left knee) and button top shoes. Pictured above are, from left to right, (first row) Raymond Stevenson, Ray Albeck, J. K. Fox, Rudge Morgan, Clarence Birdsell, Vaughn Buck, and Lurray Swartz; (second row) Clinton Frantz, Ivan Buck, Harold Boak, Howard Kauffman, Fred Kniepe, and Otto Edkin. A high school girls basketball team in the early 1930s includes, pictured below from left to right, (first row) Mary Ashkar, Vivian Robb, and Kate Sones; (second row) Elizabeth Simmons, Claudia Crossley, Grethel Hughes, Ellen Boatman, and Arlenea Starr; (third row) Grace Sones, Bob Smith (coach), Edna Robb, Peg Corson, and ? Colley. (Above, courtesy of Mary Fox Odell; below, courtesy of the East Lycoming Historical Society.)

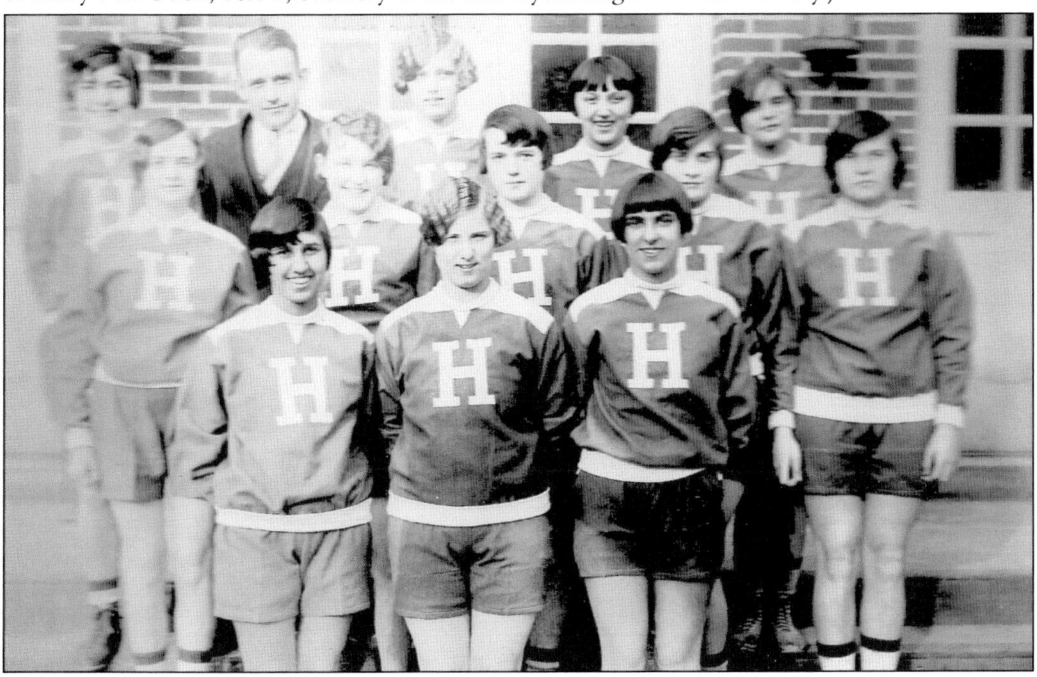

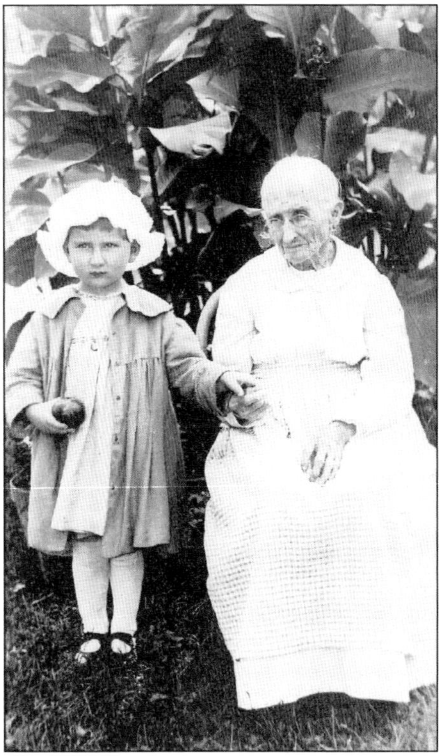

When the itinerant photographer came into the neighborhood, it was customary to request pictures of the family, such as the elderly grandmother with the toddler granddaughter or a father and daughter pose. Charlotte Houseknecht Tulley, who was born in 1835, is photographed here with her granddaughter Rose Mary Hausknecht when she was three years old in 1922. Charlotte died two years later at the age of 89.

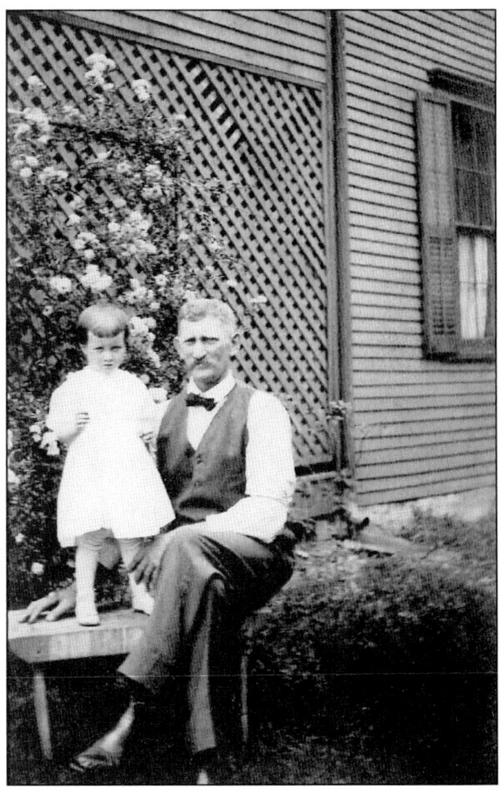

James H. Kohler, Hughesville's well-known butcher, and his daughter, Helen, are shown here in a photograph taken around 1917. Note the foliage selected as the backdrop for the photographs on this page: a broad-leafed hedge in the top image and a trellis of climbing wild roses, a mainstay in many early-20th-century flower gardens, in the photograph at right. (Courtesy of Janet Kohler.)

When Janet Kohler (seen here at right in the doorway of her father's grocery store) was a Girl Scout during the 1930s, the first commercially baked Girl Scout Cookies were sold. Until then, scouts in different parts of the country baked simple sugar cookies with their mothers. These cookies were packaged in waxed paper bags, sealed with a sticker, and sold door to door for 25¢–35¢ per dozen. (Courtesy of Janet Kohler.)

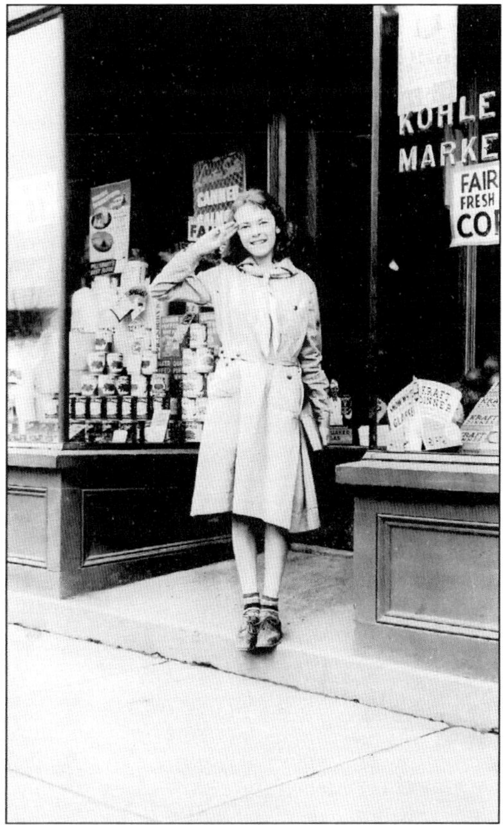

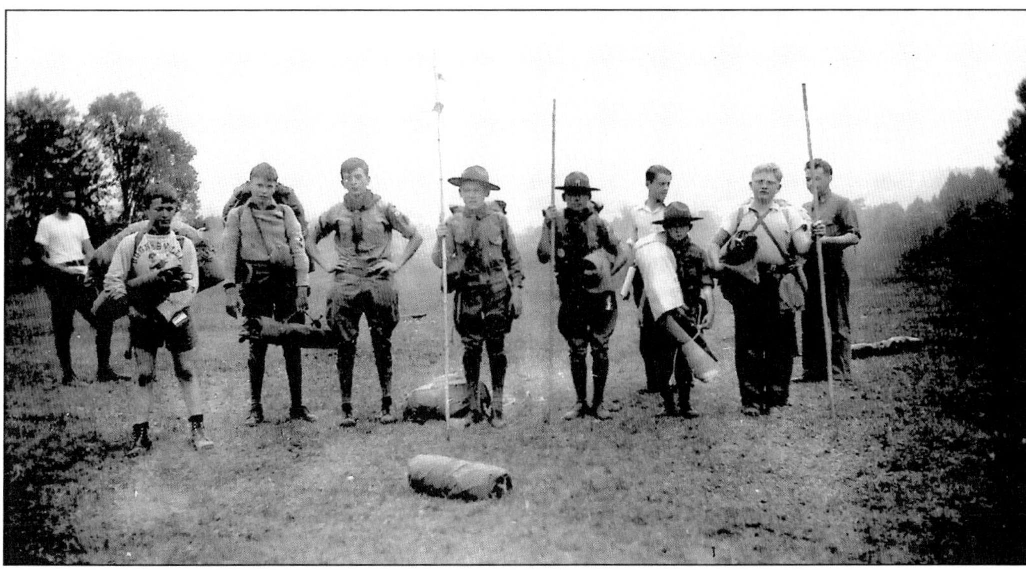

Members of the Flaming Arrow Patrol in 1938 are, from left to right, (first row) Dick Fought, Morris Egly, Robert Hess (patrol leader), Robert Odell, Harry Keller, Paul Barner, and Clifford Morgan; (second row, judges) Glenn Aderhold, Gordon McCarty, and Paul Keller. At a camporee that year, according to scout leader Lewis Creveling's notes, the Flaming Arrow Patrol "did the most grunting, complaining, and work in general." (Courtesy of Tom Crawley.)

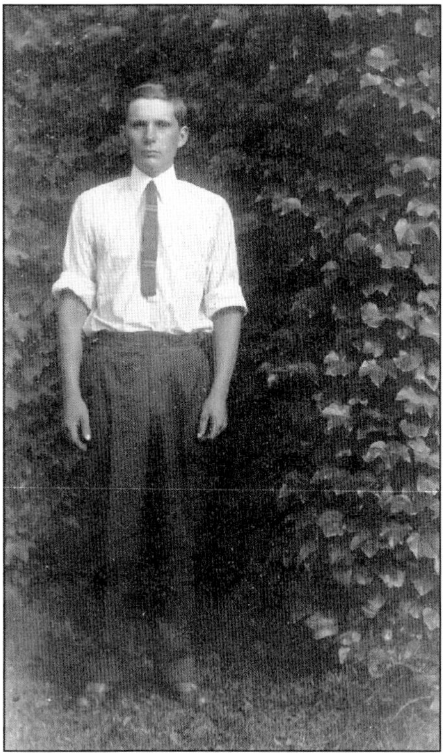

Harry L. Rogers Sr. graduated from the Muncy Normal School, taught the eighth grade at the Tivoli schoolhouse, and was in the first graduating class of the Pennsylvania State Police when motorcycles were their primary form of transportation. He is pictured here before his two-year stint in the military during World War I, and before he became Hughesville's first police chief in 1926. (Courtesy of H. Scott Knyrim.)

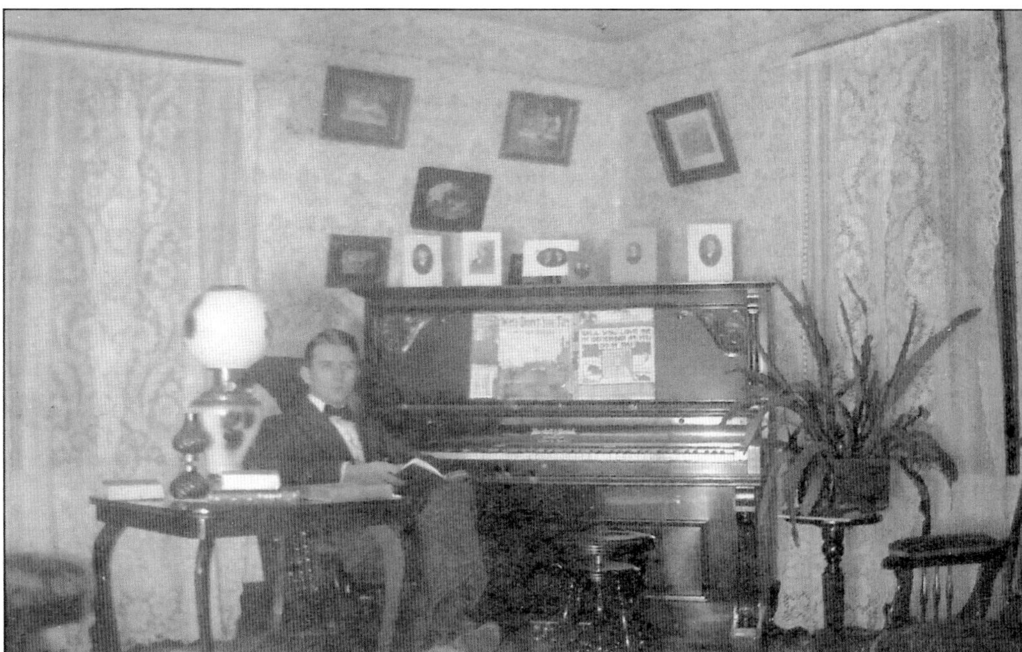

Before the widespread introduction of the radio in the 1920s and 1930s, the family piano provided much of the entertainment at home. Ralph Hausknecht is shown here seated next to a Marshall and Wendall piano, where the sheet music for James J. Walker's "Will You Love Me in December as You Do in May" is waiting to be played.

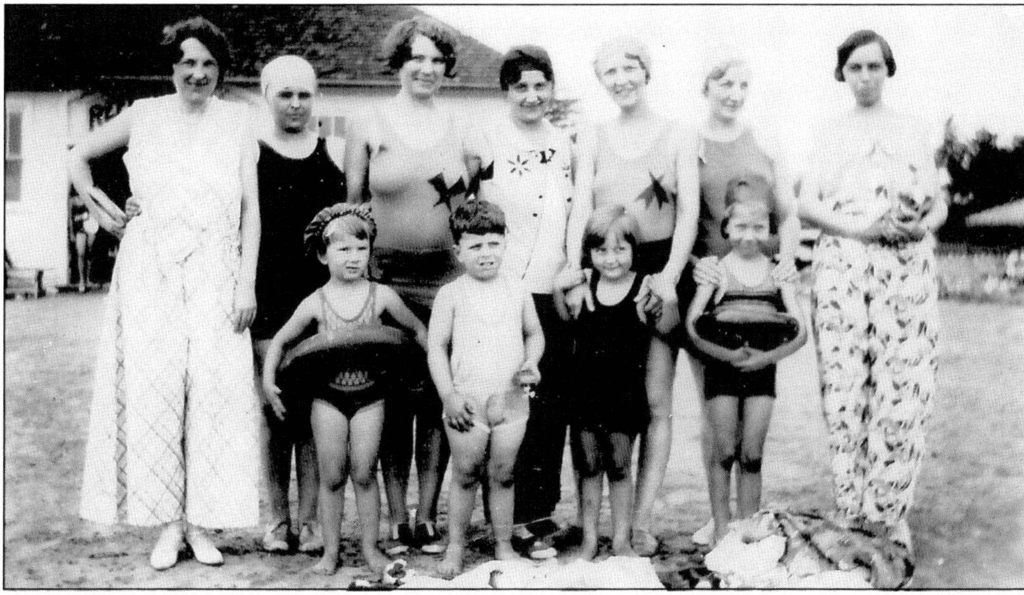

In the summertime, taking a train trip up to Lake Mokoma in Sullivan County was a fun distraction, as seen here with this group of Hughesville moms and their children around 1935. Pictured from left to right are (first row) Mary Margaret McClintock, Kenny Poust, Jean Poust, and Mary Fox; (second row) Grace McCarty Stoltz, Elizabeth Poust, Florence McClintock, unidentified, Marion Poust, Mary Fox, and Carolyn Kohler. (Courtesy of Janet Kohler.)

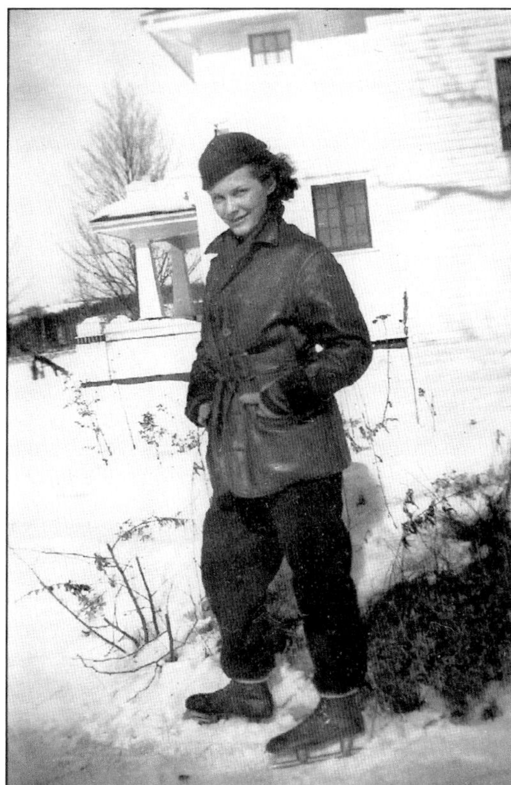

Wintertime ice-skating on Muncy Creek was also a favorite form of entertainment, as shown here by Helen Fought Barlett. It is said that once the ice froze above the mill dam, one could ice-skate "all the way to Picture Rocks and back until the first spring thaw." (Courtesy of Joe Barlett.)

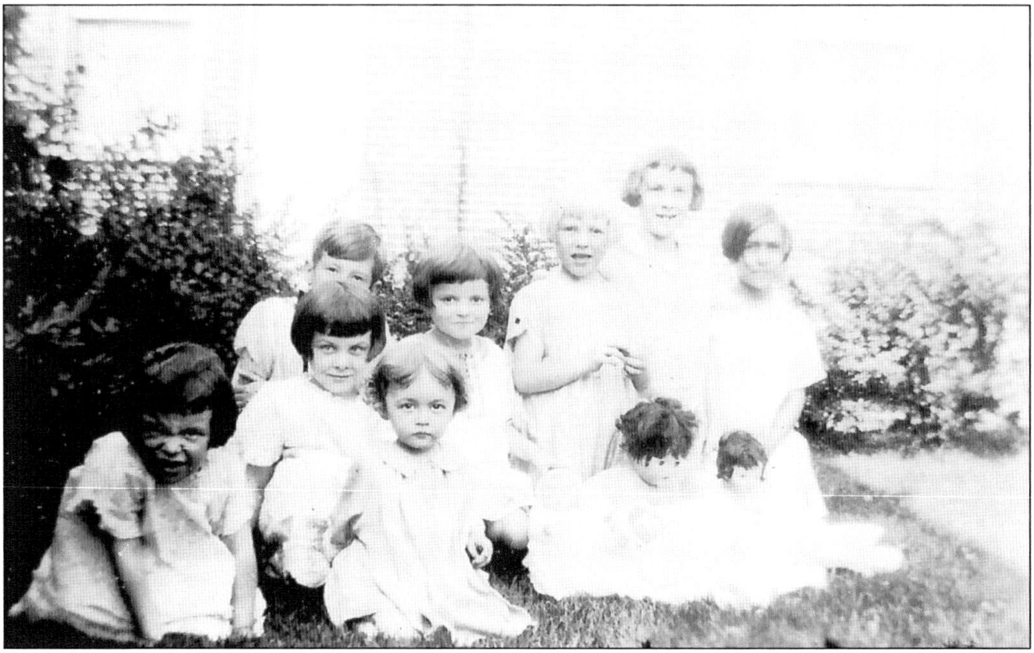

These girls enjoying a neighborhood birthday party around 1927 all lived on Water Street except for the youngest guest, 2-year-old Janet Kohler. Seen here are, from left to right, (first row) 5-year-old Helen Fought and Janet Kohler; (second row) 3-year-old Regina Fought, 7-year-old Georgianna Smith, 5-year-old Peggy Shafer, 5-year-old Thelma Siebert, 11-year-old Irene Smith, and 7-year-old Rebecca Ginter. (Courtesy of Janet Kohler.)

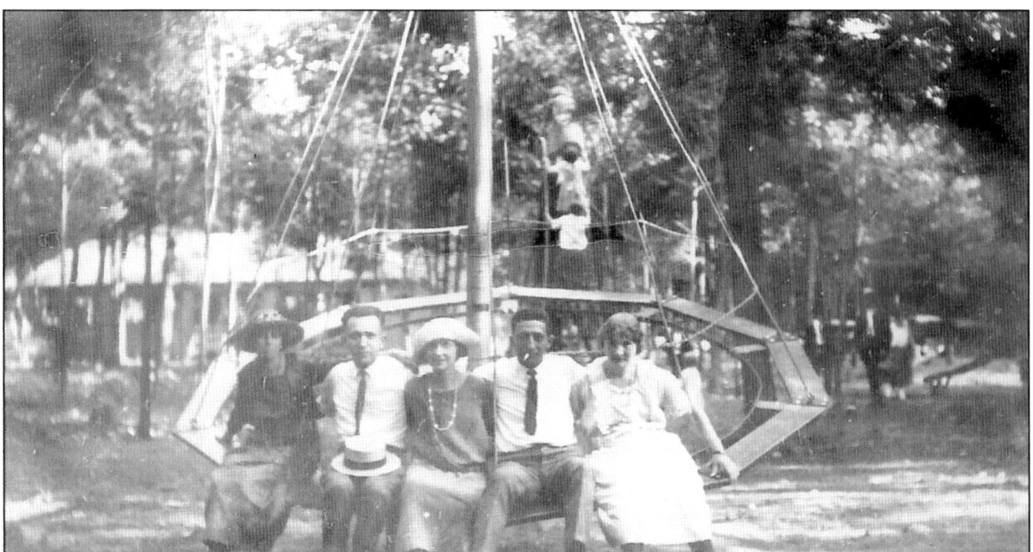

A fun Sunday outing could be a ride up to Picture Rocks' Van Rensselaer Park (named for one of the founding members of the town, A. Rensselaer Sprout) where these friends stop for a moment to get a picture taken in 1916. Seated here on the merry-go-round are, from left to right, Carolyn Kohler, Guy Arnold, Grace McCarty Stoltz, George Poust, and Ruth Arnold. (Courtesy of Janet Kohler.)

Two

The Merchant, the Miller, the Butcher, and the Banker

The first settlers in Hughesville needed supplies; seeds to plant in their fields, feed ground for their livestock, shoes for their horses, wheels for their wagons, food for their tables, and furniture for their homes. They needed hotels for their visitors and a post office for their mail. They needed a doctor for their sick and an undertaker for their dead. When the railroad tracks were laid in town, Hughesville grew even faster and provided even more opportunities. Friends became business partners, and fathers and sons worked together to start new companies.

A typical family business was one started by Hughesville's William Frontz. He began a partnership with his friend Jeremiah Kelly in the mercantile business. Their partnership ended, but Frontz continued the business, first with his brother George and then with his son Walter. Under the name William Frontz and Son, this general store sold (in 1886) items such as a coffee mill for 70¢, suspenders and razor straps for 35¢ each, 12 pounds of nails for 48¢, and a pair of overalls for $1.

Throughout the valley, descendents of the original settlers of Hughesville can still be found. Their children and grandchildren often carried on family businesses. Names such as Fought, Swisher, Freezer, and Buck are synonymous with the businesses that continue to operate today. Other names like Ed Birdsell, Wilbur Ash, Irvin Palmer, Jerry Kelly, Sandy Reed, George Gray, Kenny Poust, Granny Fought, DeWitt Bodine, John Turner, and J. K. Rishel bring back memories of stories told by a generation that will soon be gone. This chapter will take a look at how these stories began.

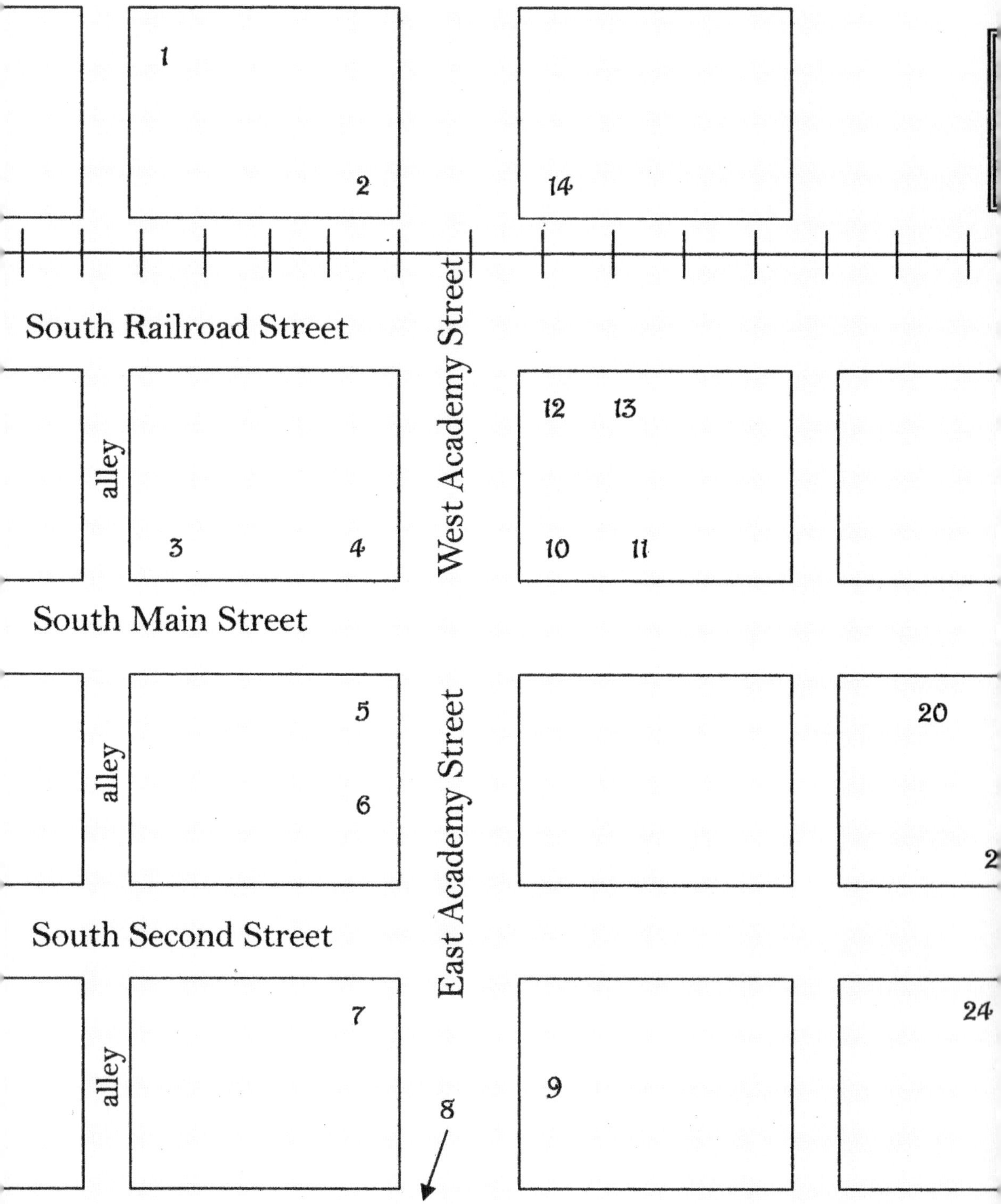

South Railroad Street
South Main Street
South Second Street
West Academy Street
East Academy Street
alley
alley
alley
1
2
3
4
5
6
7
8
9
10
11
12
13
14
20
24

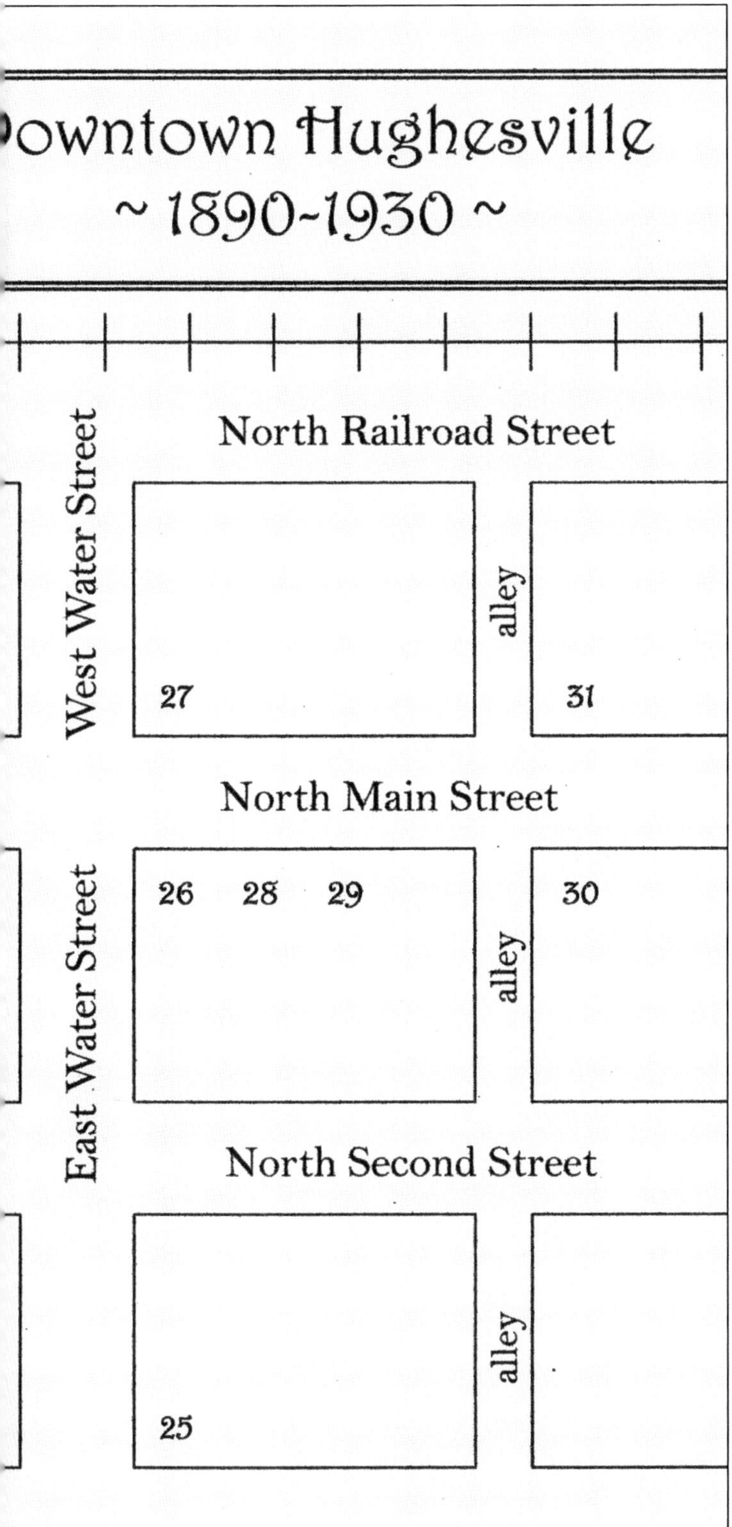

This map shows a number of businesses and community organizations in the Hughesville area: Hughesville Furniture Company (1), Shindel Silk Mill (2), Methodist Episcopal church (3), Lutheran church (4), Williamsport and North Branch Railroad office (5), Hughesville Printing Company/Hughesville Mail office (6), Evangelical church (7), Rishel's Furniture Company (8), Royal Shirt Factory (9), Hughesville Public School (10), site of first Lutheran church (11), Snowden Brothers Foundry/Machine Shop (12), Swartz Planing Mill (13), Williamsport and North Branch Railroad passenger depot (14), Reeder and Company Coal and Lumber Yard (15), jail (16), Fire Hose Company/town hall (17), First National Bank (18), post office (19), Coleman Funeral Home (20), Laird/George O. Gray General Store/Kohler's Market (21), Friends Holiness Church (22), Evangelical church around 1896 (23), Hughesville Opera House (24), Baptist church (25), Ash General Store (26), American House Hotel (27), Telephone Exchange (28), Grange National Bank (29), Jeremiah Kelly's Store (30), and the United States Hotel/Rohrhirsch Hotel/Fought's Market (31).

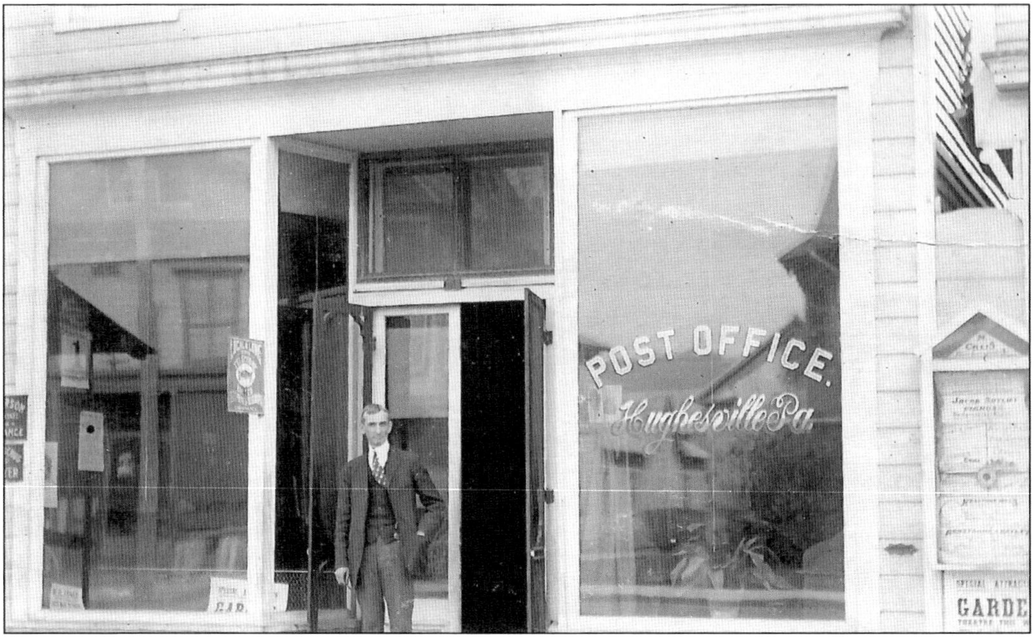

Postmaster Charles Steck Hill is shown here standing in front of the Hughesville Post Office on Main Street around 1917. He served as Hughesville's postmaster for nine years until the early 1920s, when he returned to his job as a furniture finisher at the J. K. Rishel Furniture Company, where he was first hired in 1883. (Courtesy of the East Lycoming Historical Society.)

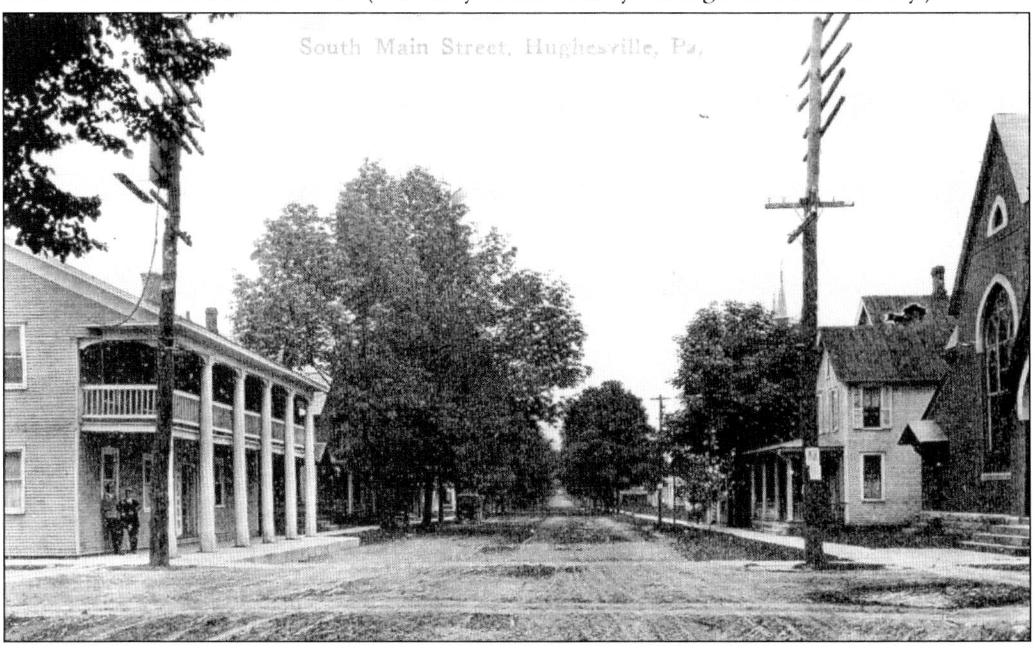

The building on the left is the former Eagle Hotel, which operated between 1868 and 1887. It was eventually remodeled into offices for the Williamsport and North Branch Railroad. The taller gentleman seen standing under the balcony is Delmar Townsend, railroad manager. In 1948, this building was moved 50 feet back from the street and still stands today at the corner of Main and Academy Streets. (Courtesy of Stewart Hill.)

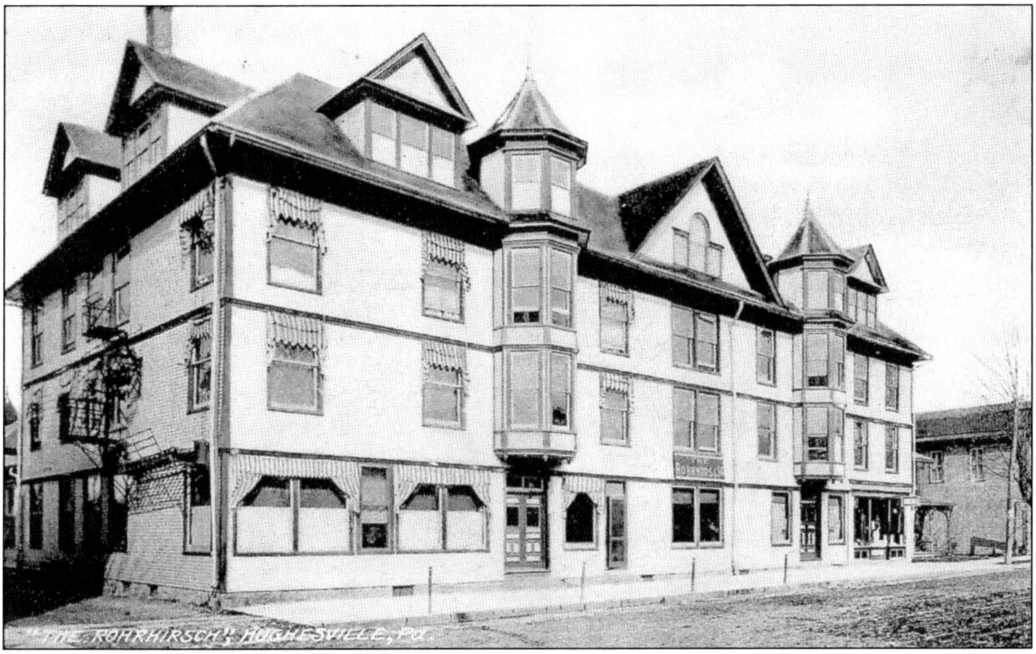

The Rohrhirsh Hotel, first known as the United States Hotel when it opened in 1820, stood on the corner of North Main Street and Strawberry Alley. In 1926, a fire destroyed the building, which by then held a number of stores including the Cadman Hardware and Plumbing Store, Fought's General Store, a small restaurant, and a number of second- and third-floor apartments. (Courtesy of Polly Hess.)

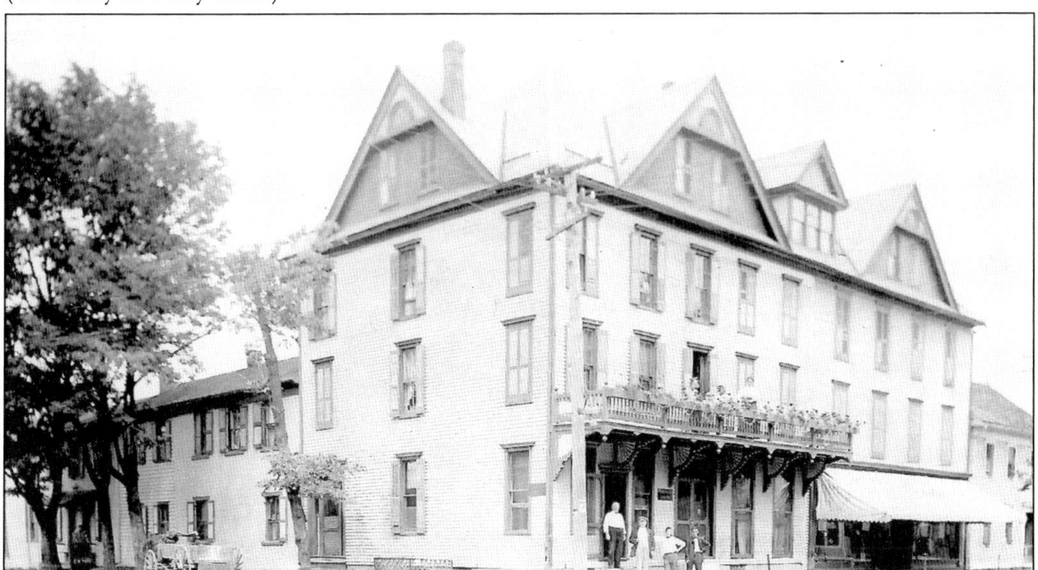

The American House Hotel was owned by Peter Ritter until 1902, when it was sold to Joseph Siegfried, who renamed it the Siegfried Hotel. This large building on the corner of Main and Water Streets burned to the ground on November 1, 1931. It was considered a total loss with damages estimated at $70,000. (Courtesy of Elizabeth Rogers Knyrim.)

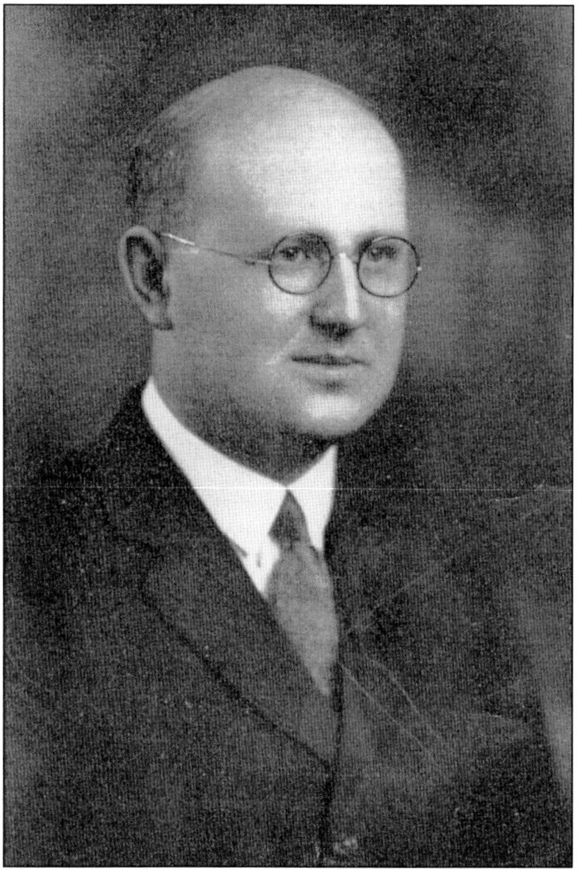

Dr. Irvin T. Gilmore (pictured at left) established his medical offices in Picture Rocks the year after he received his medical degree from Jefferson Medical College in Philadelphia in 1914. He was one of the 12 physicians and surgeons in the Montgomery, Muncy, Hughesville, and Picture Rocks area who helped establish a hospital that served the residents living southeast of Williamsport. That hospital (pictured below) was a small 18-bed facility that opened in 1922 on East Water Street in Muncy. Housed in a Victorian-style home originally owned by the Noble family, the original Muncy Valley Hospital operated until the mid-1940s. (Left, courtesy the *History of Lycoming County Pennsylvania Vol. II* by Col. Thomas W. Lloyd; below, courtesy of Janet Kohler.)

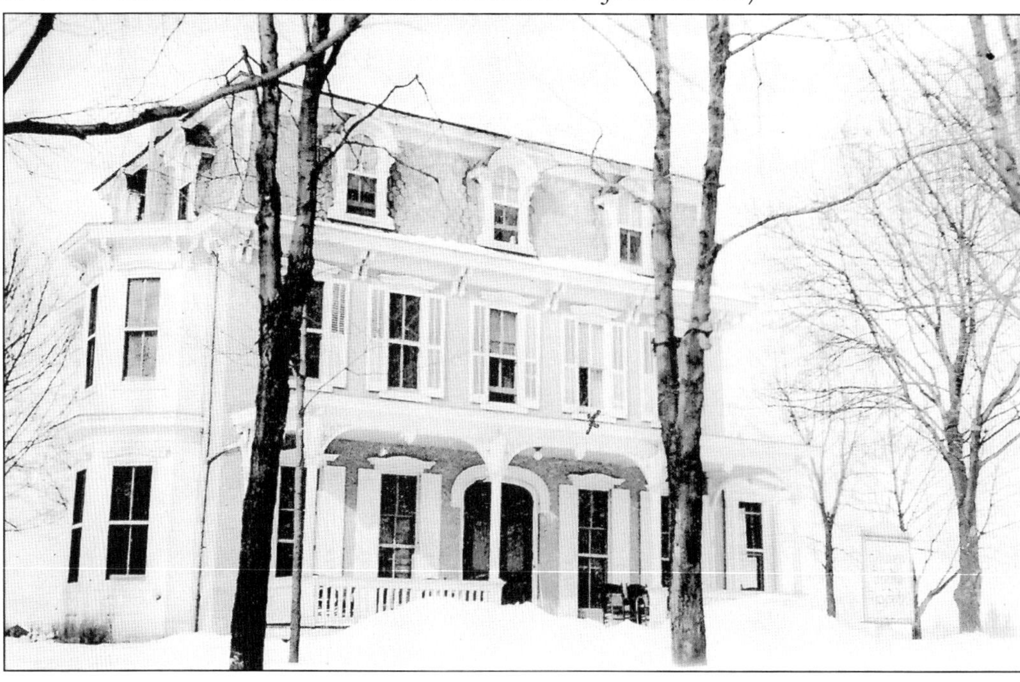

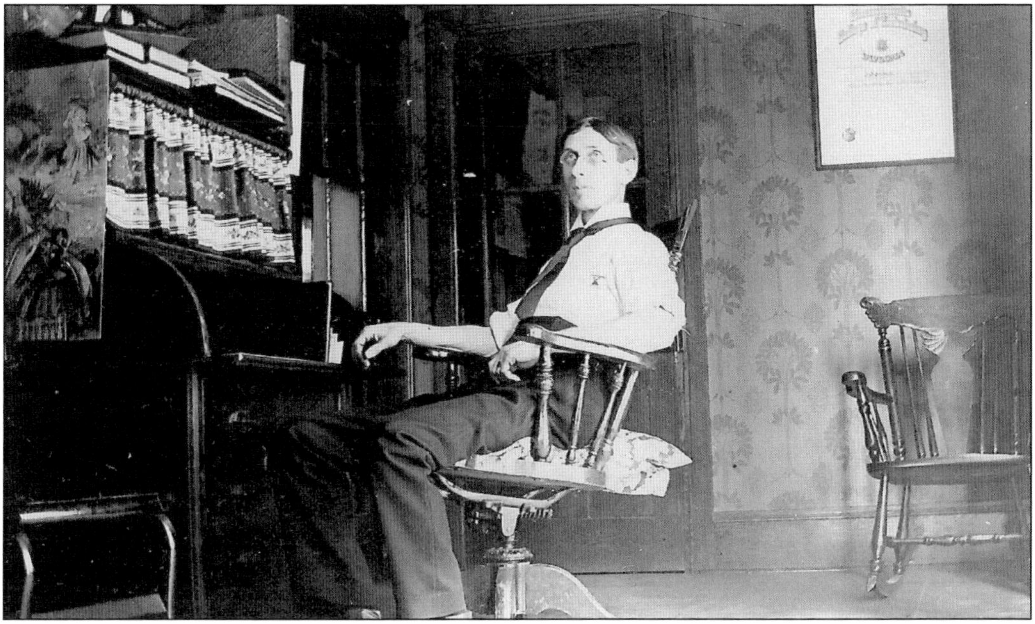

Natives of Bradford County, Judson O. Coleman and his wife, Corrine, came to Hughesville in 1906, where he established a funeral home business at their first residence on Main Street (below). Coleman is seen in the photograph above, seated in his office with a framed certificate from the Massachusetts College of Embalming hanging on the wall behind him. At the time, embalming instruction was provided by chemical companies and teachers who traveled around the country giving two-day courses. In addition to his duties as town undertaker, Coleman also helped manage the baseball team (see page 32) and ran a Bible study class at the Lutheran church. (Courtesy of the Sullivan County Historical Society and Museum.)

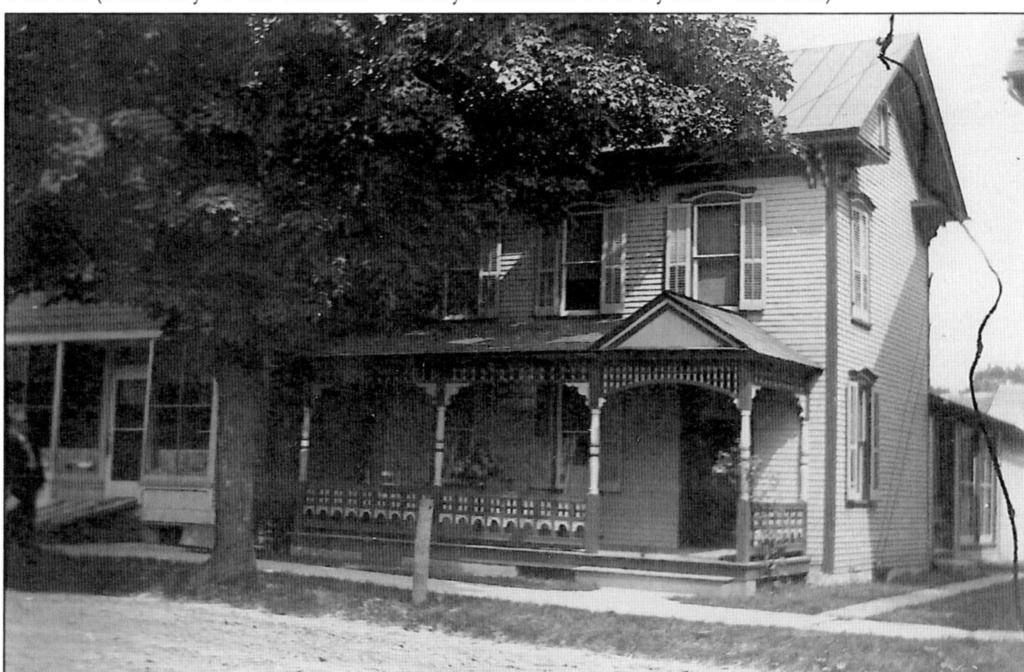

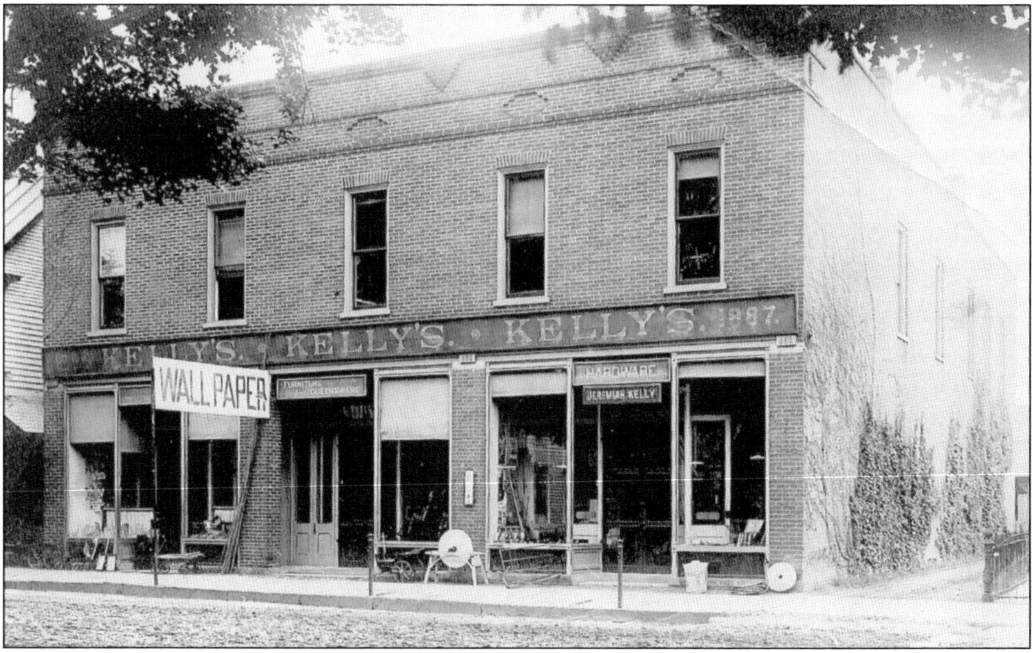

Jeremiah (Jerry) Kelly made a name for himself in Hughesville as a respected and involved member of the community. He ran this general store, the largest in town, which sold hardware, furniture, groceries, and household goods including wallpaper and Queensware dishes. Kelly also served as president of the Pleasant Hill Cemetery and was a member of the Hughesville School Board in the 1860s. (Courtesy of the East Lycoming Historical Society.)

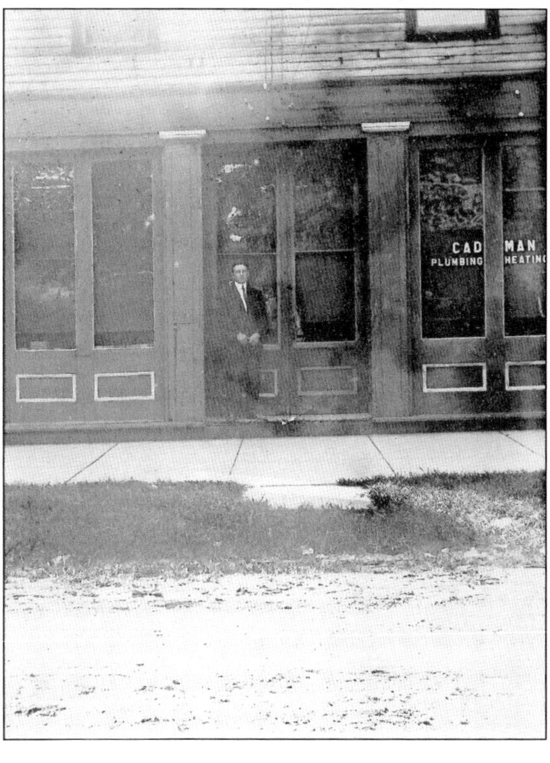

English-born Charles Cadman purchased the former Rohrhirsch Hotel building around 1923 and converted it into stores and apartments. He opened Cadman's Plumbing and Heating on the first floor and had a successful business until March 1926, when fire swept through the building, totally destroying it. (Courtesy of the East Lycoming Historical Society.)

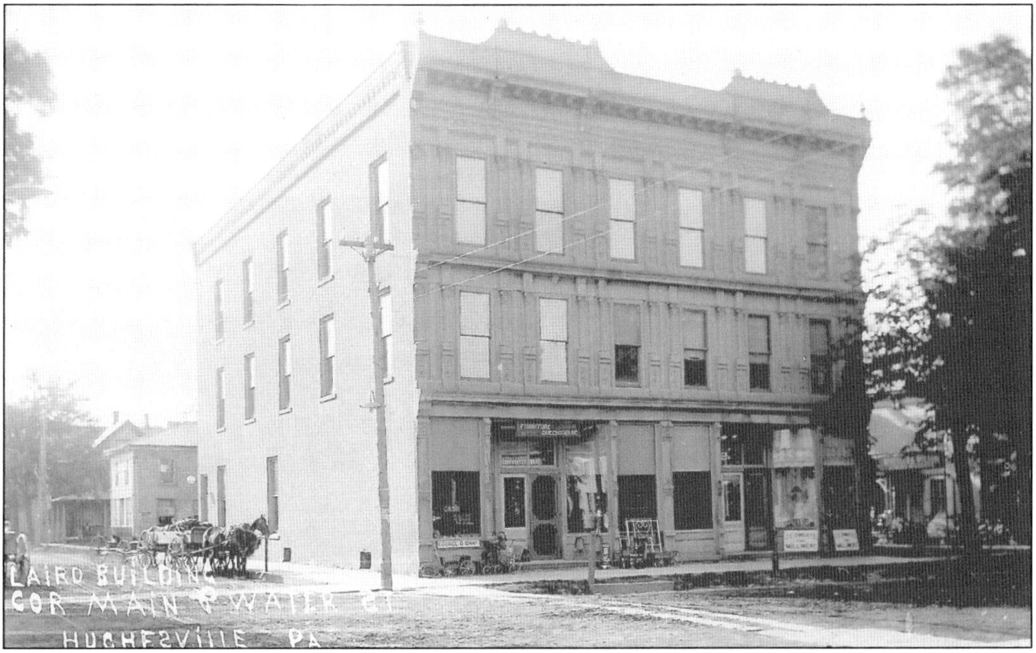

On the southeastern corner of Water and Main Streets, this three-story building (above) was known as the James Laird Company Store. George O. Gray (who was Jerry Kelly's son-in-law) bought it and opened a general and furniture store on the north side. Area residents still hold memories of the dimly lit store and the stale candy that was available for sale at Gray's store. In the southern side of the building, Charles F. Johnson operated a jewelry and optical store, and two sisters opened a millinery shop (below) where women's hats and ribbon were sold. (Courtesy of the East Lycoming Historical Society.)

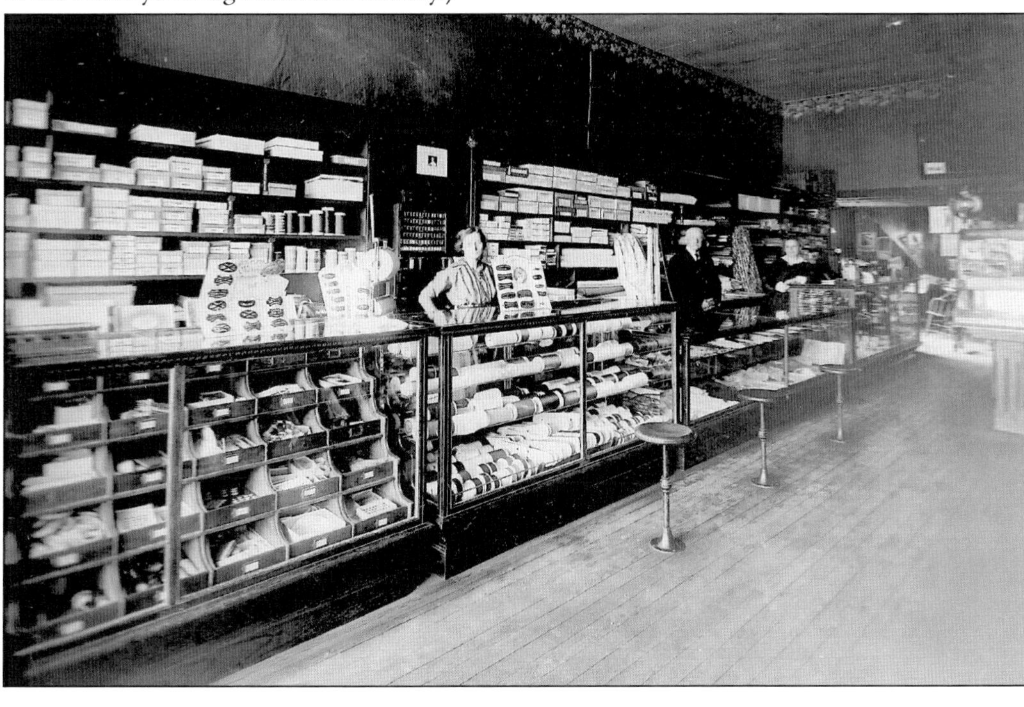

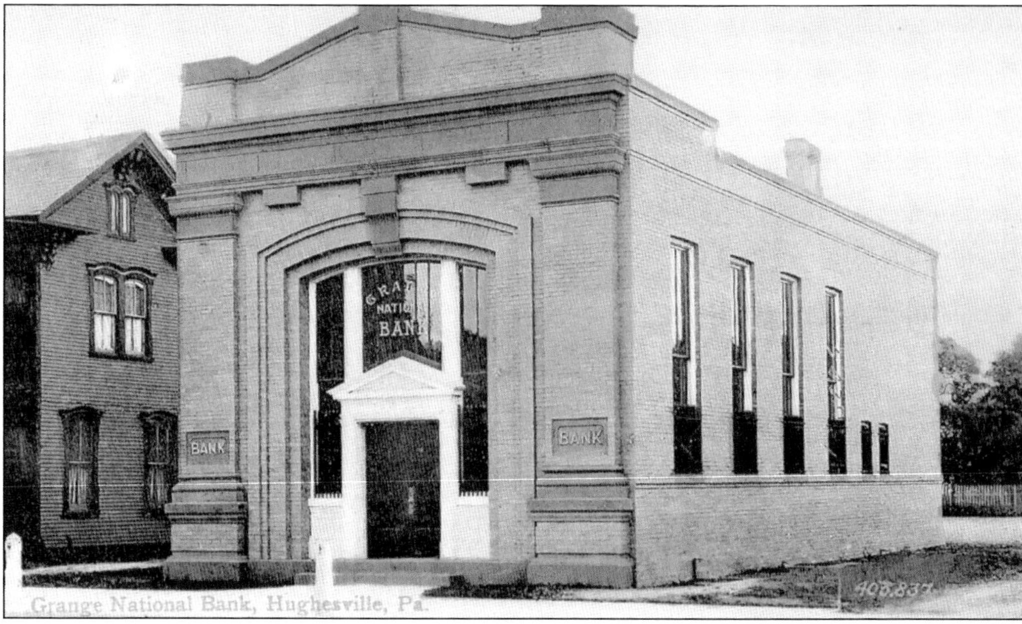

The Grange National Bank opened its doors for business on February 1, 1908, with James Boak as bank president. According to the February 6, 1908, edition of the *Hughesville Mail*, "Upon entering the bank building, one is attracted by the beauty and comfort of the main business room . . . [with] the interior furnished in red oak and counters [that] are beautiful pieces of cabinet maker's art." (Courtesy of Stewart Hill.)

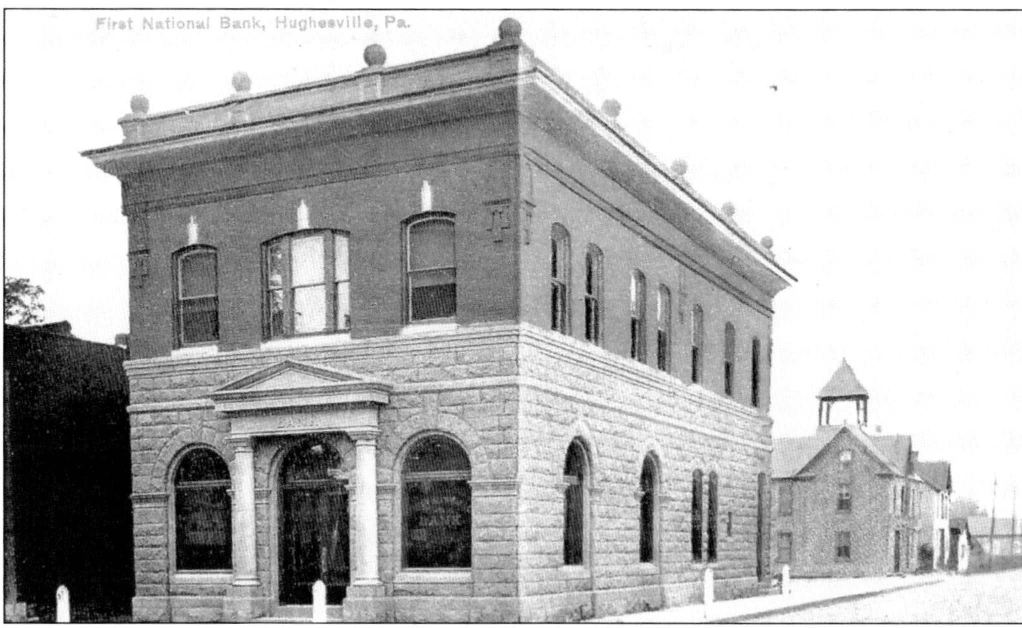

On the corner of Main and Academy Streets, the town barber cut hair and sold roasted peanuts and penny candy. In 1888, the First National Bank opened for business next door. In less than 20 years, the barber sold the corner lot to the bank, and this new building (pictured here) was erected and opened in 1907, with Jeremiah Kelly as the bank president. (Courtesy of Elizabeth Rogers Knyrim.)

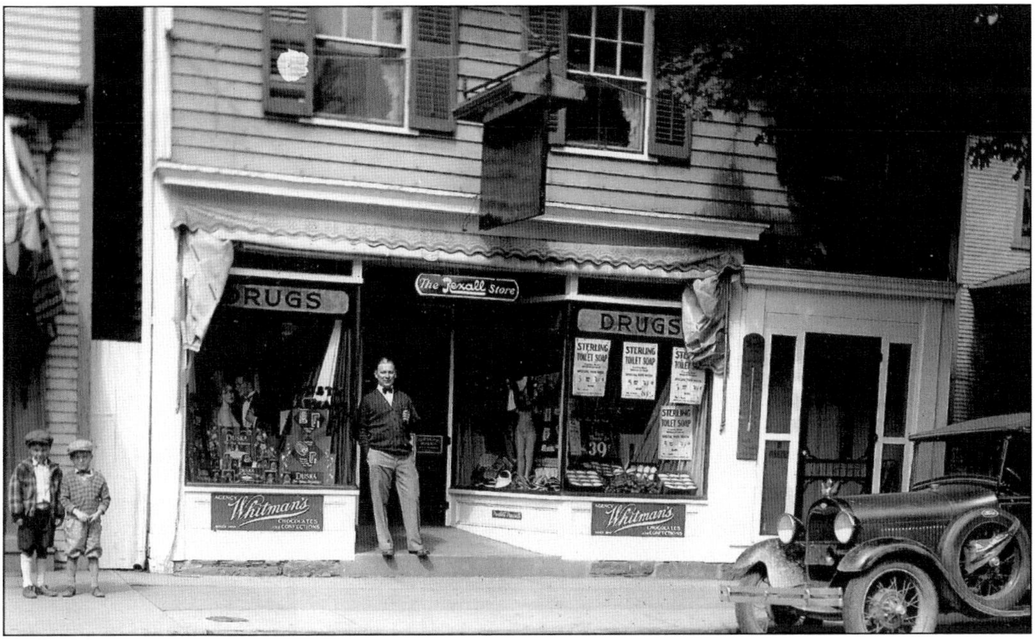

Kenneth D. Poust Sr. is pictured above at the door of his drugstore, which he established on October 25, 1925, at 17 North Main Street. Although the store and the Siegfried Hotel (formerly the American House Hotel) next door were separated by only a two-foot air space (above the two boys at left), the store survived with only water and smoke damage after fire completely destroyed the hotel in 1931. (Courtesy of Kenneth D. Poust Jr.)

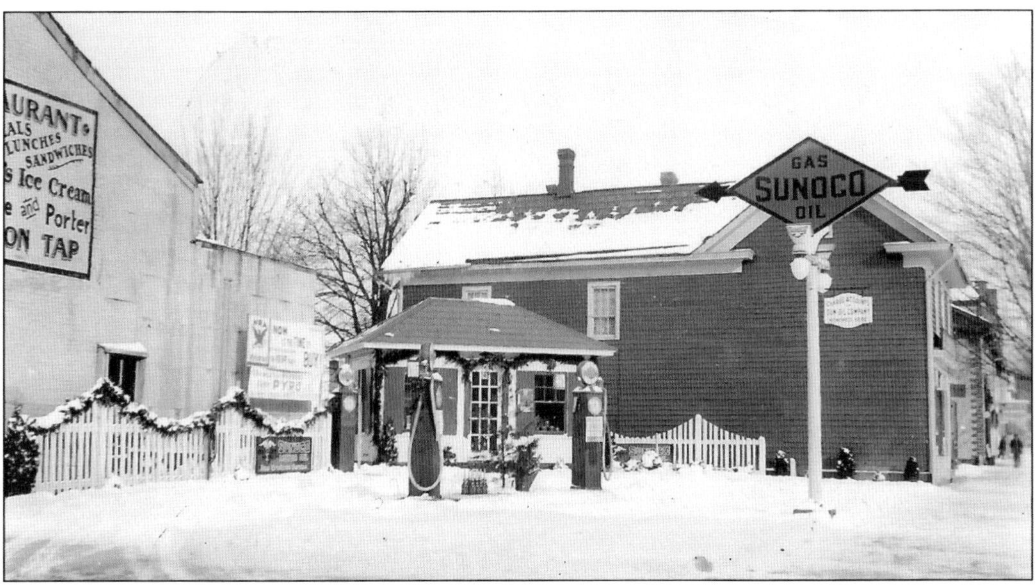

When the Siegfried Hotel burned in 1931, this Sunoco station was established on its site. An NRA Blue Eagle poster was displayed here, which meant that the owner of the business supported the efforts of Pres. Franklin Roosevelt's National Recovery Administration (NRA) programs. During the early 1930s, the NRA allowed companies to establish "codes of fair competition." (Courtesy of Lois Sites.)

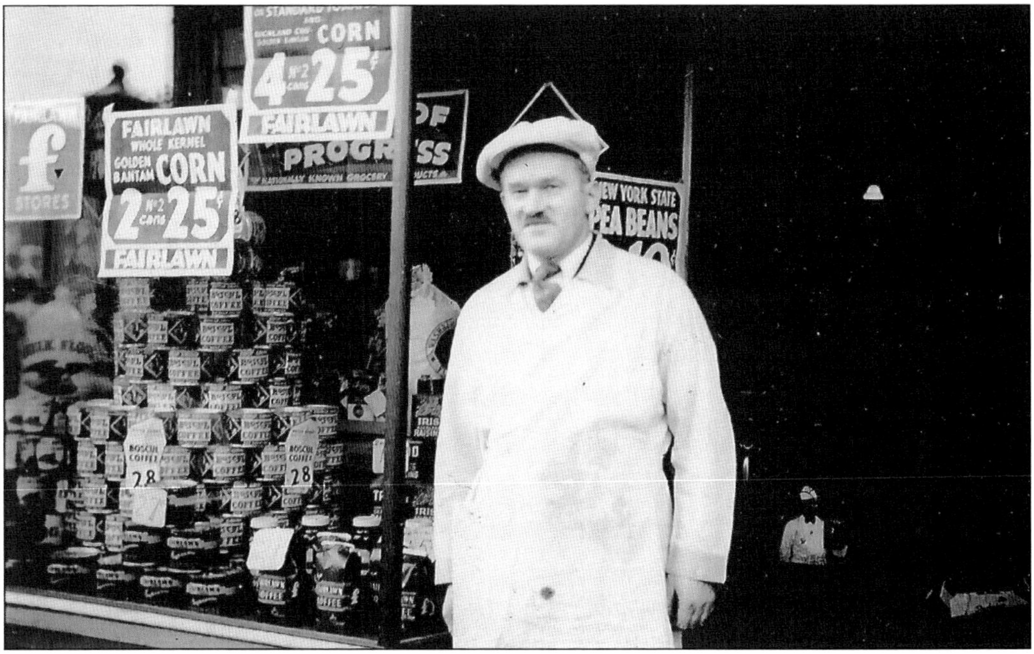

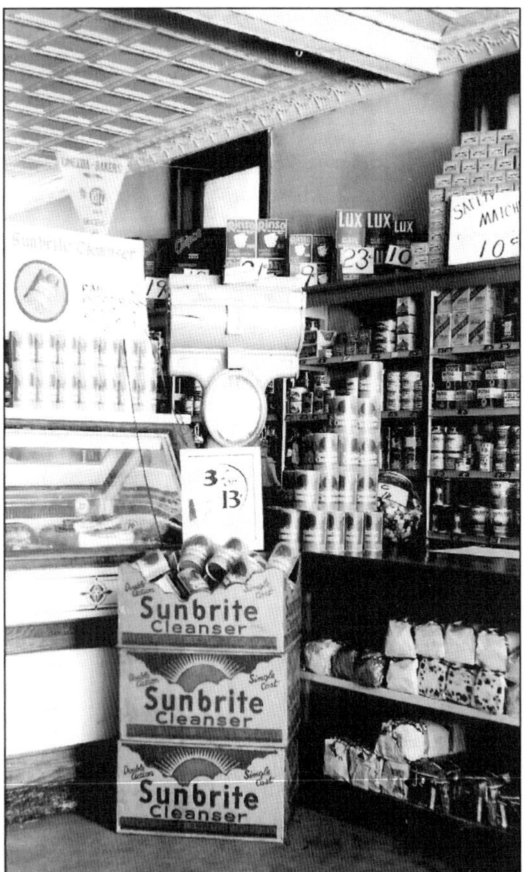

Earl Kohler is seen above standing in the doorway of Kohler's Market, first established by his father, James, in 1911. James first started butchering in Picture Rocks and then moved to Hughesville across from the George O. Gray building. James eventually moved his market to a storefront beside the Gray building. Earl and his brother LaRue continued its operation as an independent Fairlawn grocer after their father's death. At left is the interior of Kohler's Market around 1930. (Courtesy of Janet Kohler.)

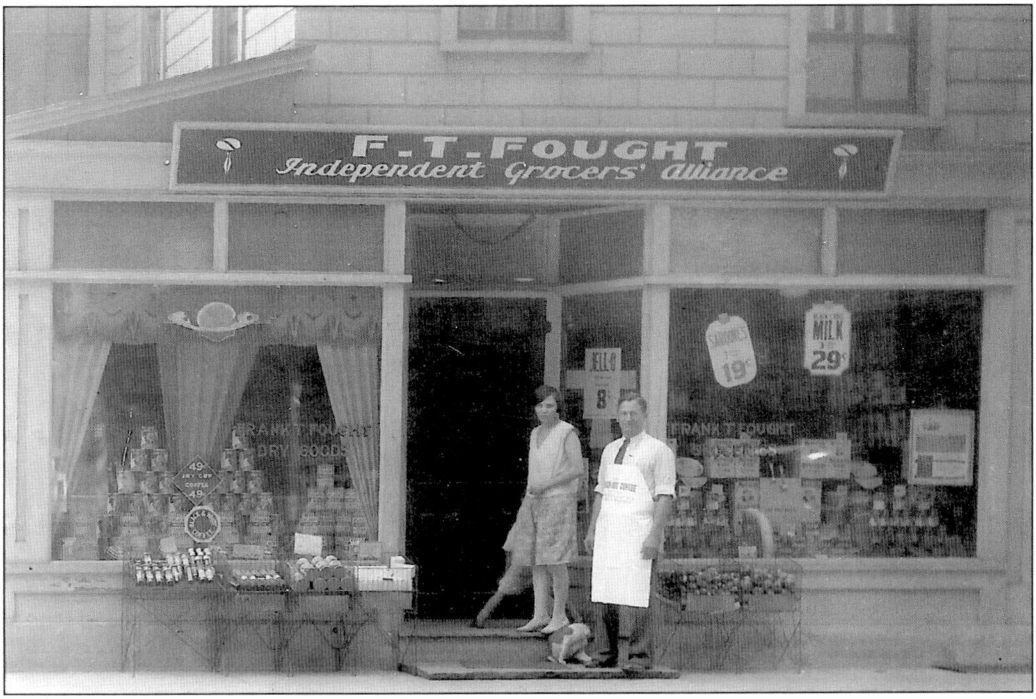

Frank T. "Granny" Fought and his wife, Valle, stand in the doorway of their store (above), which was the first place shoppers would stop when they came into town on Saturday nights. Shopping lists would be handed to Granny and Valle, who filled old banana boxes with the orders to be picked up later. The farmers returned to socialize after they did their banking and the kids were busy watching a movie at the theater. Below is Granny and his children, Dick and Mary, with the delivery truck that was used to make deliveries and to pick up local produce from farmers. And why was he called Granny? Sadly it seems that the reason has long been forgotten. (Courtesy of Joe Barlett.)

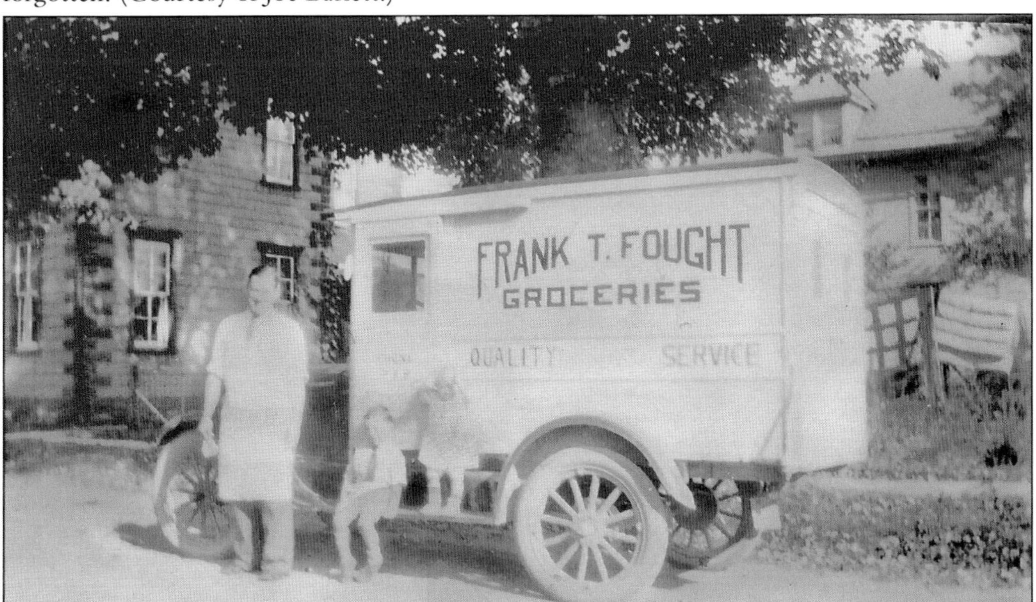

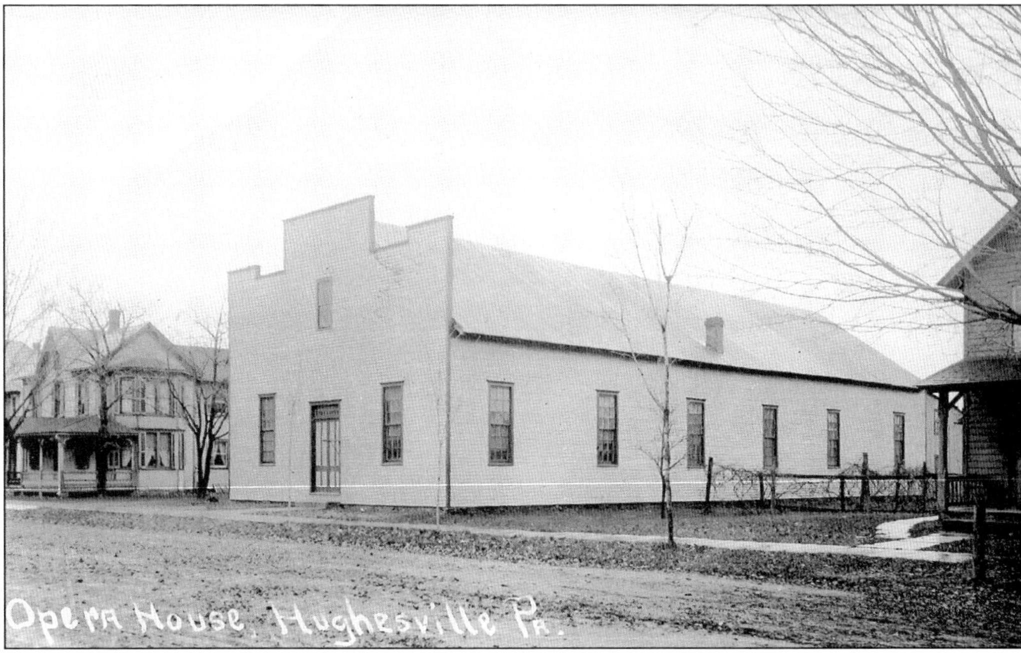

The Hughesville Drum Corp was organized in the late 1870s and raised money to build this hall in which to rehearse and perform. The Hughesville Opera House, located on South Second Street, was also the location of roller skating events, high school commencements, and talent shows. The building was sold and razed in the early 1920s, with its timber used to construct houses on the same site. (Courtesy of Mary Fox Odell.)

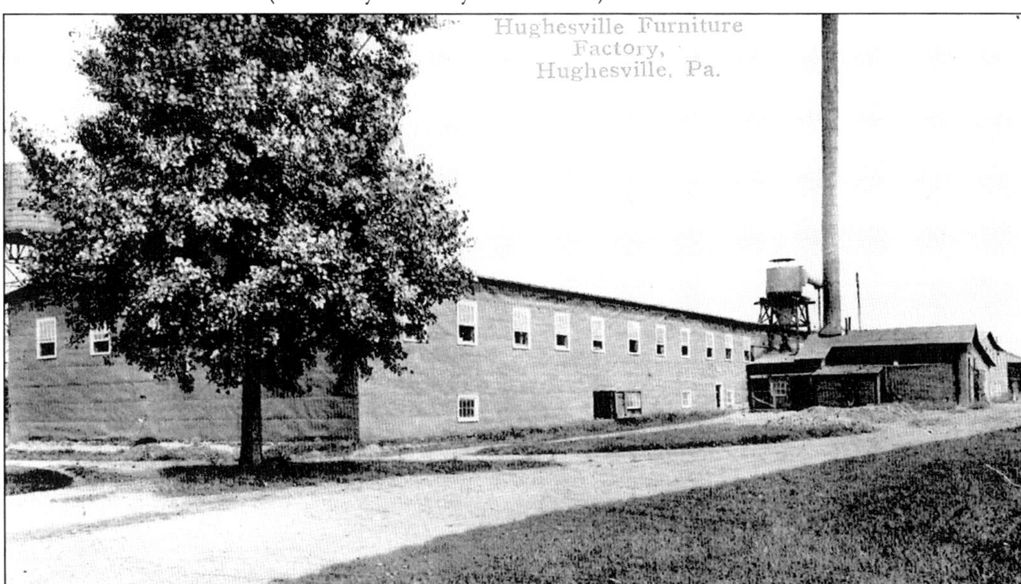

Hughesville Furniture Factory is seen here before a nighttime fire destroyed it in December 1900. Fueled by the dry timber, finished furniture, oils, and other flammable materials inside the building, the plant was quickly consumed by the fire. A number of large fires in the borough prompted the local fire company to purchase better firefighting equipment in the early 20th century. (Courtesy of Elizabeth Rogers Knyrim.)

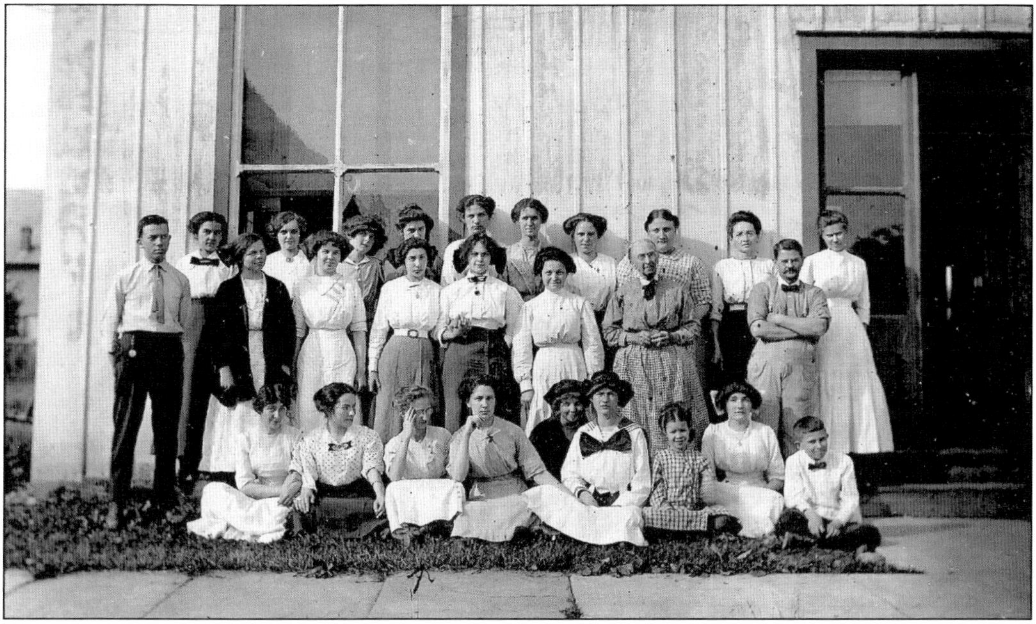

Pictured above are employees of the Royal Shirt Factory, which was located on Academy Street between Second and Third Streets. In this photograph, taken around 1912, those identified are manager William Spigelmeyer and children Annie and Kenneth, who appear at the right of the group. Charles Bubb is on the left in the second row. Others include Georgine Elliot, Ruth McClintock, Mae DeShay, Eva Wilkins, Tritta McCarty, Mabel Miller, Susie Swank, Zelpha Reese, Lois Hughes, Evelyn Johnson, Hazel Allbeck, Marie Sanders, Nora Bussler, Ethel Swartz, Cora Travlet, Breta Miller, Muriel Fague, and Eva Bussler. Below is an interior view of a factory building being erected in the early 1900s by local craftsmen and carpenters. (Courtesy of the East Lycoming Historical Society.)

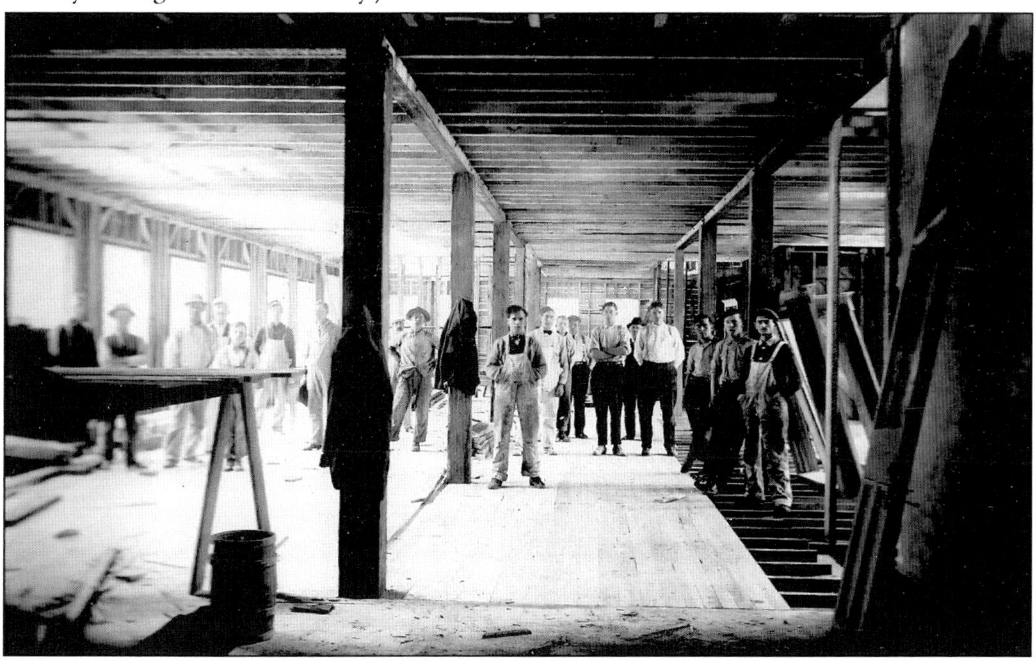

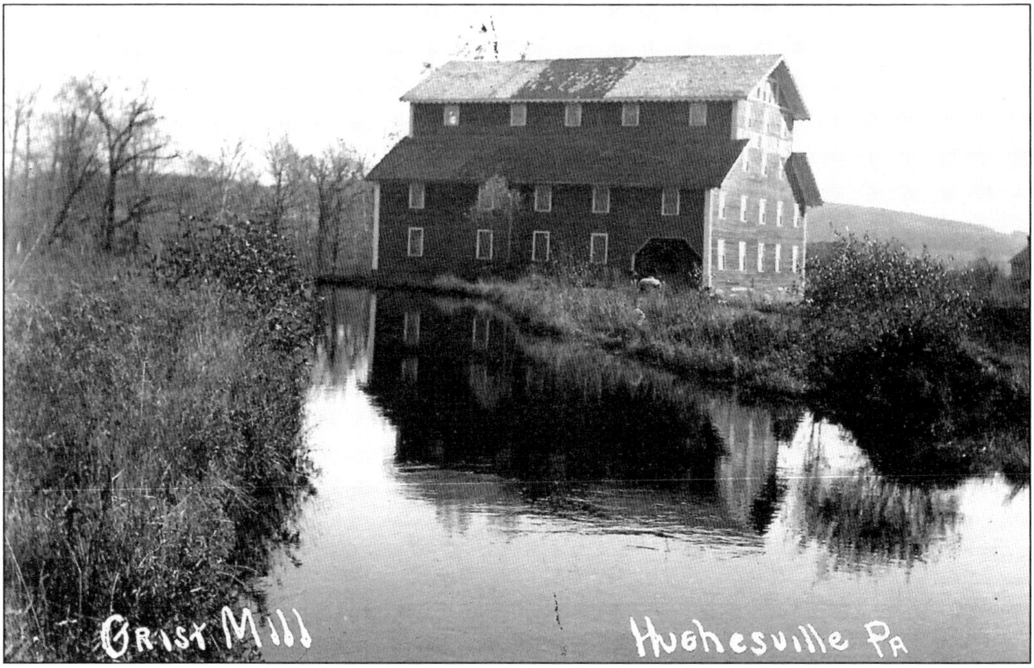

The large pond at Ball's Grist Mill (above) served as a popular swimming hole during the summer and ice-skating pond in the winter. The farmers would meet regularly at the mill—usually on rainy days so as not to interfere with fair weather farming chores—to chew the fat about crops, livestock, and the weather. But fire was always a concern at the mills. This one (below) in July 1912 quickly destroyed the Hughesville landmark. The original mill was owned by Edward Lyon but was also destroyed by fire in 1861. The threat of spontaneous combustion and fire was especially worrisome during this time of minimally effective firefighting equipment. (Above, courtesy of the East Lycoming Historical Society; below, courtesy of Stewart Hill.)

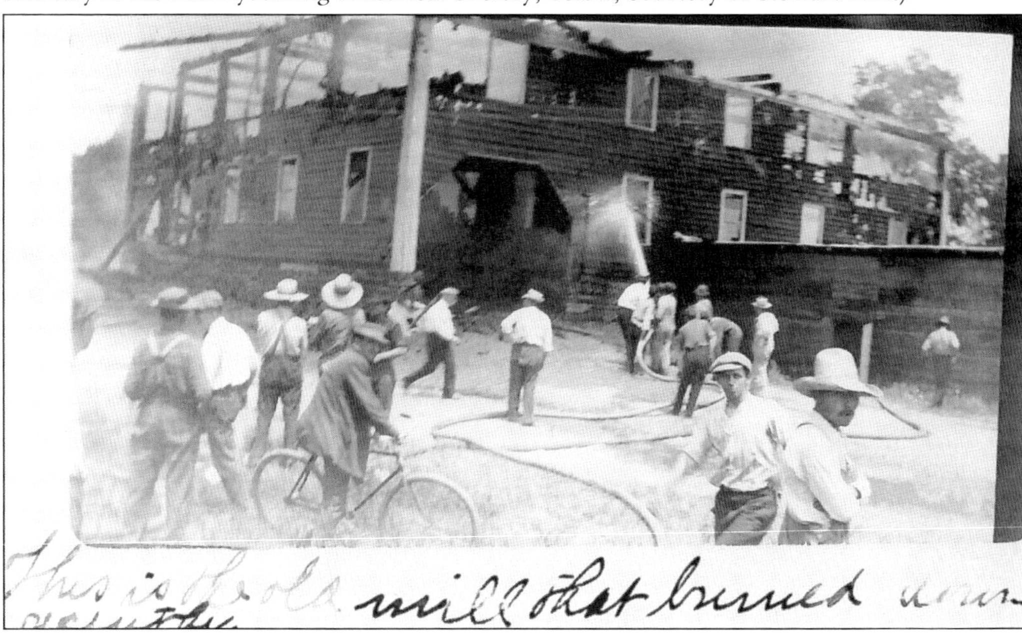

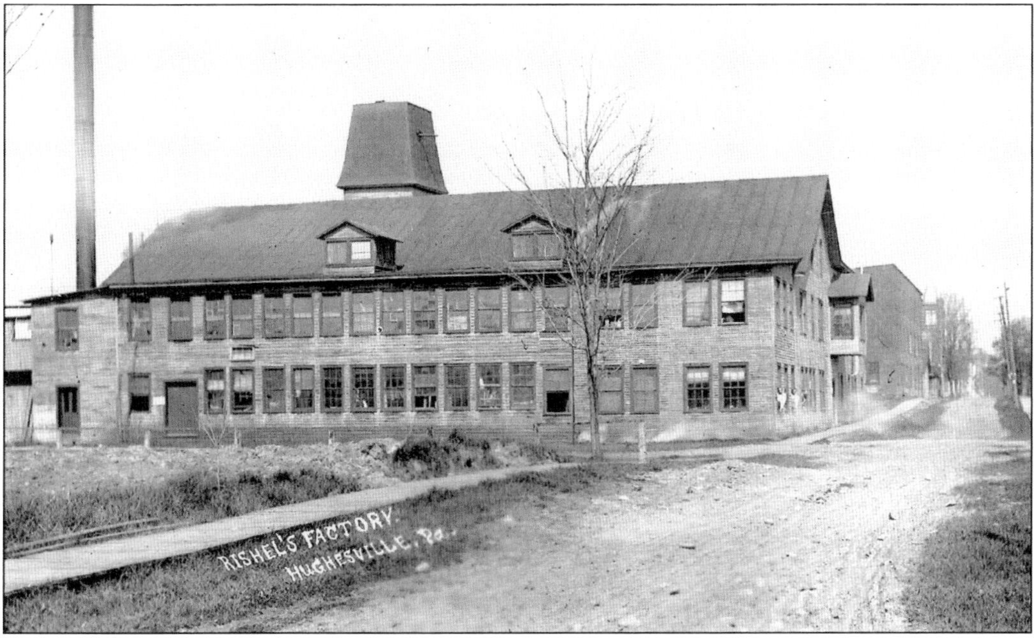

James Laird was one of the early pioneers in Hughesville who helped to establish the first Lutheran church in Hughesville and organized the first Sunday school in 1850. Making furniture was a profitable venture when Laird built this furniture factory in 1869. His son John became a partner in 1878. When the factory was sold to J. K. Rishel in 1882, John became foreman at the factory. Rishel's Furniture continued to operate successfully until a fire destroyed the plant on November 4, 1965, almost 100 years after it was founded. (Above, courtesy of Mary Fox Odell; below, courtesy of the East Lycoming Historical Society.)

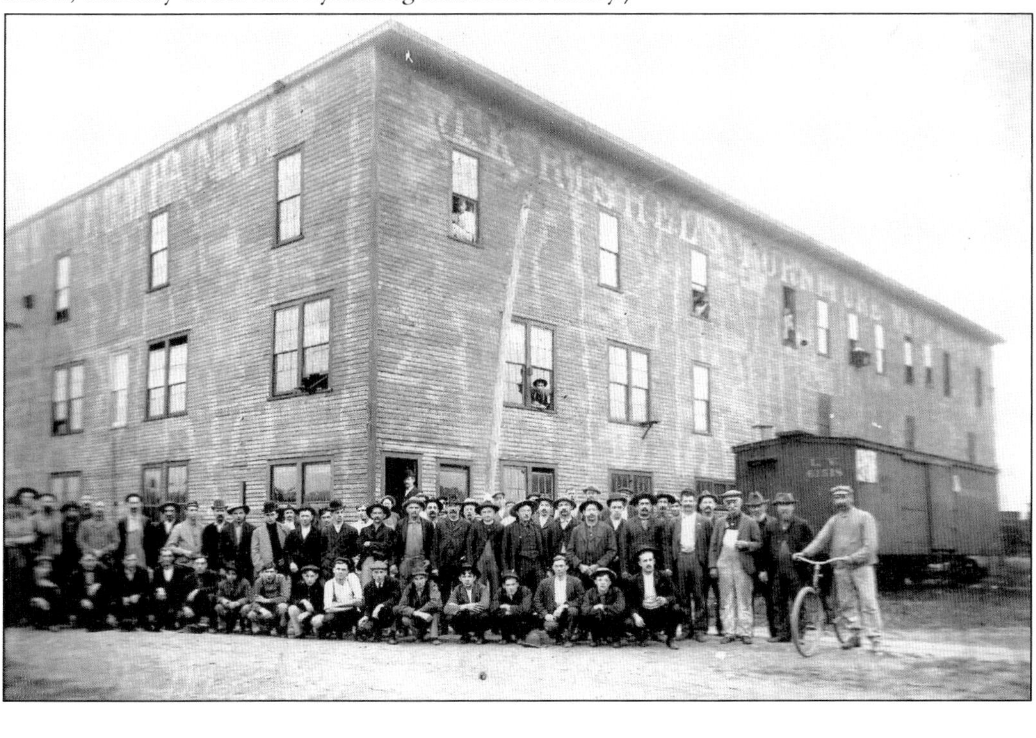

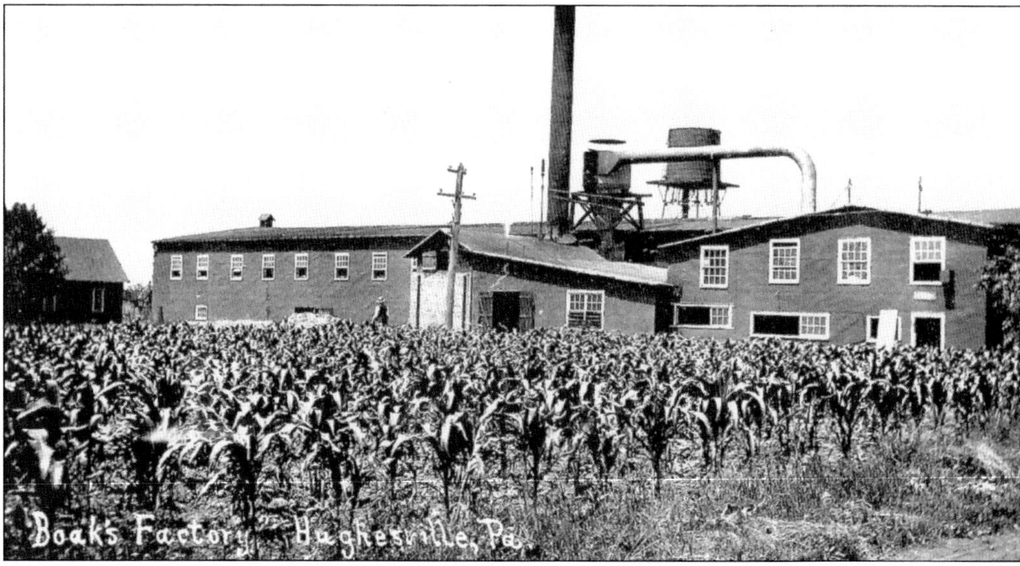

In 1879, James Boak began manufacturing furniture in Hughesville and then, with his brother Theodore, bought out the interest of Jeremiah Kelly and A. B. Worthington to take over control of the Boak Furniture Company on South Railroad Street in 1891. This factory suffered periodic outbreak of fires that caused varying degrees of damage, but it continued operation until the late 1930s, when John Mellen purchased it and renamed it the Mellen Furniture Factory. (Above, courtesy of the East Lycoming Historical Society; below, courtesy of Kenneth D. Poust.)

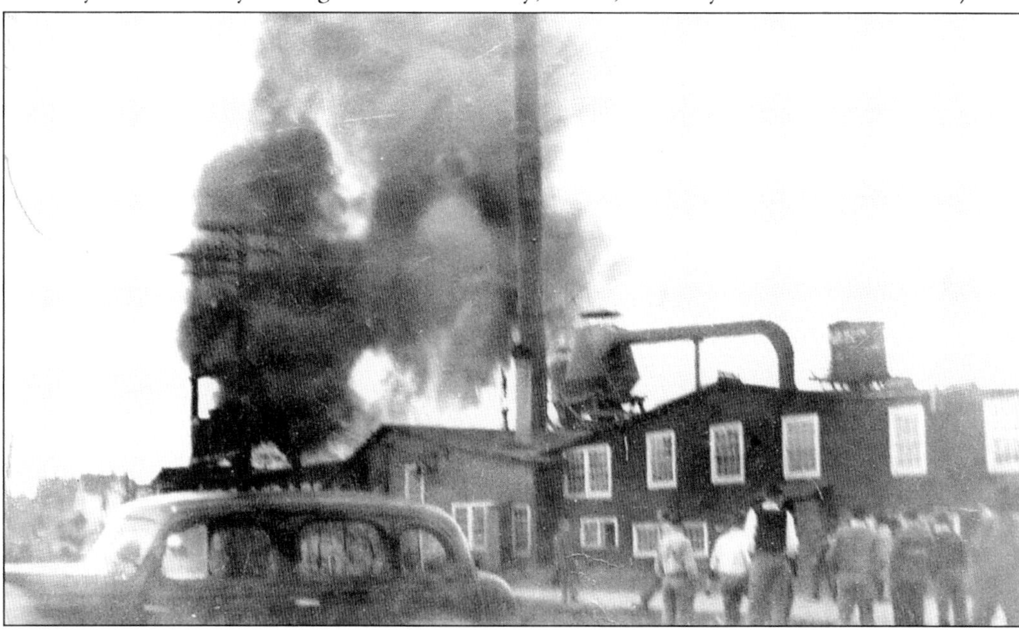

Three

The Farmers and the Fair

Families living on farms around Hughesville were hardy, resourceful souls. While they ventured into town to buy items like horse harnesses, wagon wheels, and dress fabric, these no-nonsense individuals also established their own community general stores, hotels, watering holes, dining halls, blacksmith shops, post offices, churches, and schools. There were often multiple sawmills, shingle mills, and gristmills, in addition to some kind of business that capitalized on the natural resources at hand.

Services and products were often bartered between neighbors instead of purchased. In April 1910, Earnest Fry wrote a postcard to Bert Houseknecht in response to a request for oats: "Mr. Houseknecht, We have not eny [*sic*] oats to sell but will exchange for seed if you want to." This sense of cooperation and resourcefulness originated years before, when the pioneers swapped seed potatoes for a pound of coffee.

In 1870, a group calling themselves the Muncy Valley Farmers Club gathered monthly at the Odd Fellows hall in Hughesville to discuss a variety of agricultural topics. This elicited much interest and attracted many more members to the organization, which numbered over 200 by 1873. The group held exhibitions at the southeastern edge of town that featured a parade of decorated wagons representing prominent businesses including the Laird Furniture Company; Steck's sleigh, spoke, and hub-making business; and Malony's cook stoves. The Hughesville Coronet Band played, livestock was marched down the street to the fairgrounds, and the fastest horses were raced around the trotting grounds. Produce and domestic goods, such as needlework and handmade items, were displayed and judged. The fair at Hughesville was born.

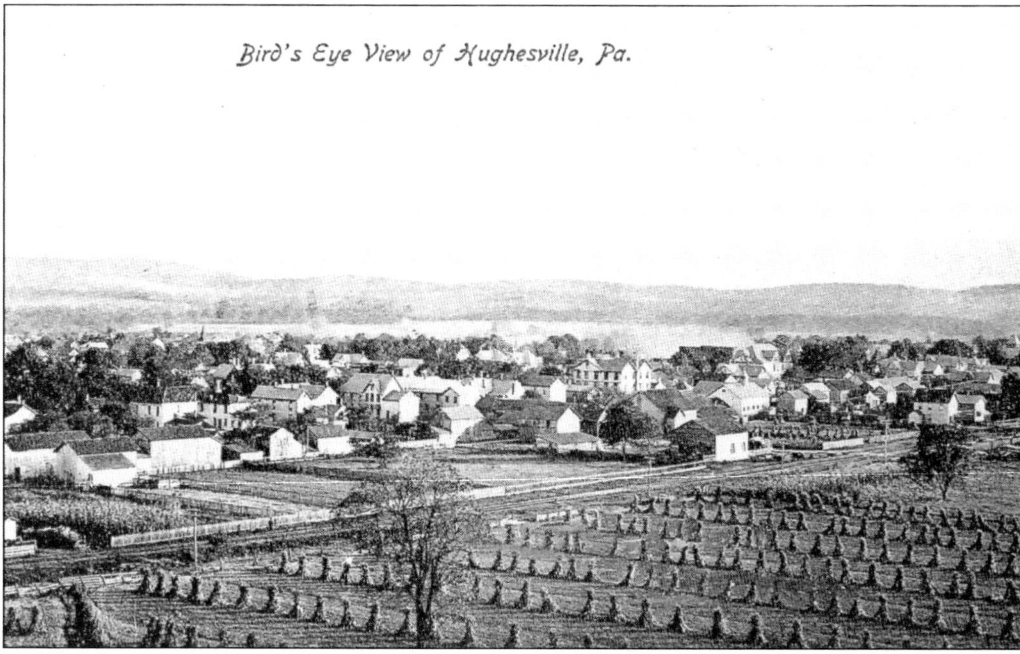

In this bird's-eye view of Hughesville, a field near the edge of town is filled with standing shocks of corn. Corn binders were used to cut the stalks of corn and tie bundles together into shocks with the ears of corn still attached. These shocks would be positioned like teepees so that the ears could dry. (Courtesy of Elizabeth Rogers Knyrim.)

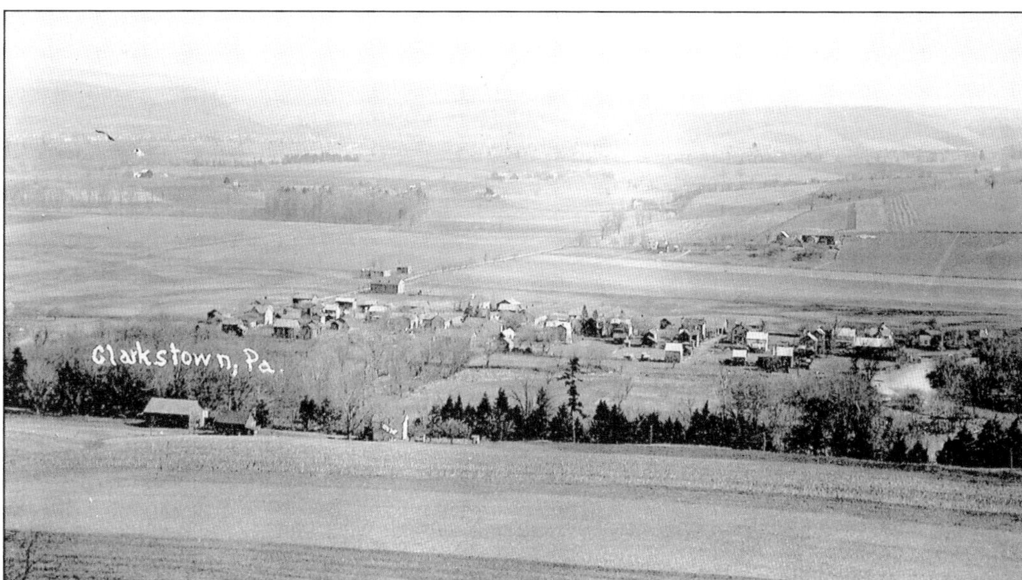

Henry Buck settled here around 1848 and called it Bucktown. Others living nearby called it Clarksville, after James Clark, an early settler who was found scalped in 1779. The name was changed to Clarkstown when a post office was established in 1869. The local shoemaker, Jacob Fiester, served as Clarkstown's first postmaster and distributed the mail from his shoemaker's bench. (Courtesy of the Sullivan County Historical Society and Museum.)

Located on Little Muncy Creek near Clarkstown in Moreland Township, this flouring mill was operated by Philip Wilson Opp. Over 125 years old, this building has survived and remains standing today. Opp was a cousin to Lt. Col. Milton Opp, Moreland Township's Civil War hero. (Courtesy of *History of Lycoming County Illustrated*, 1876.)

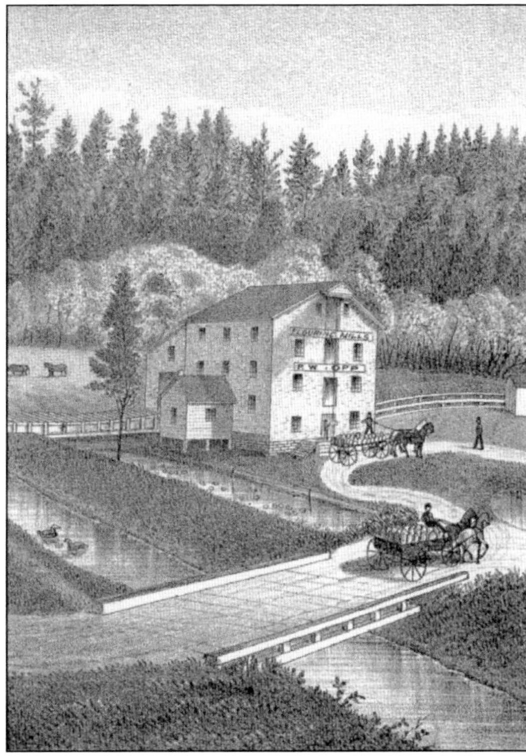

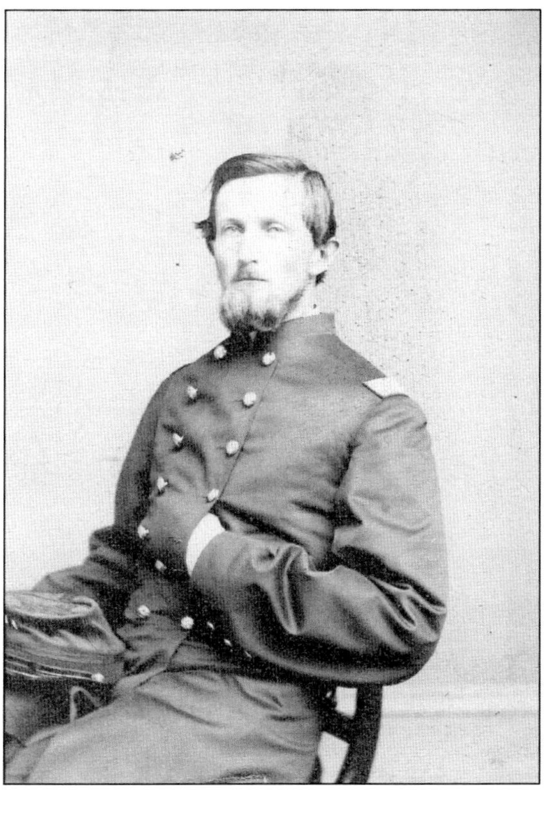

Lt. Col. Milton Opp served with the 84th Pennsylvania Volunteers, after he graduated from law school and passed the bar. He was commissioned first lieutenant of Company F Volunteers in October 1861, and served with that regiment as lieutenant, captain, major, and lieutenant colonel by successive promotion, up to the Battle of the Wilderness, where he was mortally wounded May 6, 1864, while leading his command in a desperate charge against the enemy. (Courtesy of David L. Richards.)

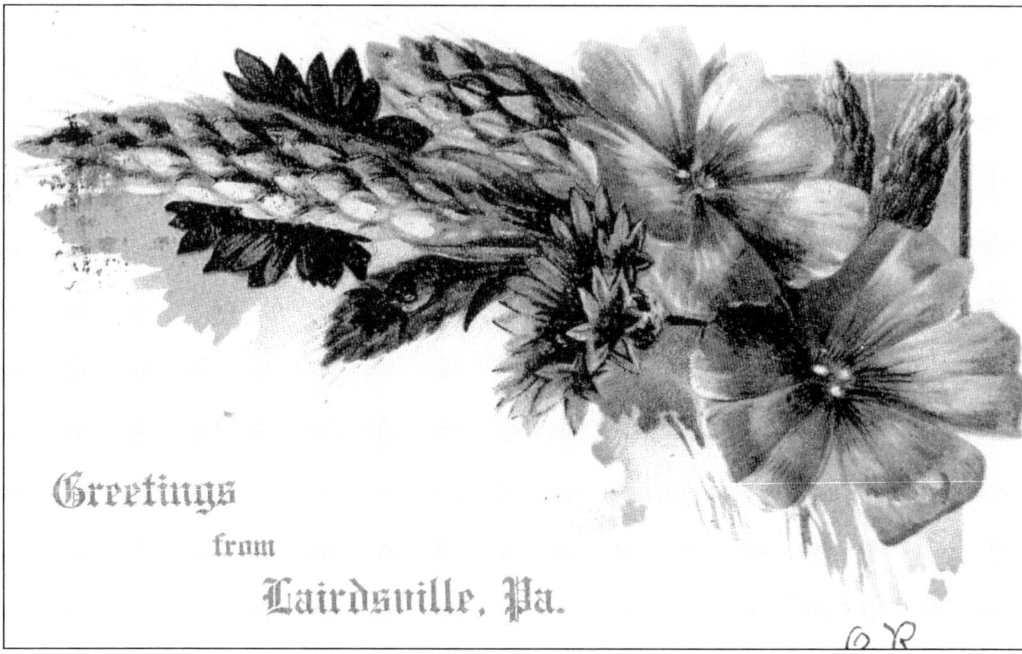

Located about a half-mile south of Lairdsville, the Franklin Tannery was regarded as one of the largest and most productive operations in the area. Tanneries such as this one used hemlock bark, which was plentiful in central Pennsylvania, as their source of tannin for curing leather. The tanning industry responded to the need for leather products, including harness and shoes, at the beginning of the 19th century. The Franklin Tannery was established in 1832 by Enos Hawley and Thomas G. Downing, who also established a leather store and shoe factory in Muncy. (Below, courtesy of the East Lycoming Historical Society.)

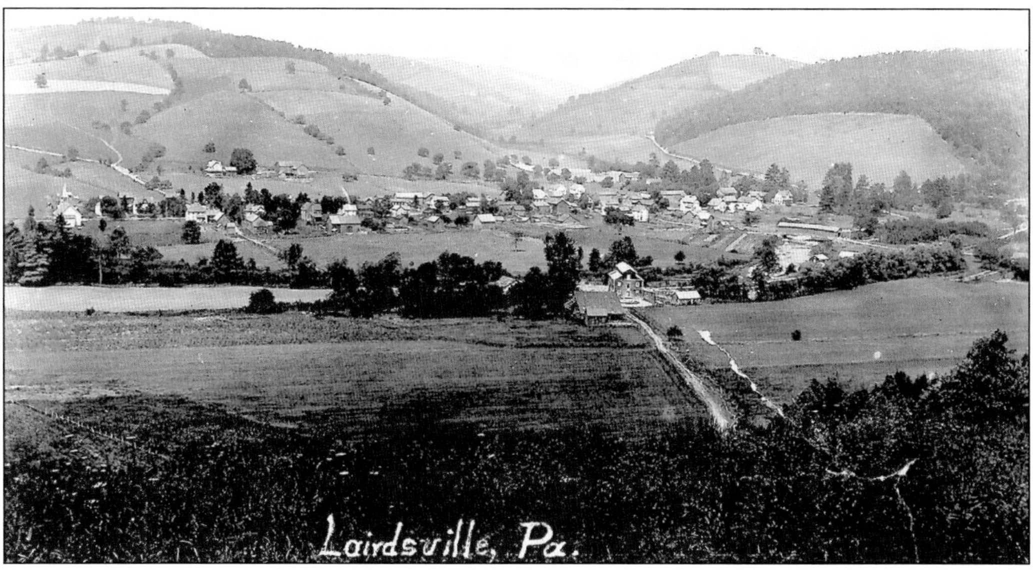

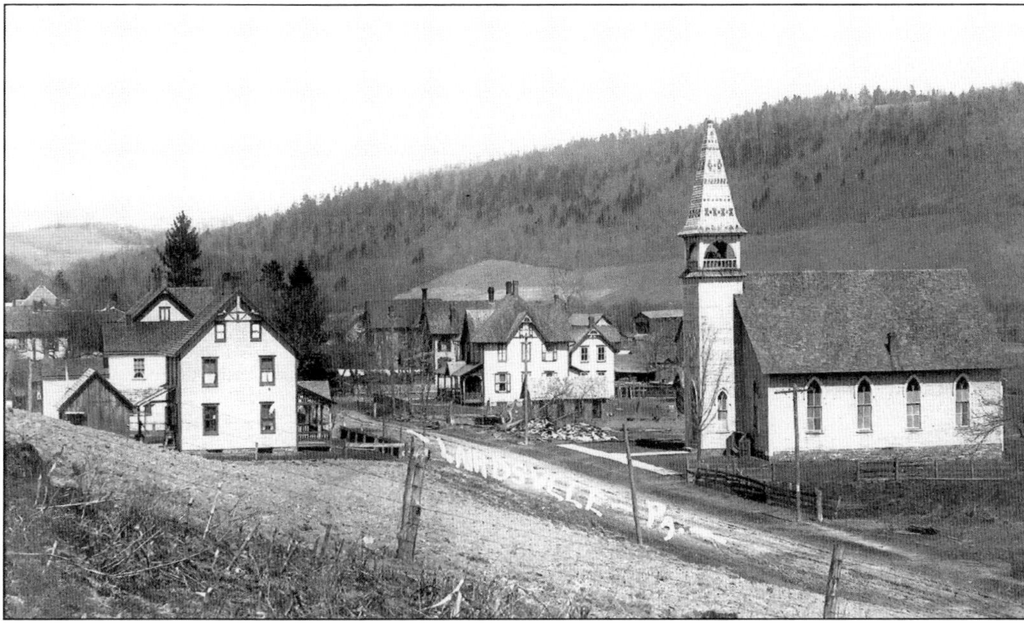

Lairdsville was, and still is, a one-road town. In the 1890s, it had two churches, three stores, a post office, one hotel, one wagon-maker shop, one steam planing mill, one gristmill, two blacksmith shops, and two physicians. Its name changed to Funstonville in 1852 and then changed back to Lairdsville in 1855. Down the road toward Hughesville was another post office, Mengwe, that opened in 1892. Below is Funston Mill, which was originally built by Henry Funston in 1825. It burned in 1858 and was rebuilt twice, the second time by Calvin Edgar Myers. The water powered wheel ground grain into mash for animal feed and wheat into flour. Buckwheat flour was also ground and sold in the area. (Above, courtesy of the East Lycoming Historical Society; below, courtesy of Sue Shaner.)

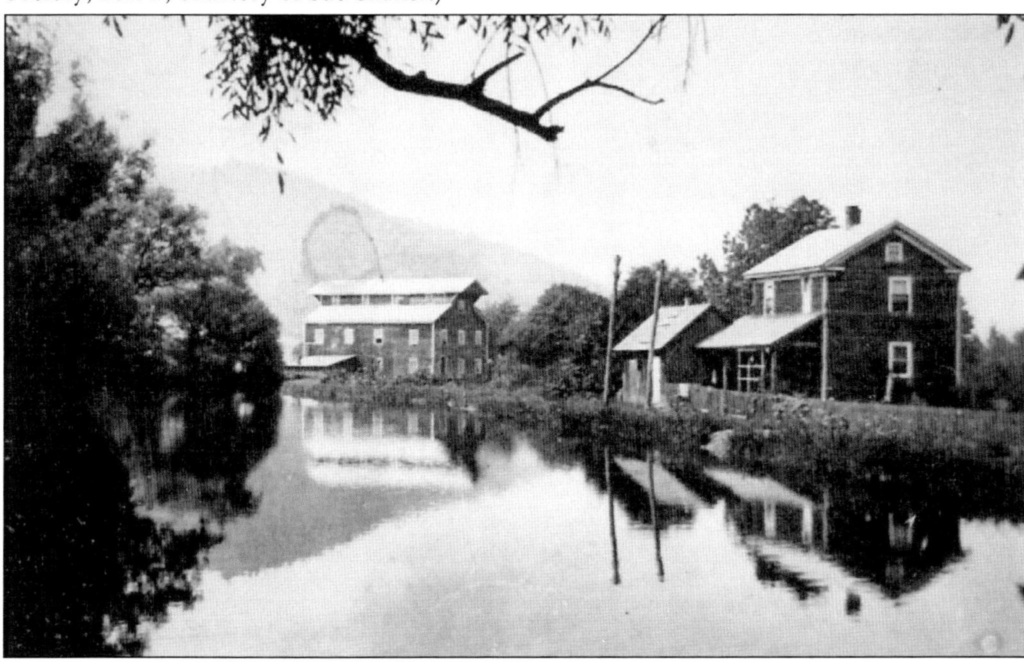

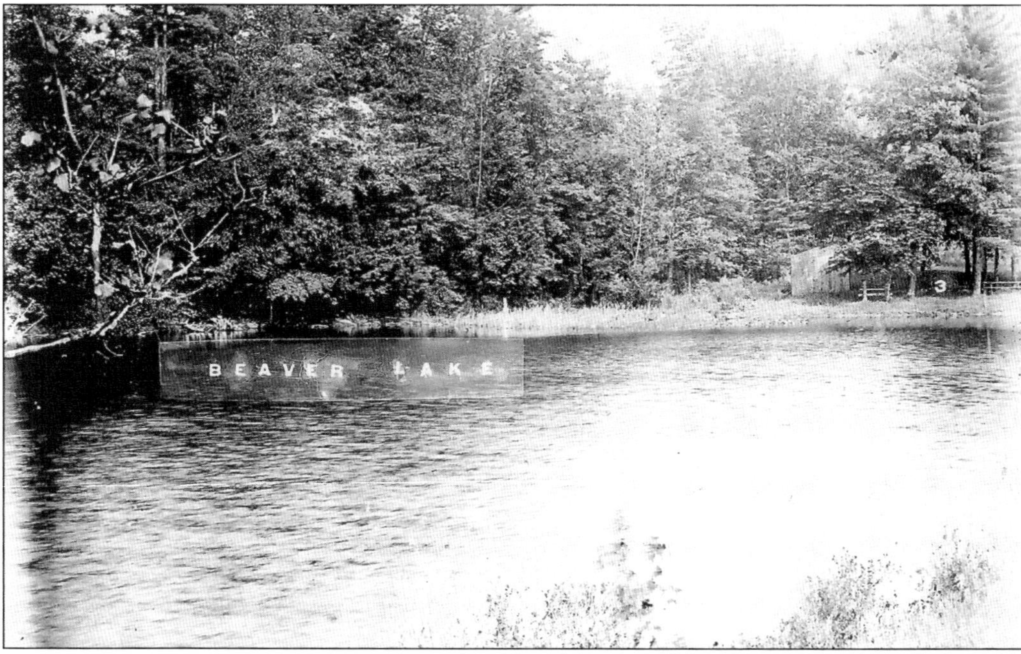

Located on the border between Lycoming and Sullivan Counties in Penn Township is Beaver Lake (above). The lake was formed in the early 1800s, when some very busy beavers blocked portions of a stream called Beaver Run. In the 1880s, a lakeside store and post office were operated by Grant Logue. In 1897, a three-story hotel (below) was built on the lake with 12 bedrooms on the second floor and 6 bedrooms on the third floor, while the first floor featured a large ballroom and dining room. Dances and the natural scenery attracted visitors from Williamsport and other areas. The cost for room and board plus the use of a boat was $1 a day. The hotel burned in 1927. (Courtesy of the East Lycoming Historical Society.)

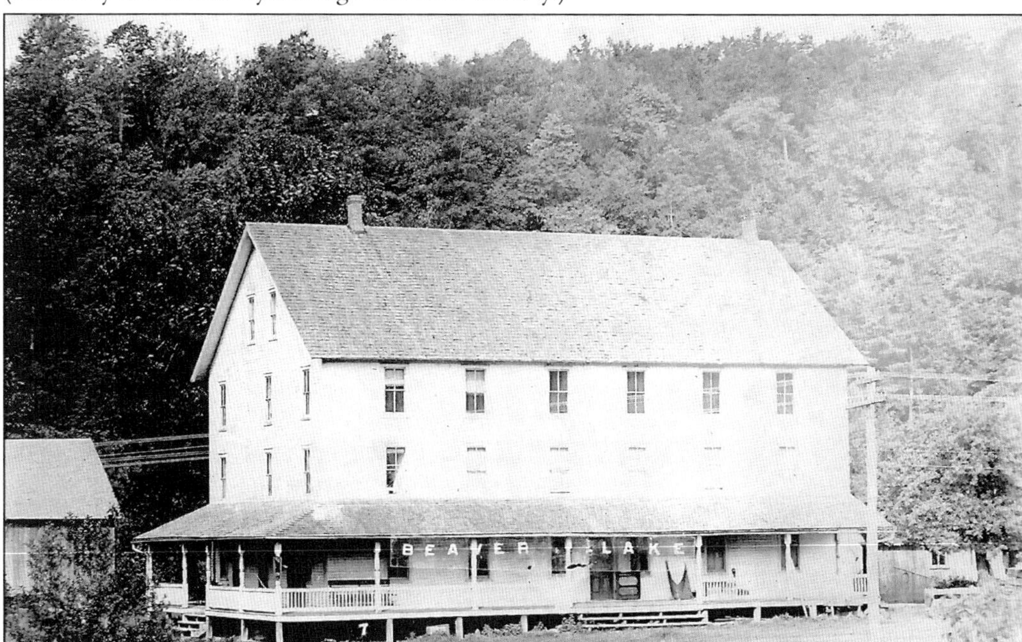

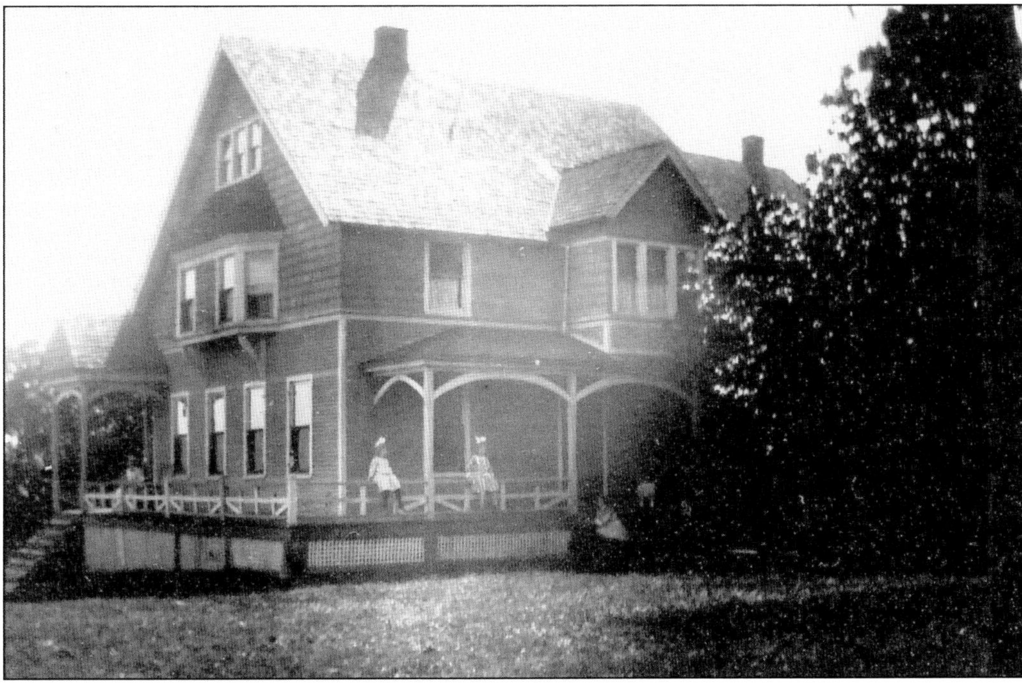

During the late 1800s, Shrewsbury Township was "celebrated for its delightful summer resorts," according to John Meginness in his 1892 account the *History of Lycoming County*. He goes on to say, "Near the northern border is Highland Lake, adjacent to which three large summer hotels are now attracting many pleasure seekers. The first erected was the Highland House, then followed Hotel Grand View, and later, The Essick [below]. They are spacious buildings, furnished with all modern conveniences. There is also a cottage boarding house [as well as] private cottages [above]." (Above, courtesy of Sue Shaner; below, courtesy of David L. Richards.)

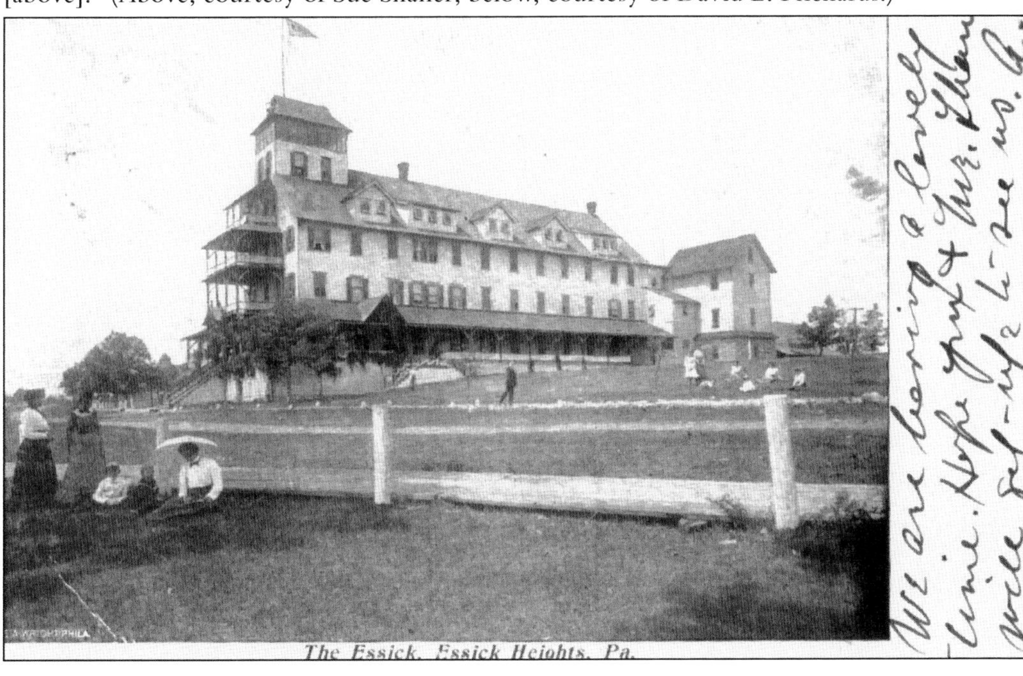

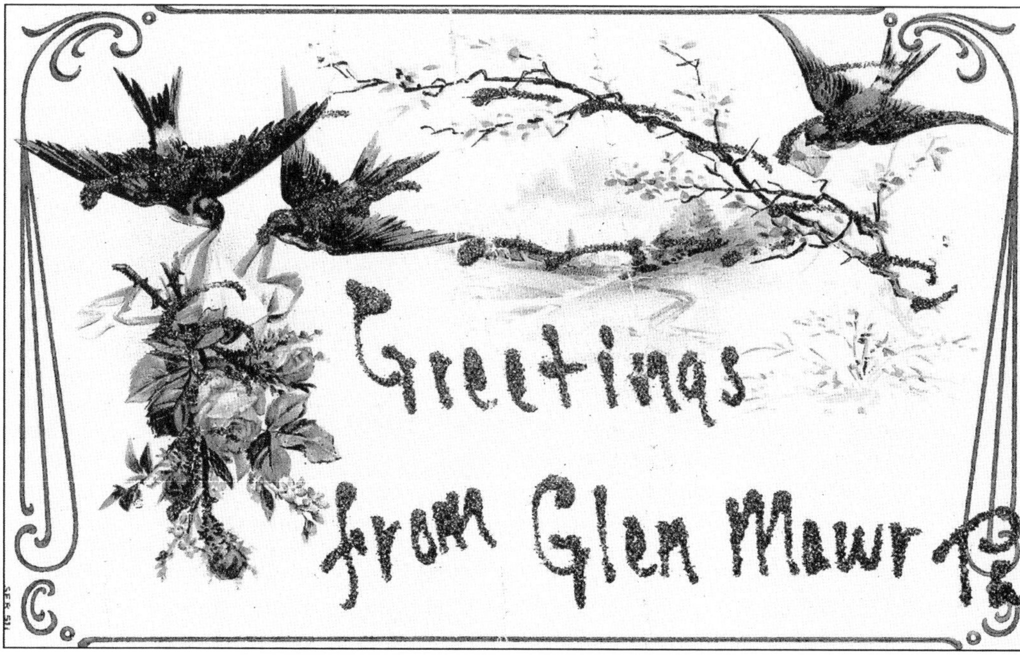

Which is it, Glen Mawr or Mawr Glen? It could depend on which side of town one is talking about, or it could depend on the time period. In his 1892 history of the county, Meginness called it "Glen Mawr" when he was referring to the establishment of its post office in 1886. In Thomas W. Lloyd's 1929 history, Lloyd stated that a post office existed in "Mawrglen." Apparently the northern (and oldest) side of town is Mawr Glen, which is also the side that the railroad station was located. The south side of town, where the newer buildings and homes were built, is known as Glen Mawr.

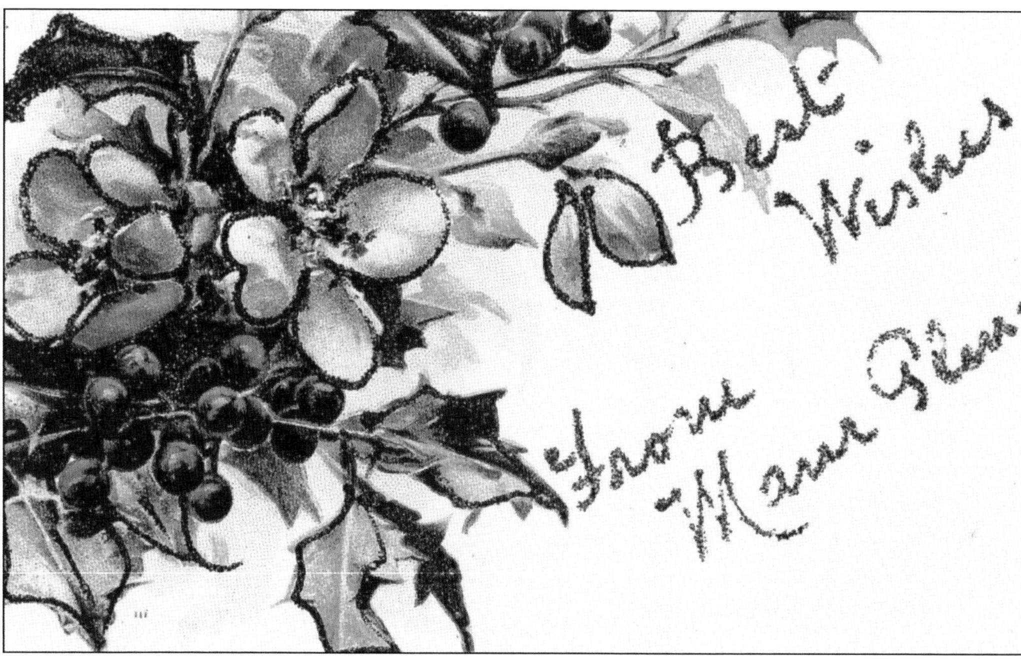

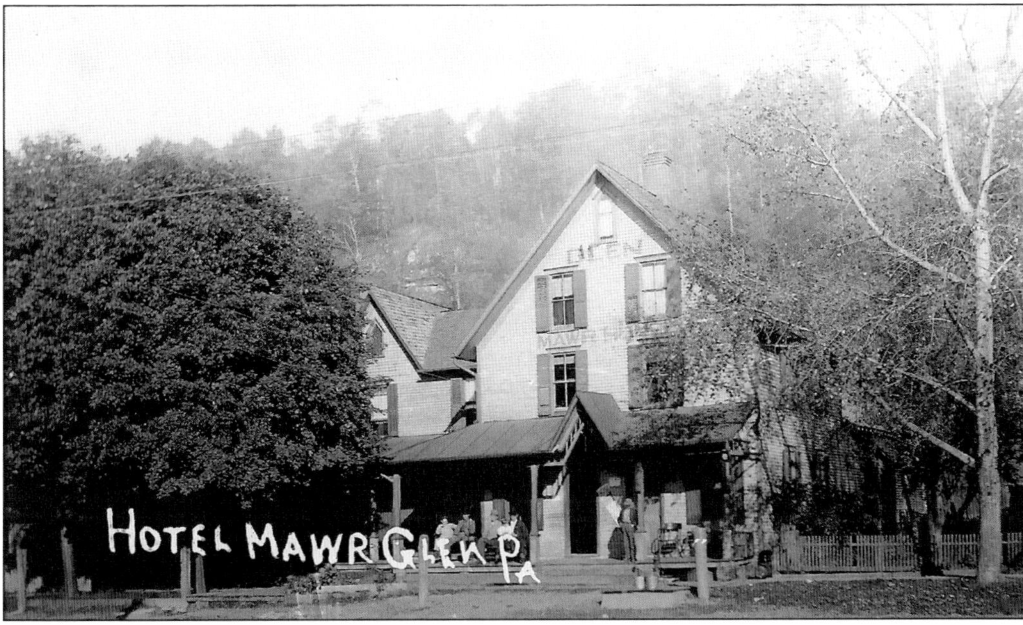

Although the sign painted on the building (above) says "Glen Mawr Hotel," the building is identified by the photographer as "Hotel Mawr Glen." The hotel can also be seen in the center of the photograph below, behind the trees. The large white buildings to the left were the home of Lewis and Clara Secules. Attached to their home was a store, which has since been torn down. When young Gladys Montague Lovell and her parents lived with her grandparents in their home near the store, she remembers taking baskets of eggs there each week to sell. (Above, courtesy of Stewart Hill; below, Courtesy of Elizabeth Rogers Knyrim.)

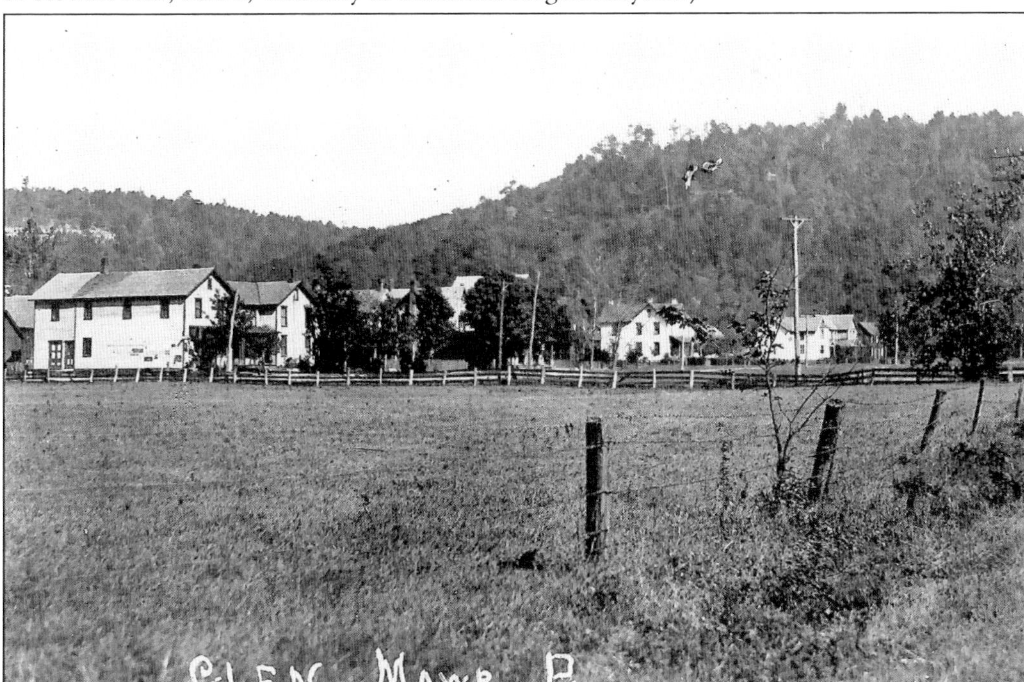

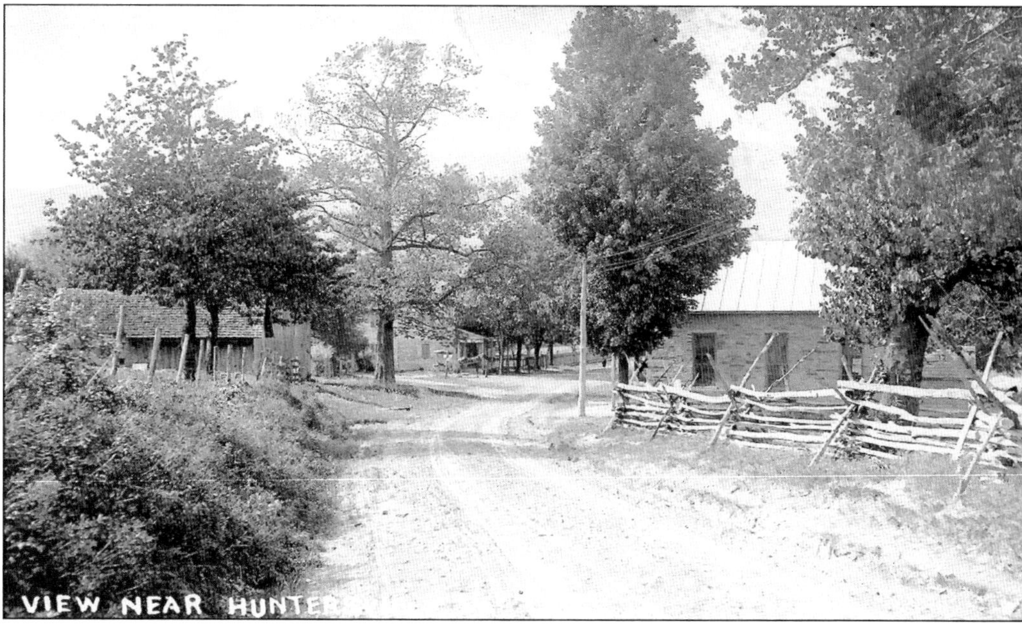

In 1879, Mill Creek Township was formed from Muncy Township, with Huntersville its only village, located on its eastern border next to Wolf Township. Iron ore and copper were mined, as well as flagstone being quarried. Editor John Meginness reports that Huntersville had "one store and one blacksmith shop, and three houses comprise the balance of the improvements. The substantial looking stone schoolhouse might be claimed by the village, but it is in Wolf Township, as the public road here is the line that divides the provinces." Therefore the left side of the photograph below is Wolf Township, while the right side is Mill Creek Township. (Above, courtesy of Stewart Hill; below, courtesy of Howard "Mick" Hill.)

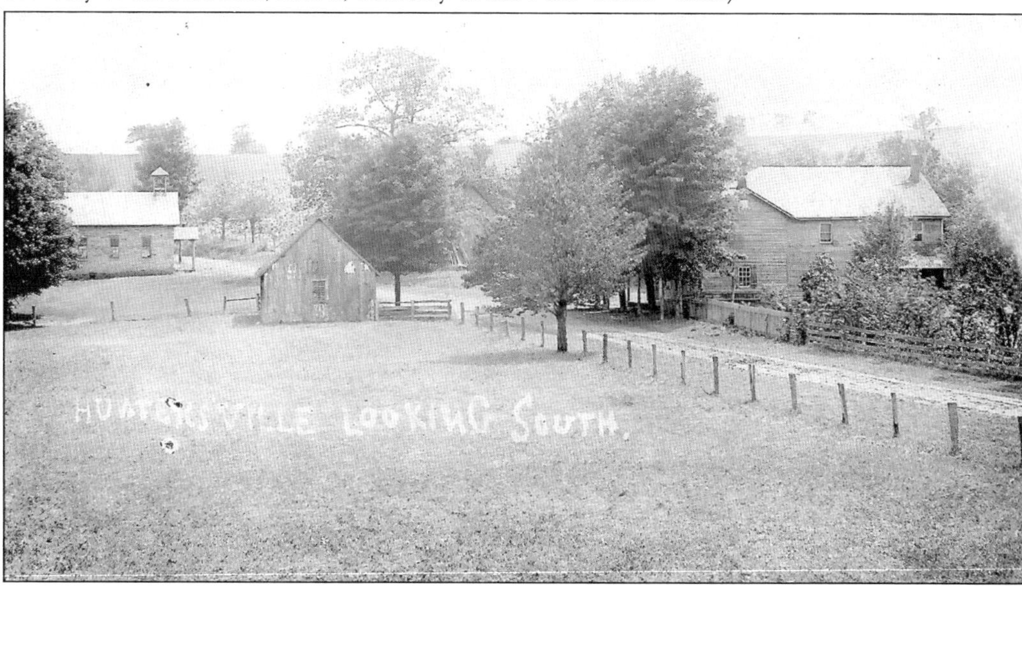

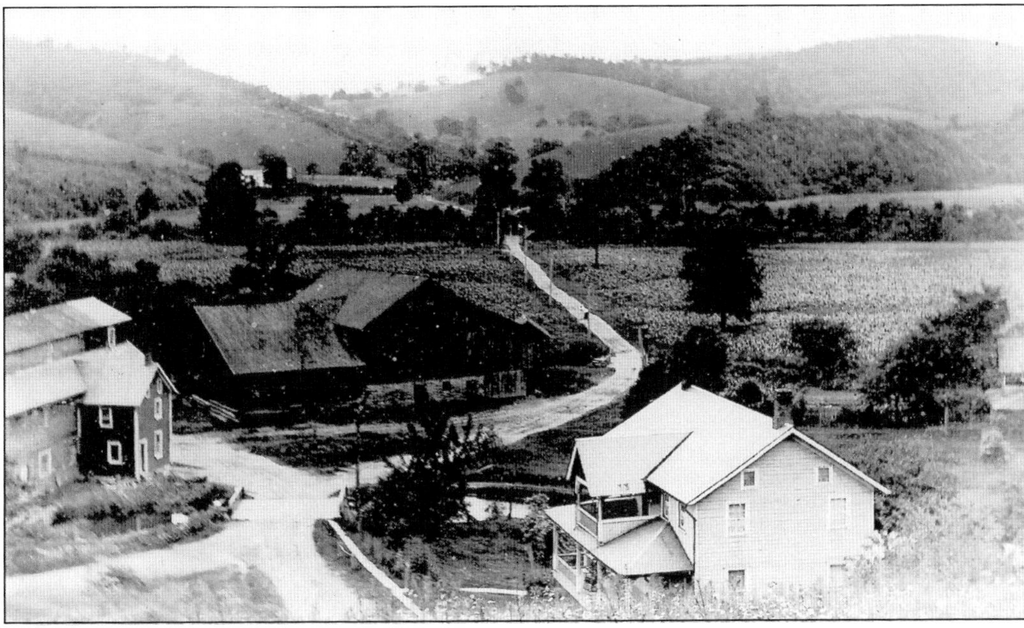

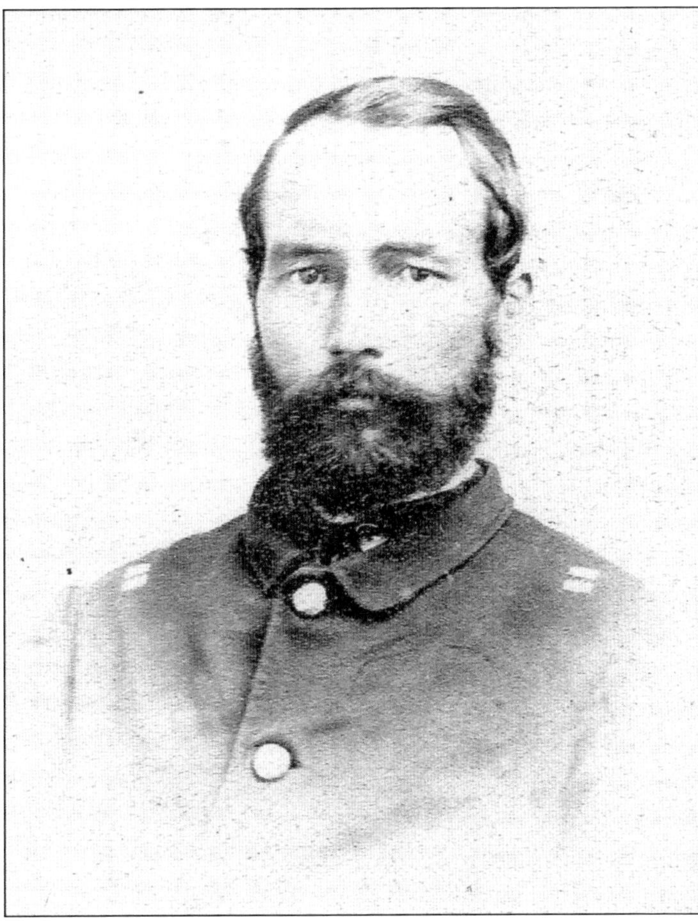

Between Hughesville and Picture Rocks is Bryantown (also referred to as Bryan Mill), the site of the woolen mill that was built in 1842 by Ellis Bryan. While the mill (above, left) has been town down, the house (foreground) still stands today. Bryan's son Sam (right) took over the mill's operation after he returned from service during the Civil War. He enlisted in Company B, 84th Pennsylvania Volunteers, served over three years, and was wounded twice; once in 1862 at the battle of Winchester and again in 1864, at the battle of Spotsylvania. (Above, courtesy of Joe Barlett; right, courtesy of David L. Richards.)

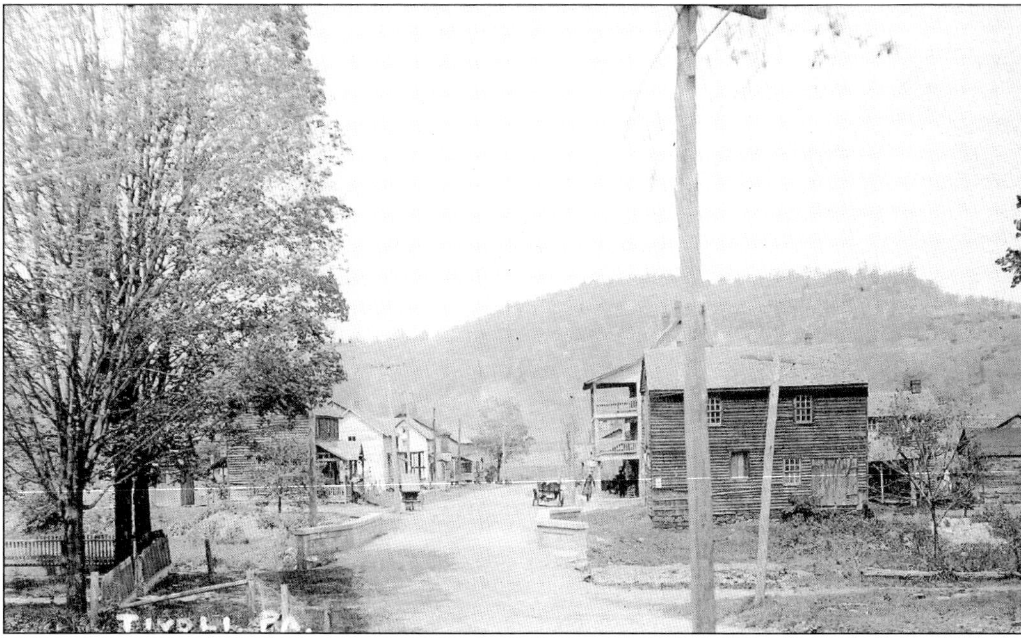

When the post office at Tivoli was established in 1854, the town was called Corson's as Daniel Corson was appointed postmaster. The name of the town was changed to Tivoli in 1861. The townspeople, however, called it "Dog Town" because of the constant din of howling dogs owned by resident George Taylor. (Courtesy of Stewart Hill.)

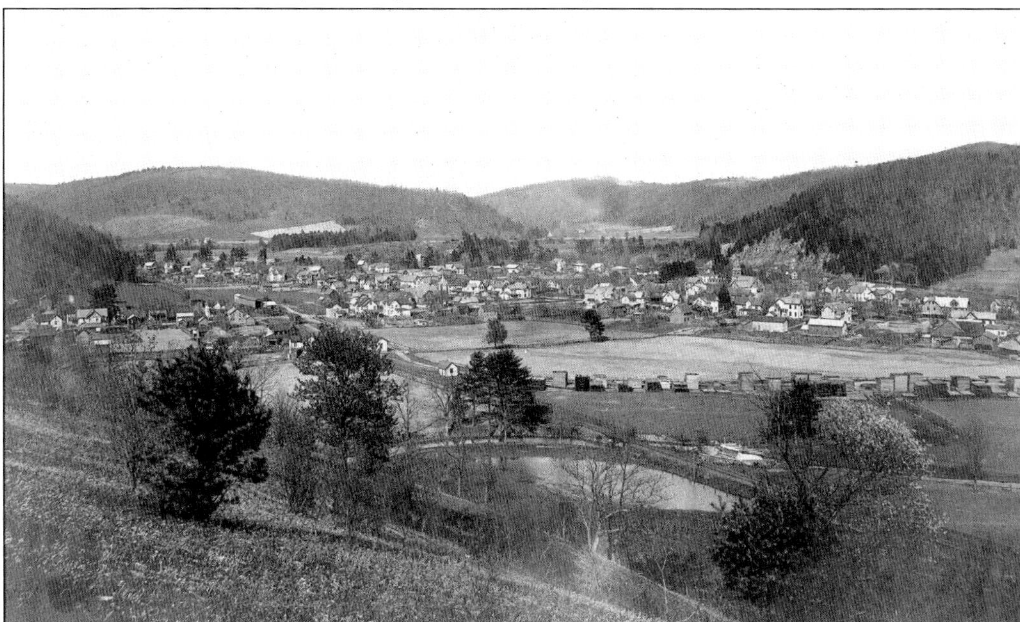

When Picture Rocks was incorporated into a borough in 1875, the railroad had not yet reached this tiny community located north of Hughesville. In less than 10 years, however, tracks were laid to the edge of town and eventually connected with Tivoli, Glen Mawr, and points north. Spurs (foreground) were laid to deliver wood products for the furniture- and door-making factories in town. (Courtesy of Aaron Houseknecht.)

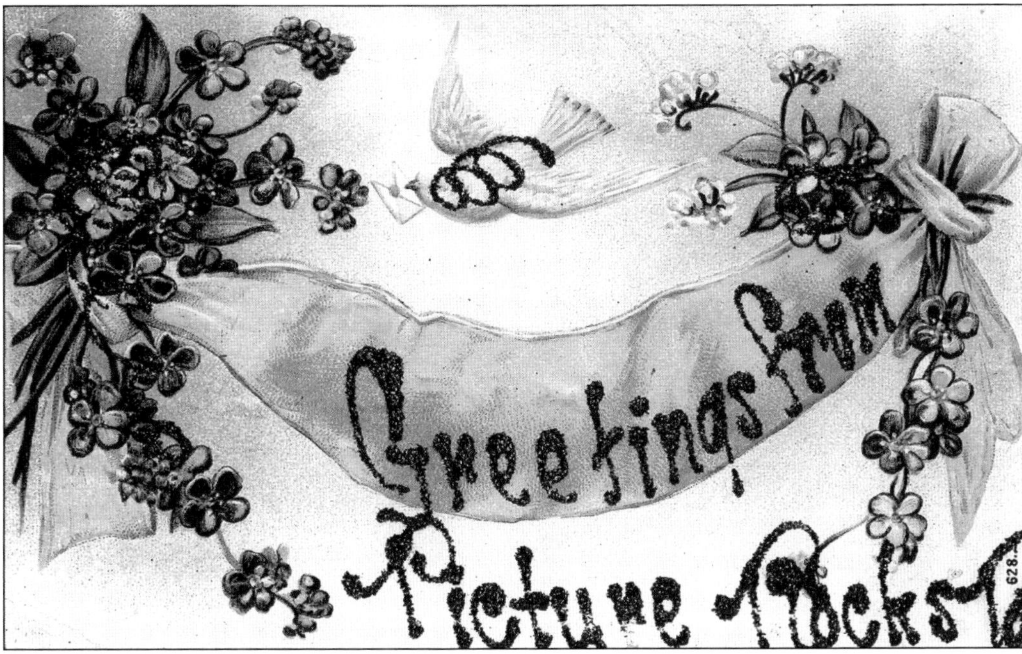

Amos Burrows entered into a partnership with A. R. Sprout in 1848 when they purchased a sawmill and 58 acres of land along Muncy Creek. The men came to the Picture Rocks area and moved their families into the one cabin that stood near the sawmill. They also brought machinery with them to make window sashes, blinds, and doors. Amos's son, Sabin, began making bedroom furniture in his father's factory, and then helped his father move the business to South Main Street. They added dining room furniture, other members of the extended family joined, and the name became Burrows Brothers Company. The Burrows family continued manufacturing high quality furniture and other wood products until the 1930s. (Above, courtesy of Harold Hill; below, courtesy of the Sullivan County Historical Society and Museum.)

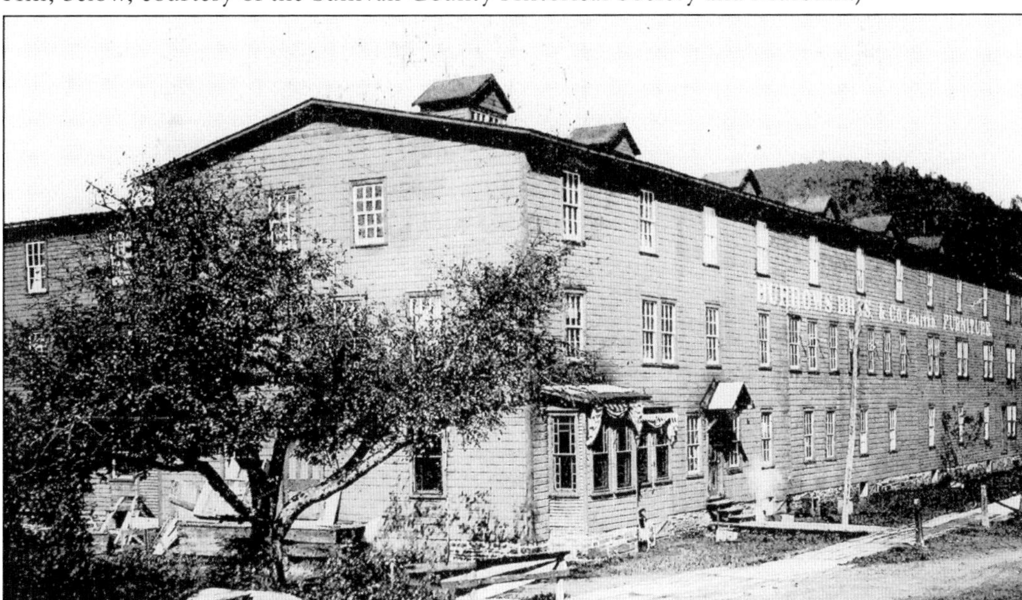

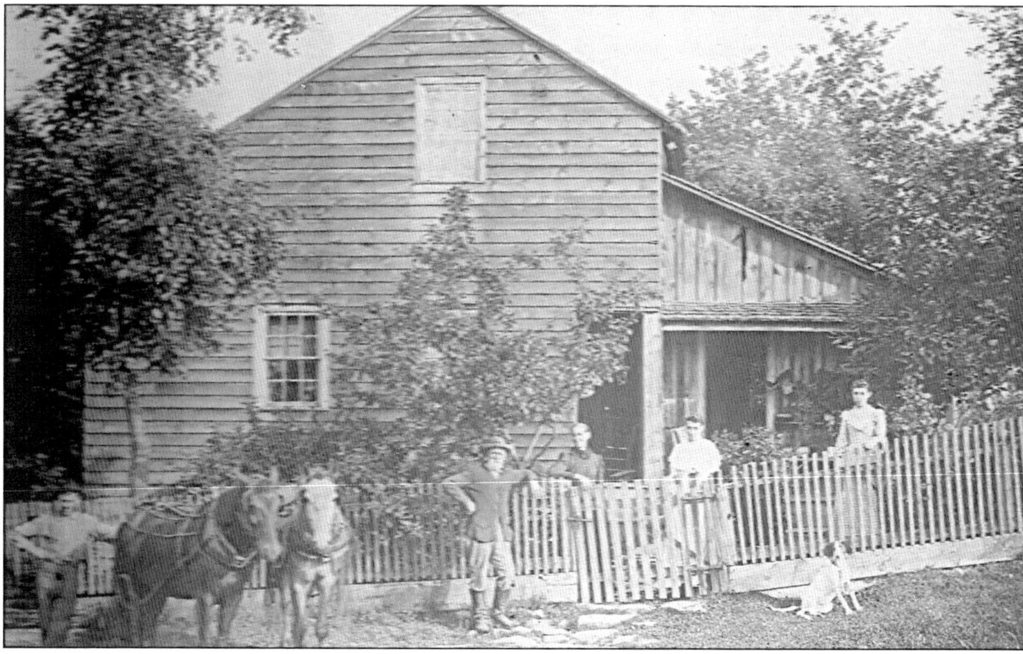

Compared to the houses that were built in Hughesville (see pages 13–27), the farmhouses seen on these pages (pages 70–71) illustrate the practicality and thriftiness of these families. There were no turrets or arched windows, no dormers or banistered porches. Farmhouses were made of wood and shingles cut at local sawmills and left unpainted and unadorned. Above is the Houseknecht family—one of many in the valley—namely (from left to right) Amandus Thompson (Tom), William, Matilda, Sarah, and Mabel at their farm near the Hilltown schoolhouse in Moreland Township around 1885. Below are Cyrus and Isabella Holmes, with their daughter Hazel at their home near Glen Mawr in Penn Township around 1897.

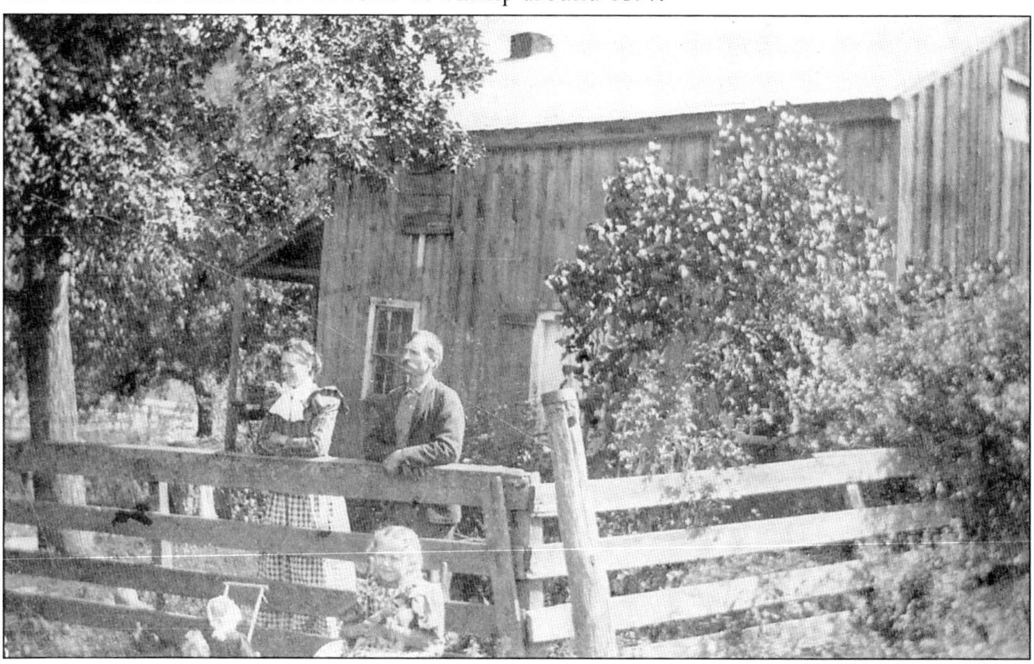

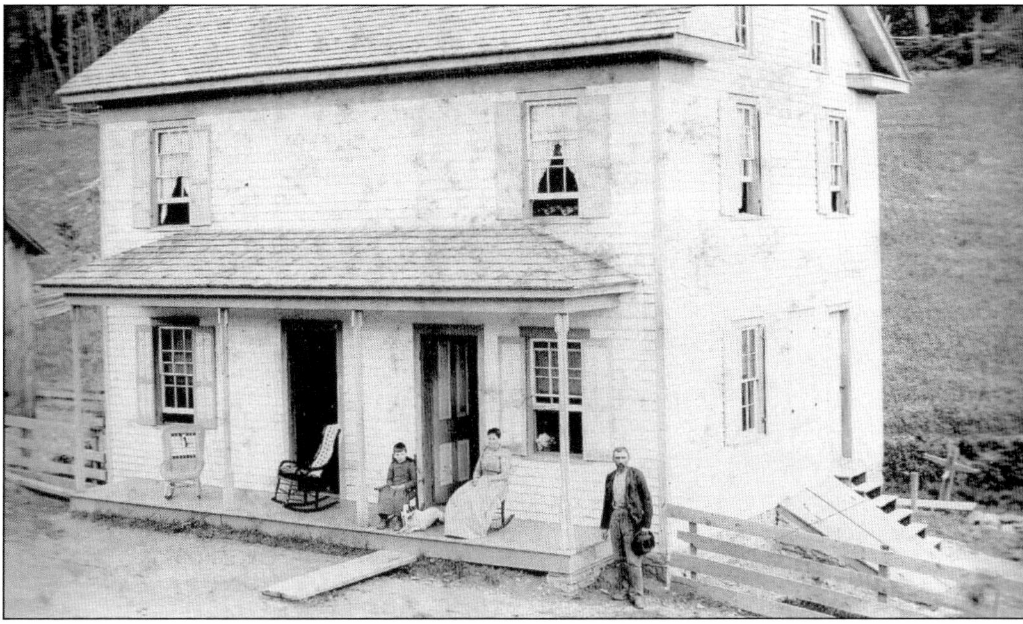

The builders of both homes on this page chose sites that were not exactly flat. Bert Houseknecht erected this house (above) in Penn Township during the 1880s for his wife, Martha. They are pictured with their dog and Minnie Castleberry, a neighbor girl who lived with them for a time. Another house that required careful leveling was this one (below) in Unityville, the home of Thomas Benton Minier and his wife, Margaret. Thomas was the town blacksmith and also served as justice of the peace in Unityville. Seen are, from left to right, Wilson W. Minier, Margaret (mother), Sara Matilda "Tillie" Minier Whitmoyer, Thomas Benton Minier Jr., Tura Minier Hess (or perhaps Crist), Anna Margaret Minier Lore, and Thomas (father). (Below, courtesy of Aaron Houseknecht.)

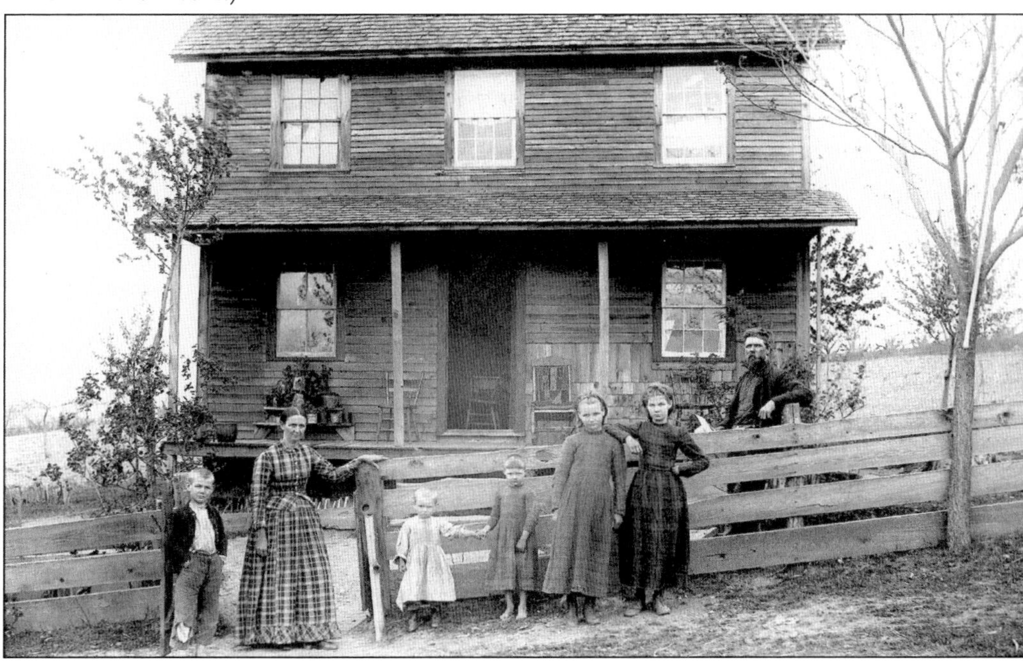

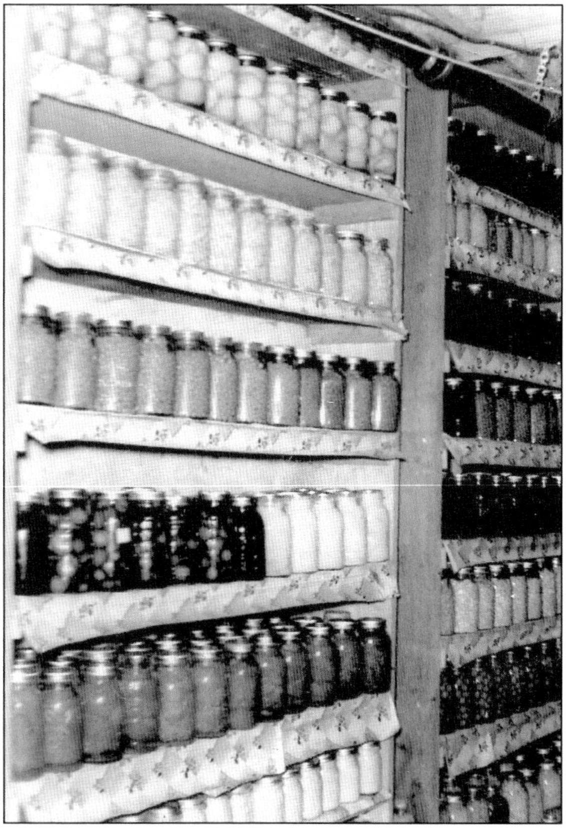

The farm women took pride in the fruits and vegetables they grew in their large gardens and the number of Mason jars lining their pantry shelves. This innovation, a wide-mouthed glass jar with a screw-on zinc lid, was designed by a man named John Mason from New York. This method of preservation provided a longer shelf life for a variety of foods. (Courtesy of Sue Shaner.)

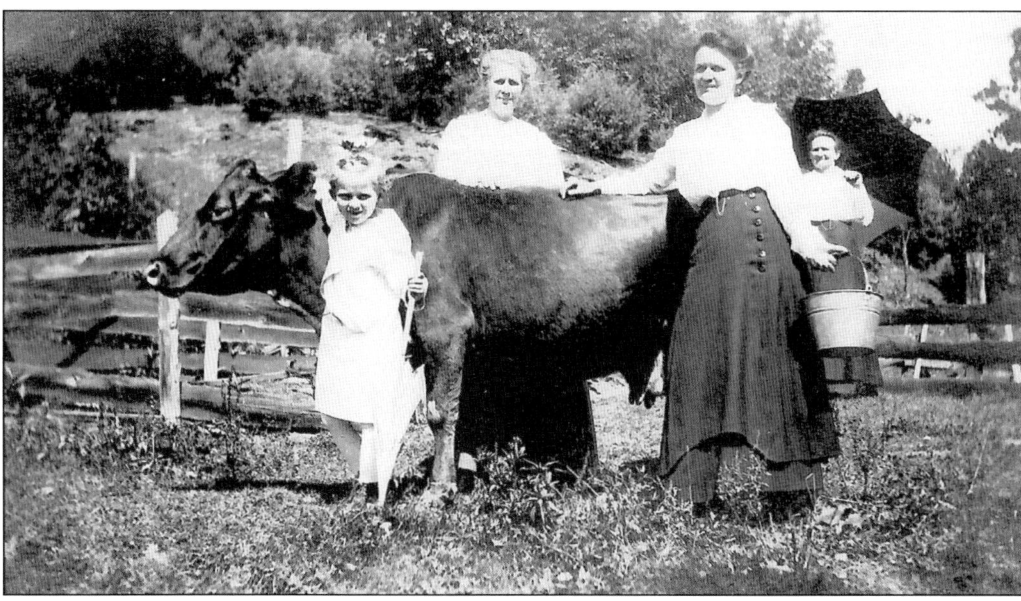

Young Elva Holmes (left) is carrying one and her aunt Martha Phillips Fry (right) has opened one over her head. Why are they carrying umbrellas out in the cow pasture? One can only imagine, but they seem determined to go home with milk in their bucket. Elva's mother, Isabella, is standing behind the cow, and her aunt Clara Phillips holds the bucket.

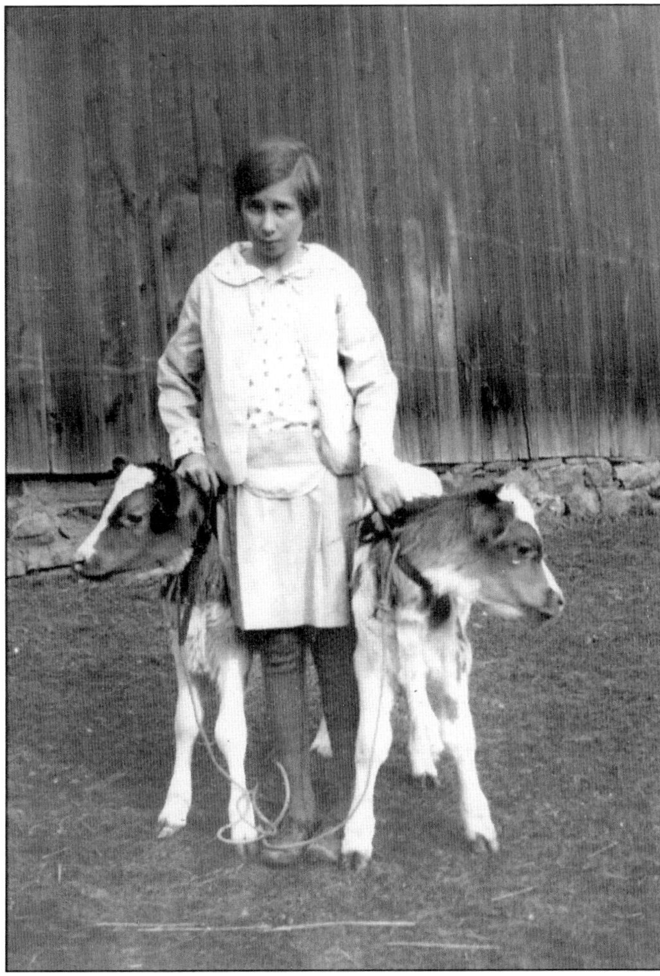

Farm girls grew up caring for animals and often profited from it, too. Clara Houseknecht Wheal (right) proudly shows her twin calves, King and Queen, born in 1929. In the years that followed, Wheal would receive $10 for each calf sold that was a descendent of the twins, an arrangement she had made with her father. Chickens were also a source of food and income on the farm. Wheal is shown below with some of the laying hens that she and her mother tended. They sold about 50 dozen eggs per week to an egg contractor.

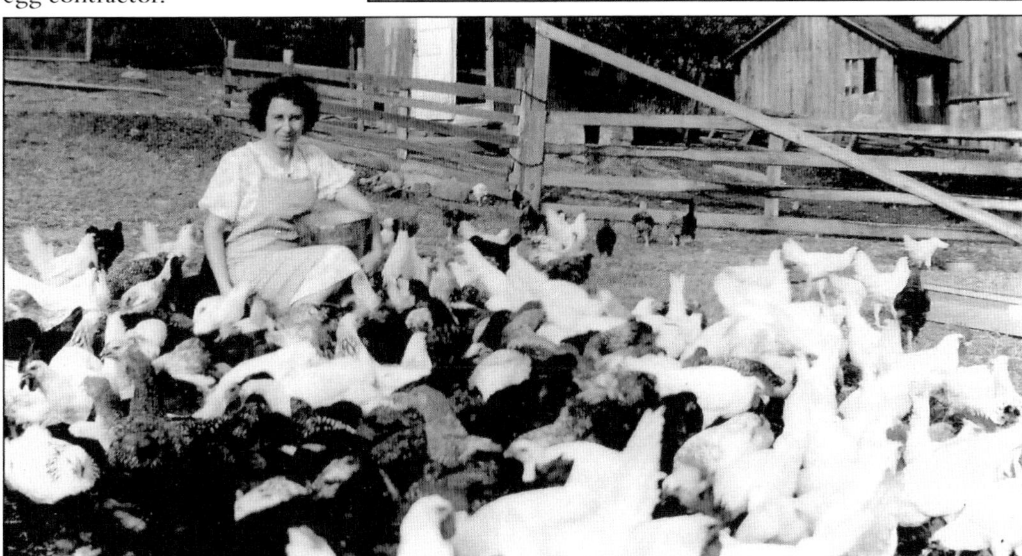

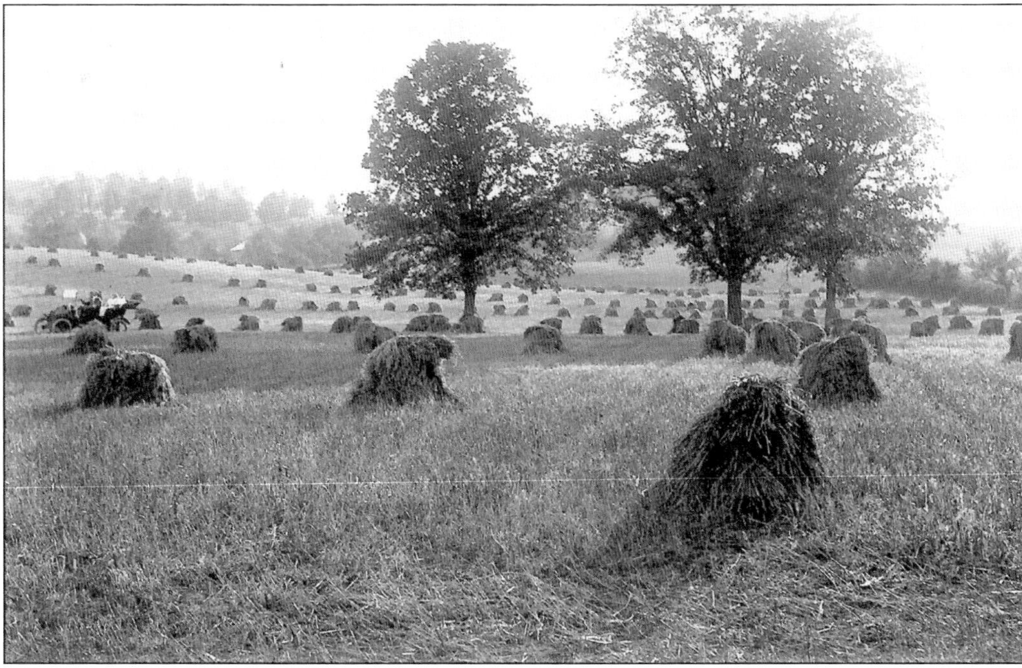

Crops were grown close to town, which is where this field is—on the site of the present junior/senior high school. The author of the note on this postcard mailed August 1914 boasted, "This is a portion of our oats field. Over 4,000 sheaves. Put them in the barn last week. Everything looks fine this year. You can see Pleasant Hill Cemetery in the distance in this picture." (Courtesy of Stewart Hill.)

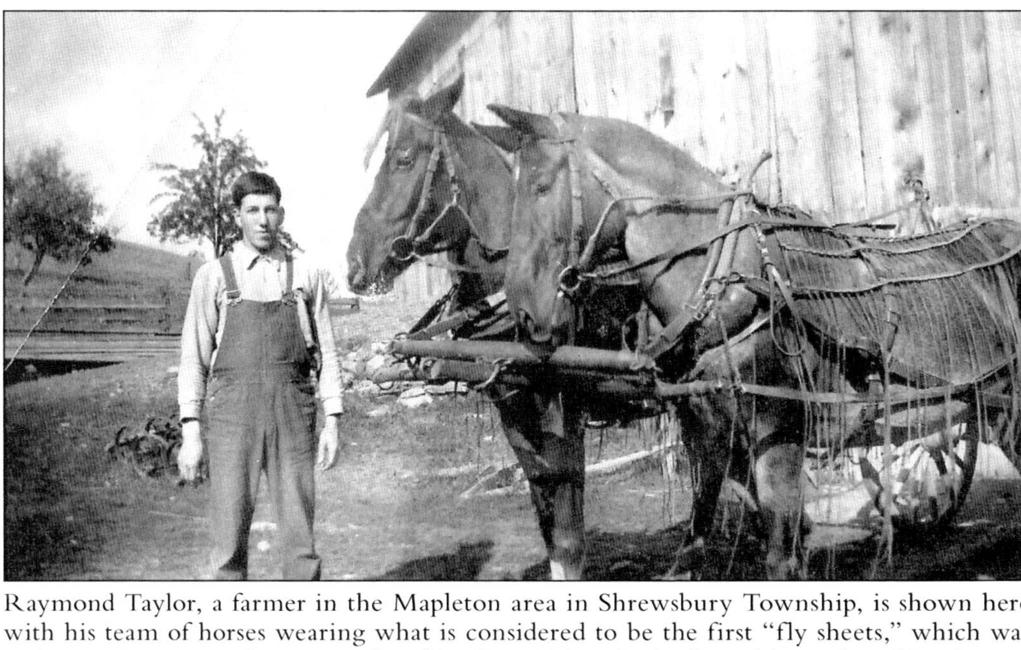

Raymond Taylor, a farmer in the Mapleton area in Shrewsbury Township, is shown here with his team of horses wearing what is considered to be the first "fly sheets," which was an innovative way to keep annoying flies from biting the backs and legs of working horses. (Courtesy of Sue Shaner.)

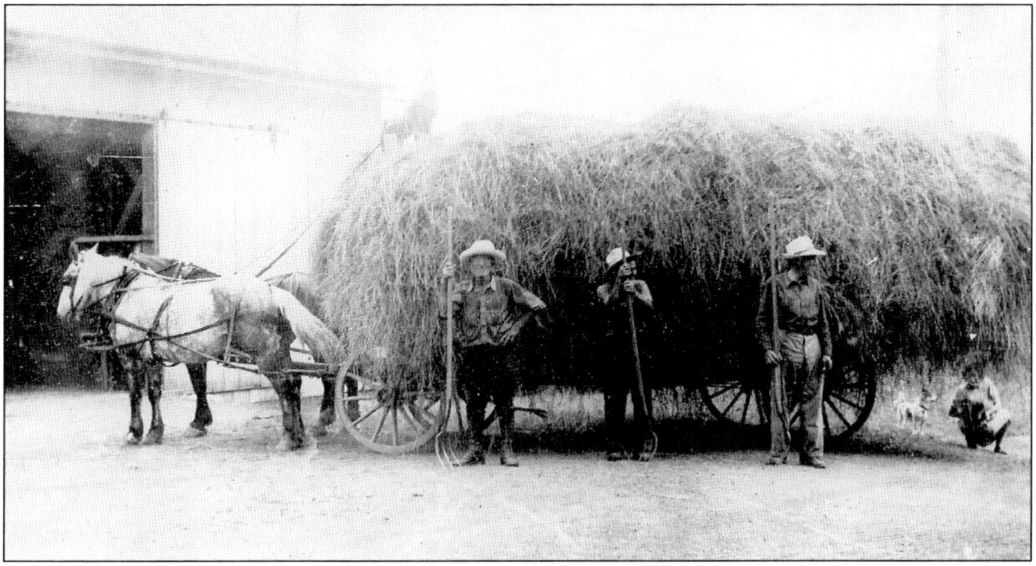

This scene took place in the Highland Lake area, where hay was cut and loaded onto horse-drawn wagons to be hauled to and stored in the barn. The workers are identified as follows, from left to right, ? Sheets, Raymond Taylor, John Warner, and David Price (crouching under the back of the wagon). (Courtesy of Sue Shaner.)

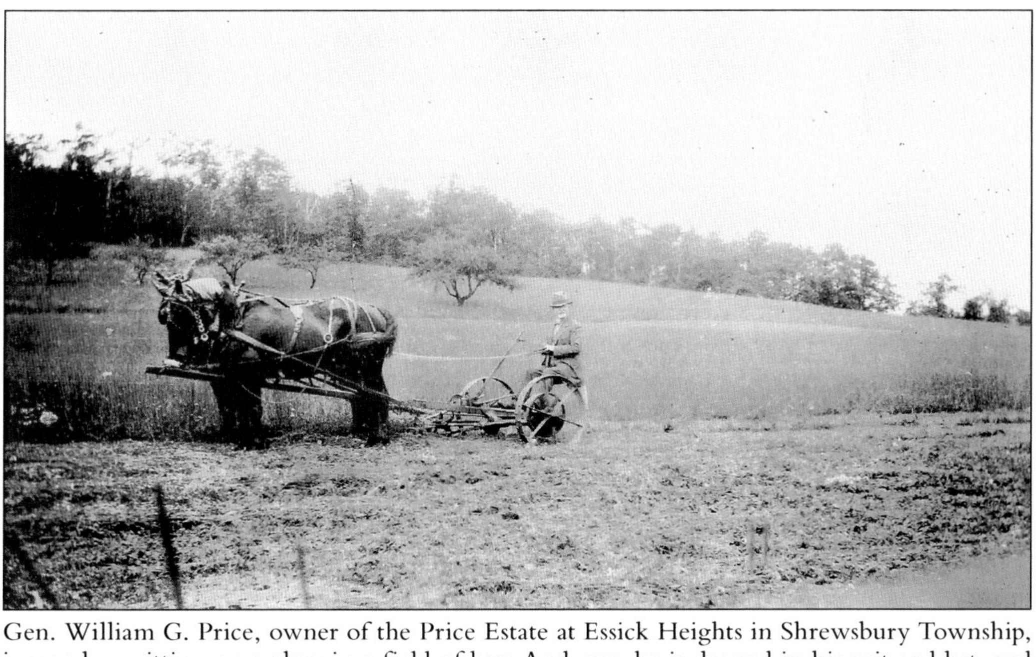

Gen. William G. Price, owner of the Price Estate at Essick Heights in Shrewsbury Township, is seen here sitting on a plow in a field of hay. And, yes, he is dressed in his suit and hat, and wearing a bow tie, in this obviously posed photograph. (Courtesy of Sue Shaner.)

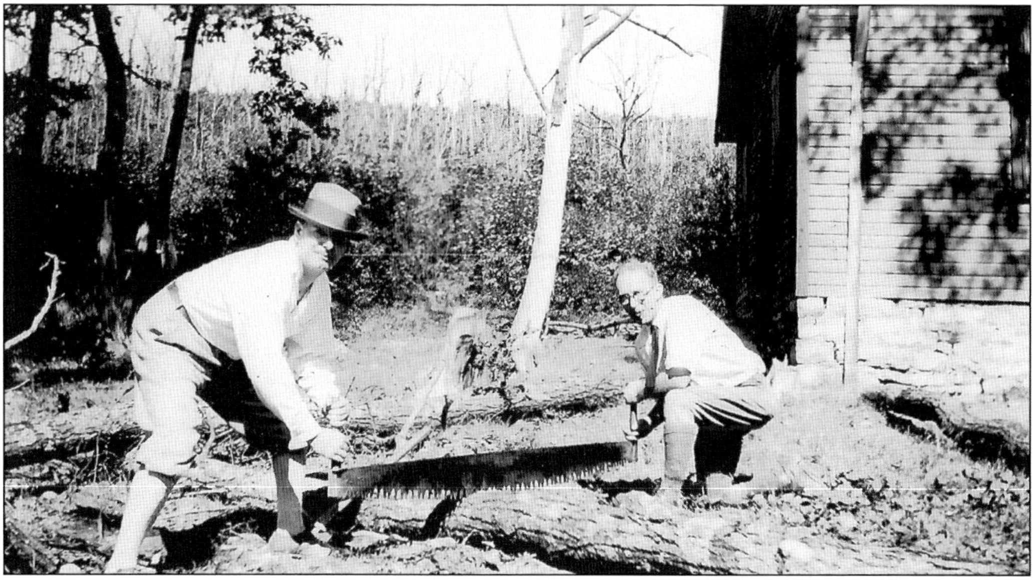

While farmers tilled the soil, gangs of loggers worked in the woods in Lycoming and Sullivan Counties. Knowing how to handle a crosscut saw was a necessity to provide the logs needed for wood stoves and fireplaces. Here is Roscoe Burrows with an unknown friend wielding a crosscut at the Wind Whistle Inn at Essick Heights. (Courtesy of Sue Shaner.)

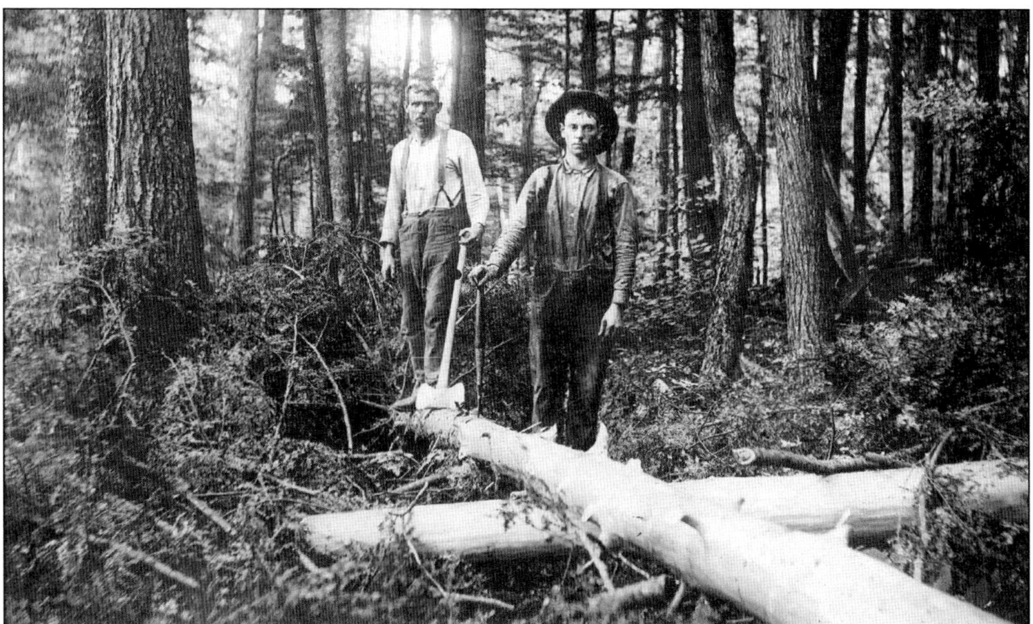

Many Hughesville-area men seeking an honest day's work joined logging gangs working in surrounding counties. There they stripped bark from hemlock trees to be used in the tanning process. Often a father and son worked together, as seen here with father Monroe Stroup (left) and son Aaron. Monroe is also pictured on the opposite page, at top left, with an unidentified logger. (Courtesy of Aaron Houseknecht.)

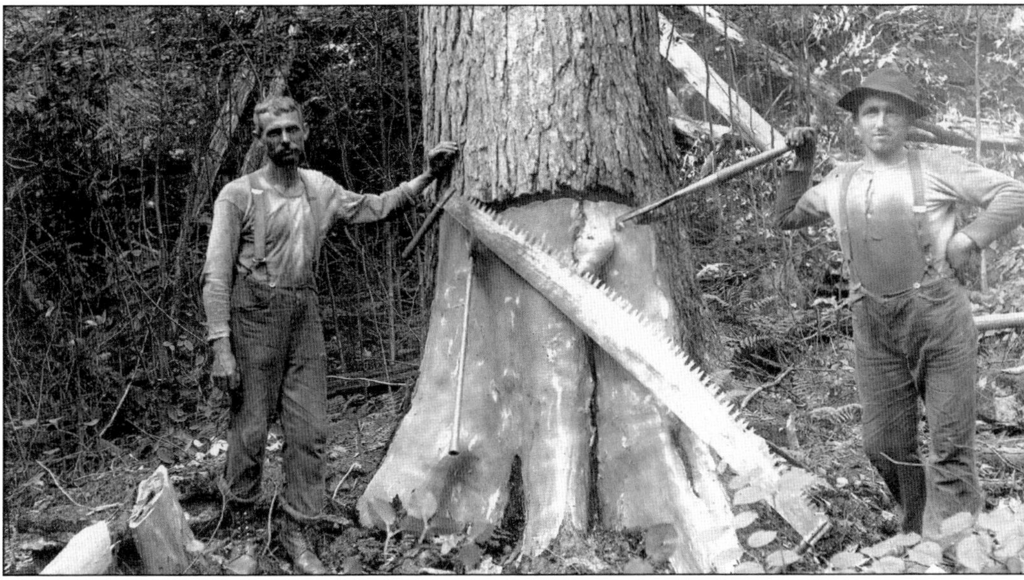

Nolan's Lumber Camp is seen below in 1915. Shown are, from left to right, (center, first row) Mac Houseknecht, Harv Smith, unidentified, Brady Whitmore, Jess Bryan, Carl Rightmire, and George Brown; (second row) Bill Wolf, unidentified, Lloyd Miller, Gene Shoemaker, "Pegleg" Sherman, unidentified, Joe Ambs, Harry Brown, next three unidentified, Less Horn, unidentified, Gust Bennett, unidentified, Arch Rider, unidentified, unidentified, Flem Bradley, Johnny Critter, and George Nolan; (third row) unidentified, George Cooper, George Swank, Harry Flick, Bucky Minnier, Joe Nolan, John Annable, unidentified, ? Balos, Jim Davis, unidentified, George Oranger, Charlie Howard, unidentified, George Sherman, and two unidentified; (fourth row) unidentified, Jim Bradley, Snap Norris, unidentified, Sam Sherwood, Roe Houseknecht, unidentified, Bill Taylor, John Braker, Amos Wank, unidentified, Ray Sullivan, Izai George, unidentified, ? Rooker, unidentified, Aaron Monroe Stroup, unidentified, unidentified, Norman Brown, and two unidentified; (fifth row) four unidentified, Jack Kating, Sam Rider, unidentified, and Clarence Sullivan. (Courtesy of Aaron Houseknecht.)

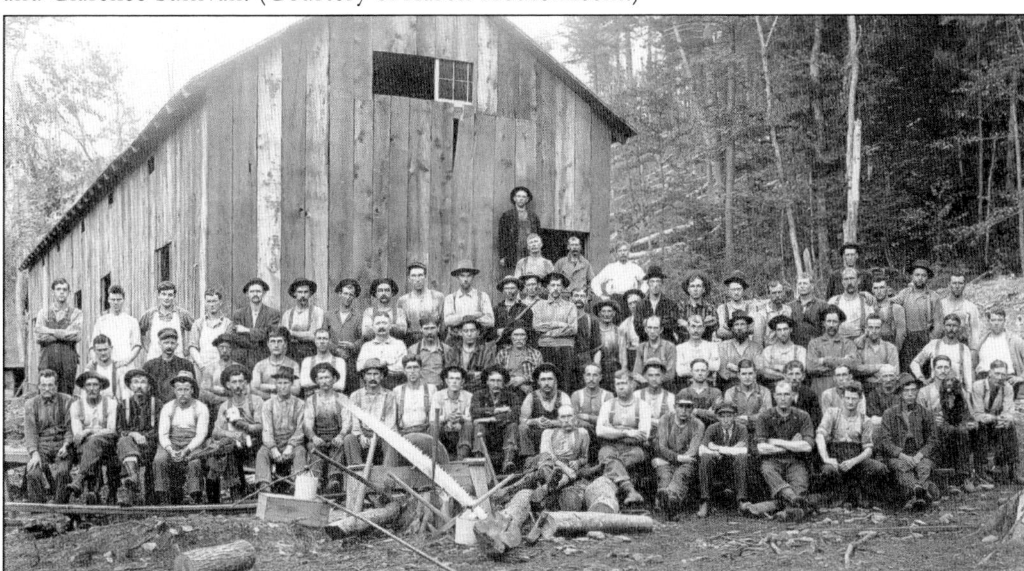

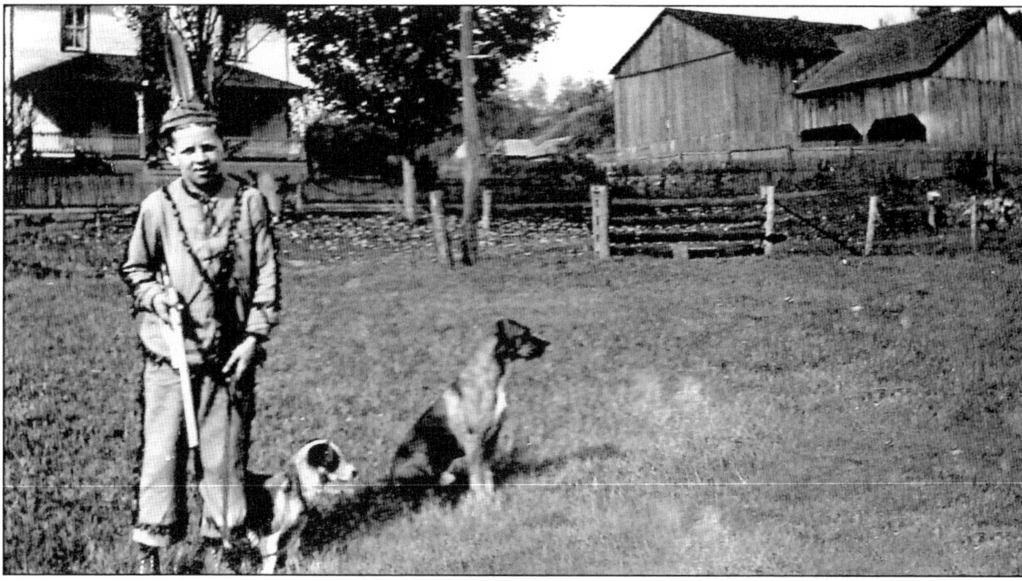

Country boys grew up to be hunters, so learning to handle a gun and dogs came early in life. Here young Justin Rynearson plays a dress-up, feather-headdress game with his toy gun and dogs in the fields of his home near Highland Lake around 1915. The dogs appear to have caught the scent of a rabbit, perhaps? (Courtesy of Sue Shaner.)

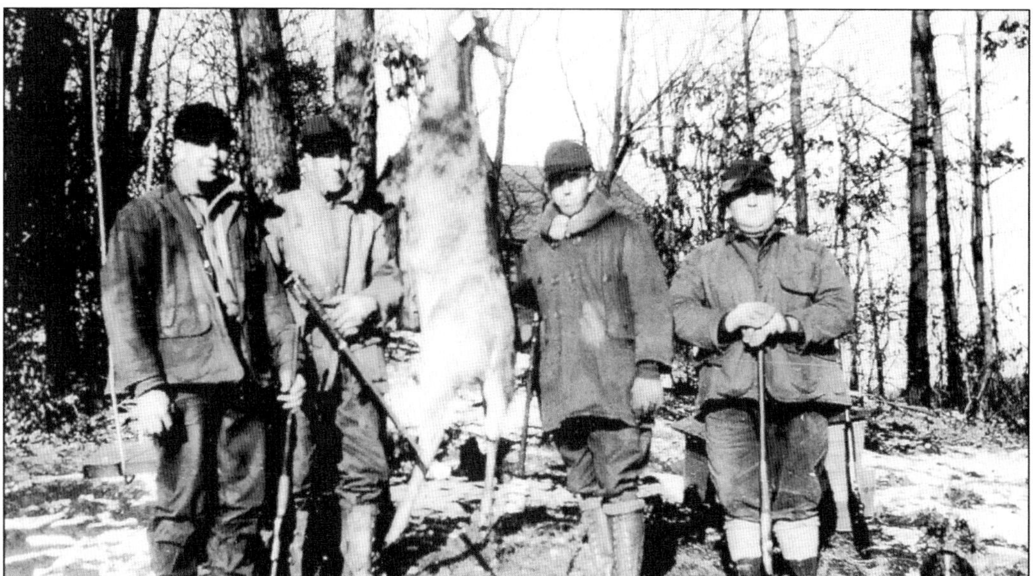

Deer hunting was an annual ritual for the men and boys. They dressed in their warmest wool coats, filled their pockets with shotgun shells, and trudged out before dawn to their tree stands to wait. This successful hunt at Camp Genesee shows, from left to right, Ernest Taylor and Raymond Taylor (next to deer) with two unidentified hunting buddies. (Courtesy of Sue Shaner.)

During the early 1890s, ring-necked pheasants raised in England were purchased by private citizens who released them in Lehigh and Northampton Counties. Through stocking and private game farms, the pheasant population increased locally, especially after 1923, when laws were enacted that restricted season and limits. Torrence Houseknecht was thrilled when he bagged this pheasant on his farm in Penn Township.

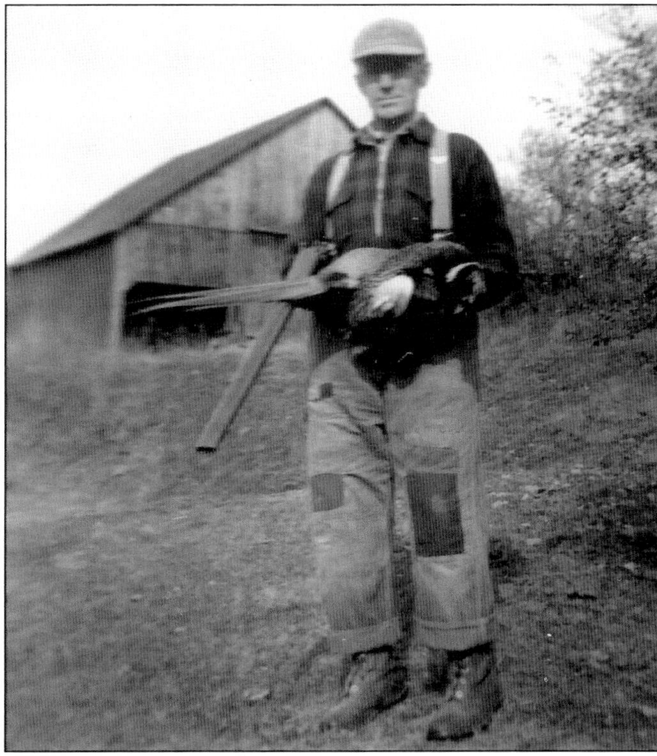

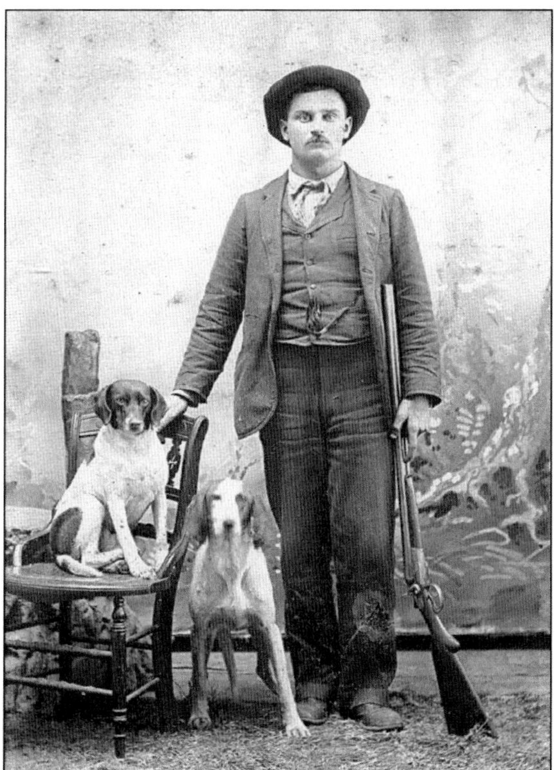

Posing with his dogs and rifle in this undated portrait is Rem (also known as Remmie or R. C.) Bussler, who was born around 1871 in Hughesville. By 1920, he and his wife, Alta, were raising their five children as he continued to operate his own butcher shop on Main Street, which he established during the early 1900s.

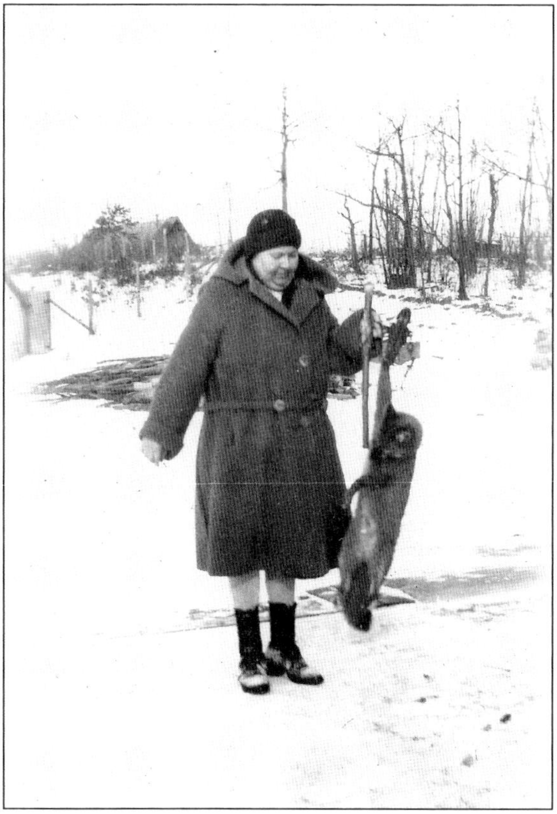

Although the women did the majority of the work around the house, tended the garden, and fed the chickens, many also helped out by setting traps to catch game, as Nan Bennett Taylor is seen here with the gray fox she trapped at Camp Genesee on Highland Lake. (Courtesy of Sue Shaner.)

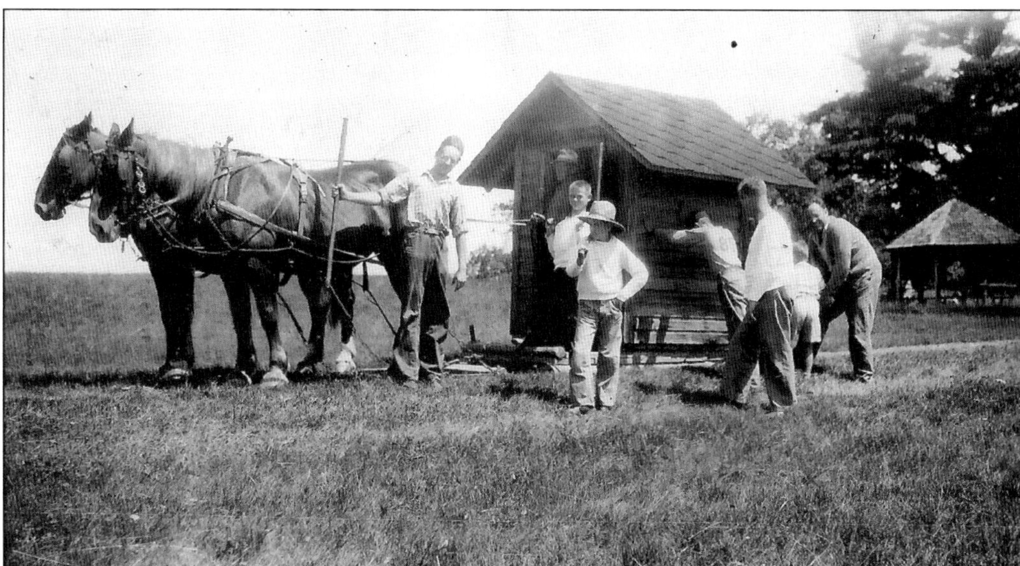

Figuring out a way to make a difficult job fun is evident here when these men were confronted with the job of moving an outhouse at the White Cloud Cottage to the Bellevue Cottage at Camp Genesee. Pictured are, from left to right, Bill Price, Raymond Taylor (standing inside outhouse), Gilroy Daymon, Bob Price, David Price (pushing against the building), Alrich Price, Bob Granger Jr., and Bob Granger Sr. (Courtesy of Sue Shaner.)

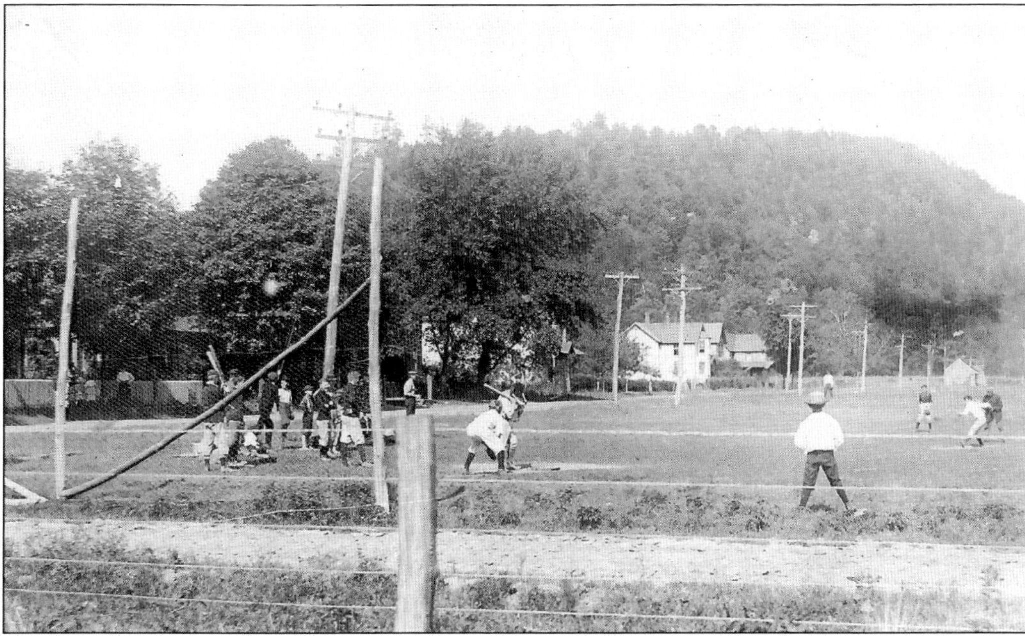

Participating in some form of sports or outdoor recreation was commonplace. Here a baseball game is being held in one of the fields outside Glen Mawr. Spectators watch the game from the cool shade provided by the trees along the fence, and the next batter aims for the corn field just past left field. (Courtesy of Stewart Hill.)

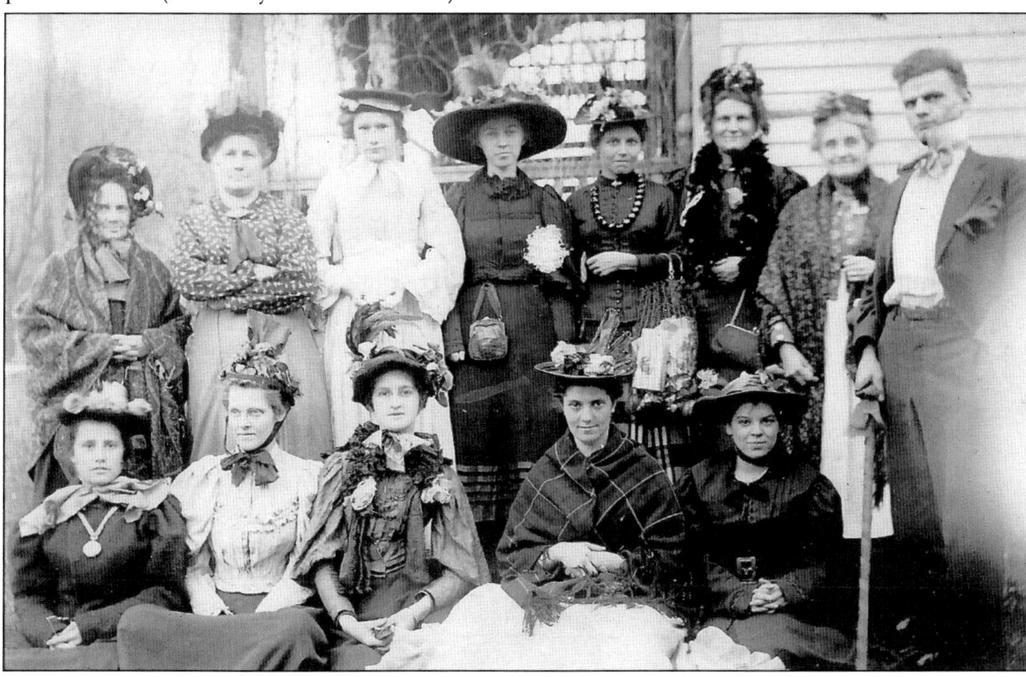

These amateur thespians pose for a photograph as they prepare for their production's dress rehearsal. Rev. William Wilson Reeder, the gentleman on the right, is the only person identified in the photograph. He was born in Huntersville and served as a Methodist pastor in Trout Run and the Eagles Mere area. (Courtesy of Sue Shaner.)

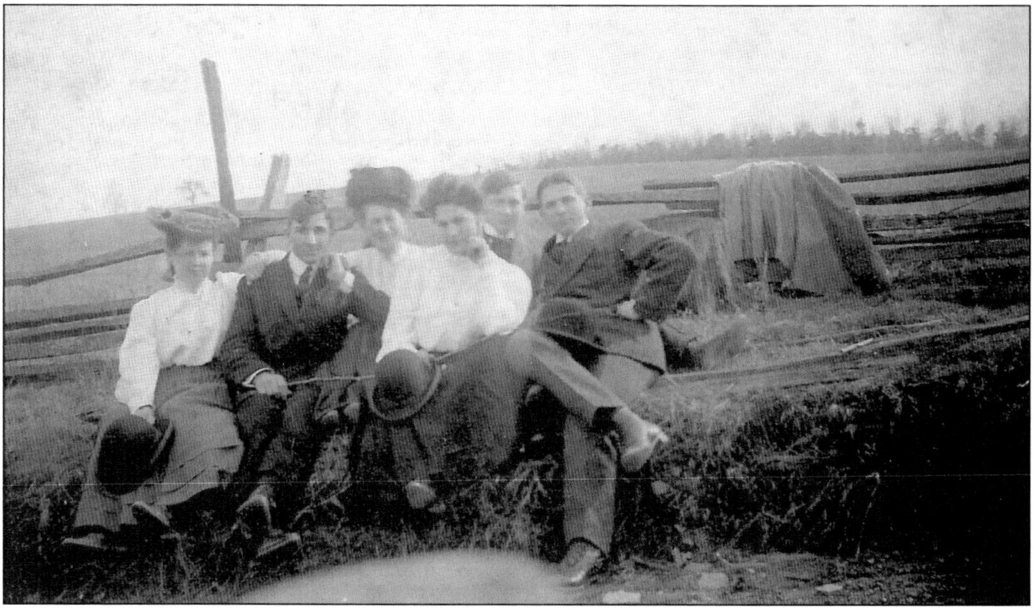

Young people took advantage of every church service, box social, or Sunday school picnic to relax and enjoy the company of friends and relatives. Here a group from the Hughesville area lounges on bales of hay. Seen above are, from left to right, an unidentified young lady sitting next to Chester Houseknecht, Ocie Houseknecht, Elsie Houseknecht, unidentified (in back), and Ralph Hausknecht. And these young ladies (below) are dressed in their Sunday best. They are, from left to right, Mame Poust McClain, Hazel Holmes Houseknecht, and Jane Holmes Myers as they pose for a picture before joining Lavina Poust Montgomery in the buggy for a ride home from church or possibly a ride to the fair?

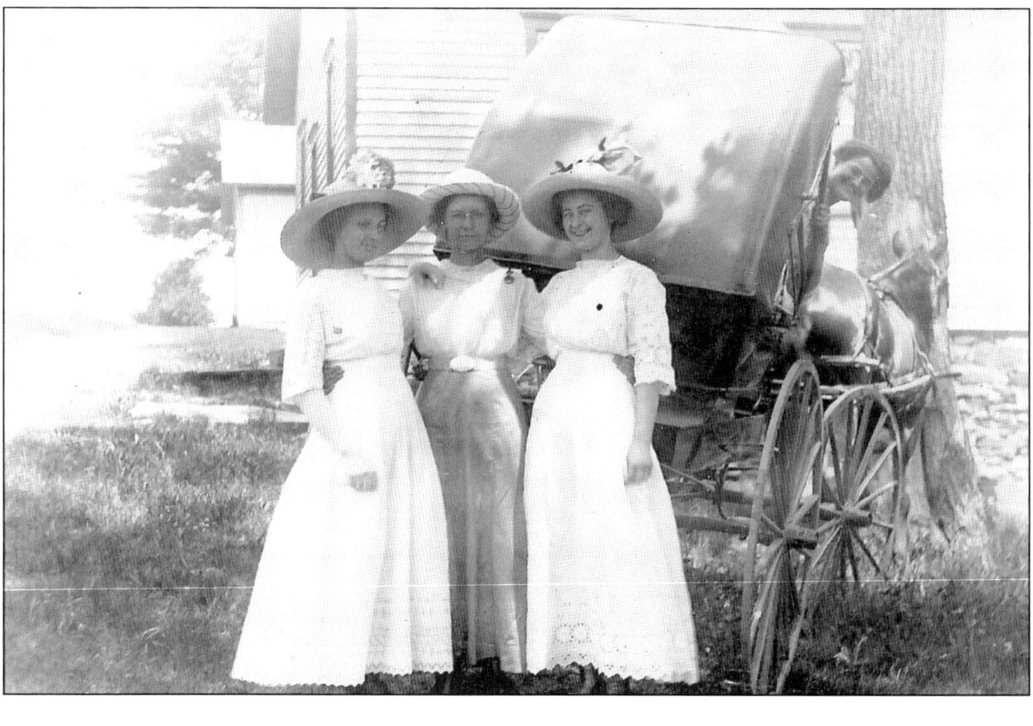

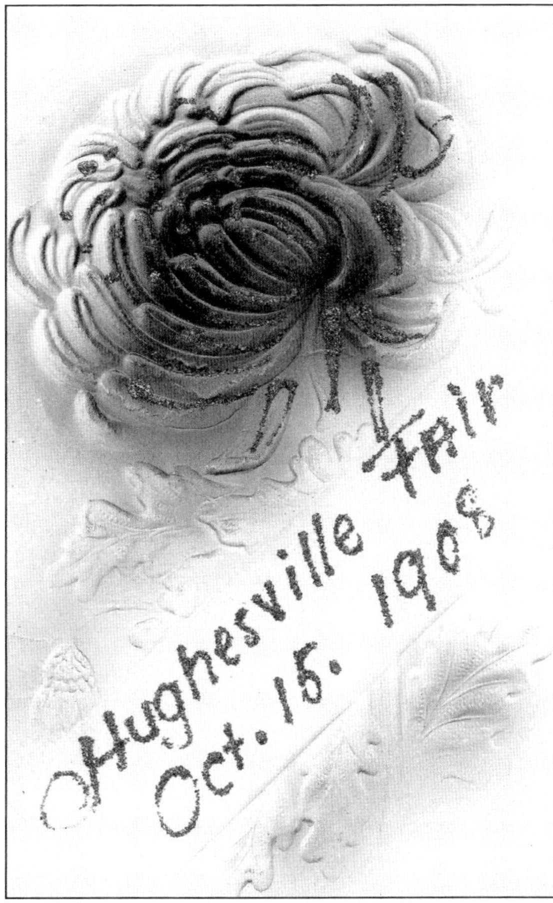

In the fall of 1870, the 10-member Muncy Valley Farmers' Club held its first agricultural exhibition on the grounds of its club, located on the eastern edge of town. Within a few years, the club's membership grew to over 200, and the annual event featured a decorated wagon parade and the judging of livestock, produce, flower arrangements, and women's handcrafted items. In February 1908, the farmers requested a delay of the beginning of the fair from mid-September to mid-October. According to the *Hughesville Mail*, "this, it is believed, will work to an advantage all around, permitting the farmer to get through with his fall work and also have his crops and fruits all gathered so that he may be able to attend the fair." (Below, courtesy of Polly Hess.)

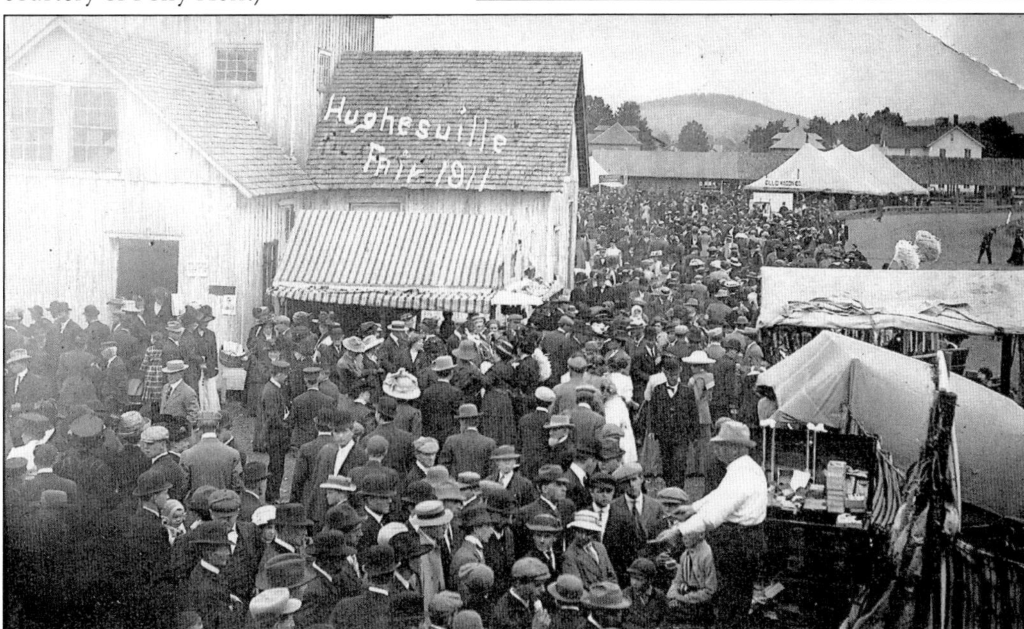

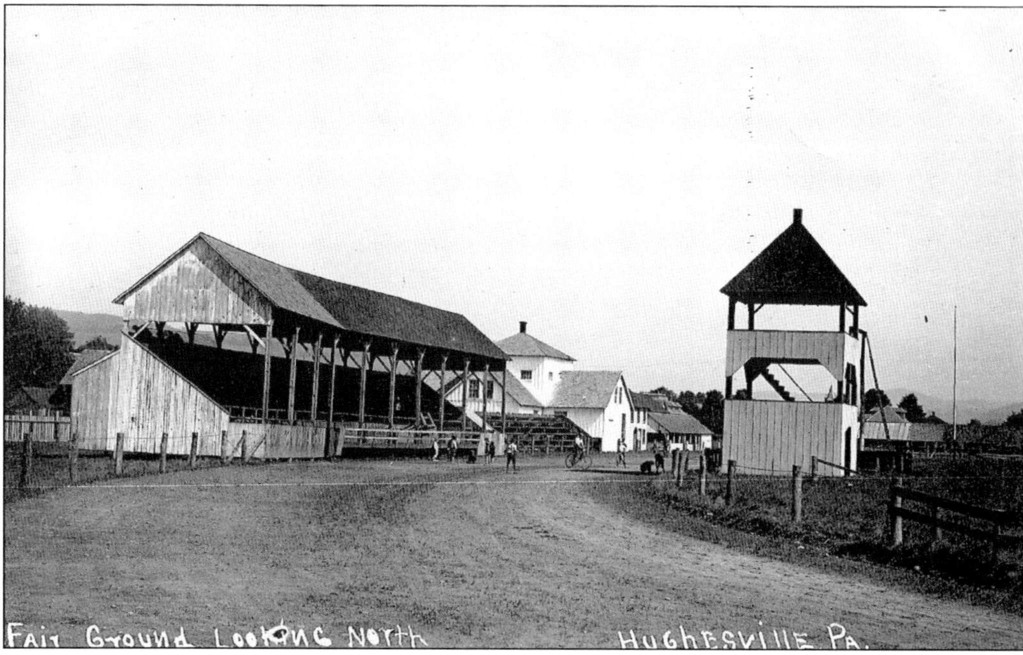

A grandstand was eventually built on the fairgrounds to help fairgoers view the trotting horses that had become a popular event at the fair. As early as 1873, it was reported in the *Canusarago Daily Herald*, a special paper printed during the fair that year, that "the trotting against time for fastest trotting horse or mare . . . created considerable amusement, and was witnessed by a large crowd." The horse stables and the cow barns were popular places for fairgoers to meet and start their day at the fair. These fields would overflow with families who arrived early in the morning, dressed in their best clothes, with picnic lunches to eat throughout the day. By early evening, the grounds would again empty as the crowds returned home. (Above, courtesy of Mary Fox Odell; below, courtesy of the East Lycoming Historical Society.)

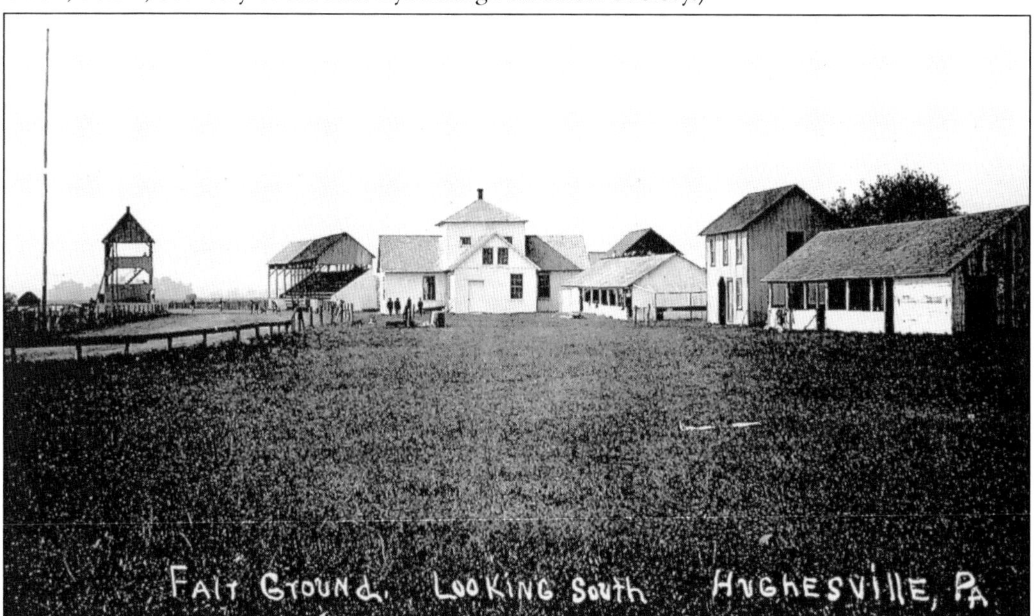

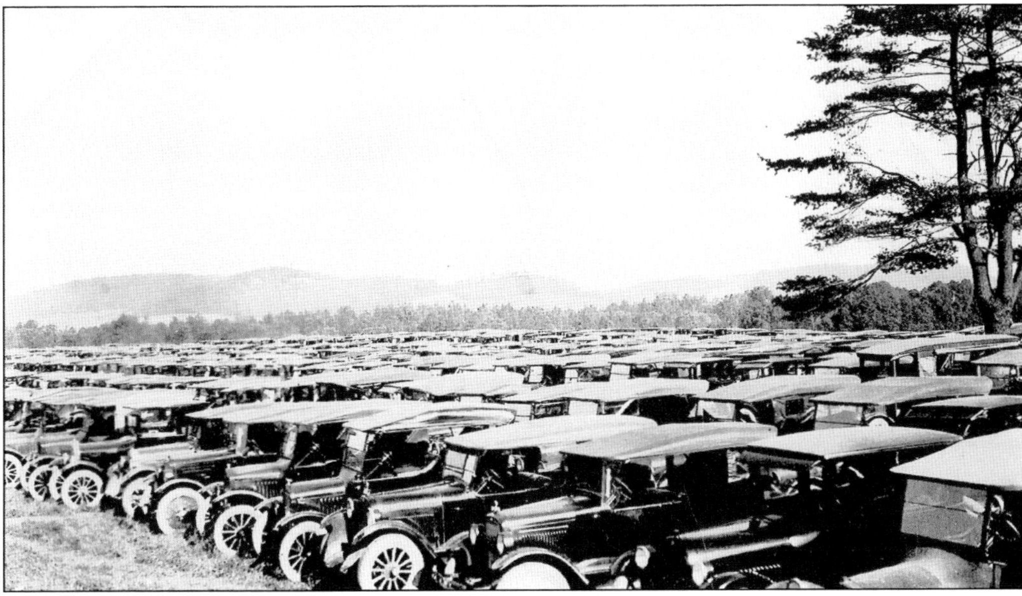

Transportation to the fair could have been a cart pulled by an ox, as seen on the front cover, or it could have been a wagon or carriage pulled by a horse or two, but by the 1930s, the parking lot at the fair would look like this (above)—filled with motorized automobiles. And what would one see at the fair? There were games along the midway, gypsies telling fortunes, penny-pitches, the merry-go-round, and the ever-popular judging of agricultural items. (Above, courtesy of Kenneth D. Poust; below, courtesy of the James V. Brown Library Archives.)

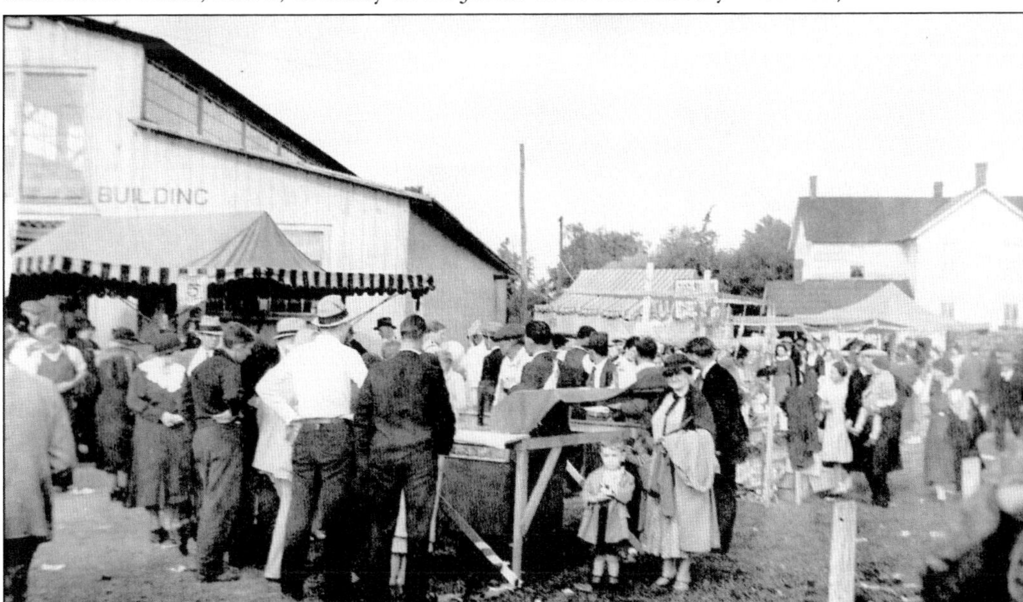

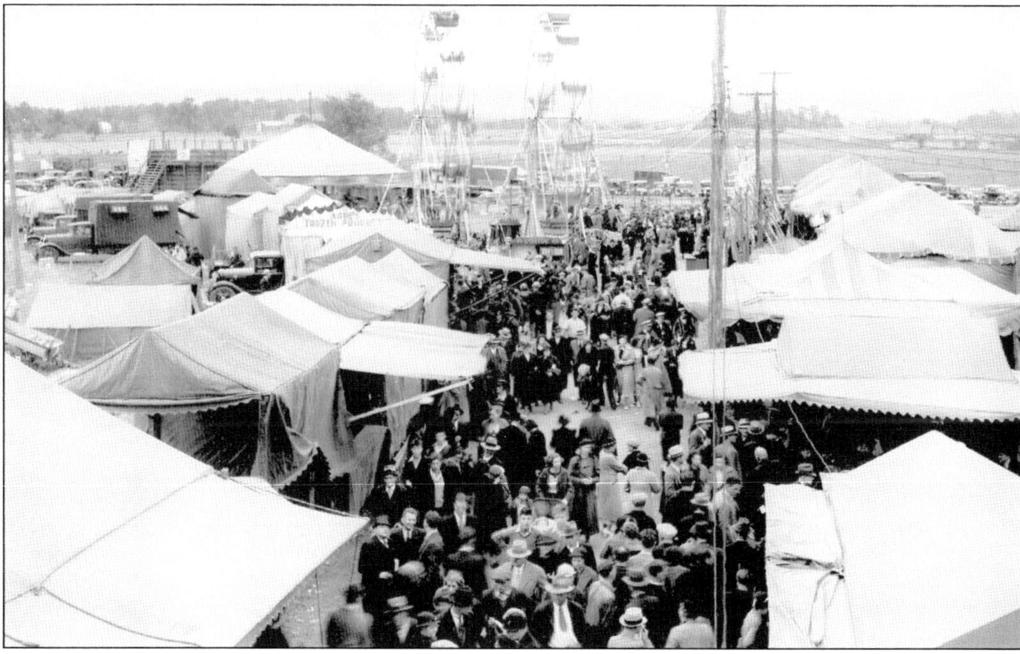

As the fair grew, more and more people would attend, with some coming from other counties on Williamsport and North Branch Railroad excursion trains. The midway would become a throng of bodies moving through the narrow pathway. This would provide wonderful opportunities for pickpockets to help themselves to wallets and ladies' bags. (Courtesy of the James V. Brown Library Archives.)

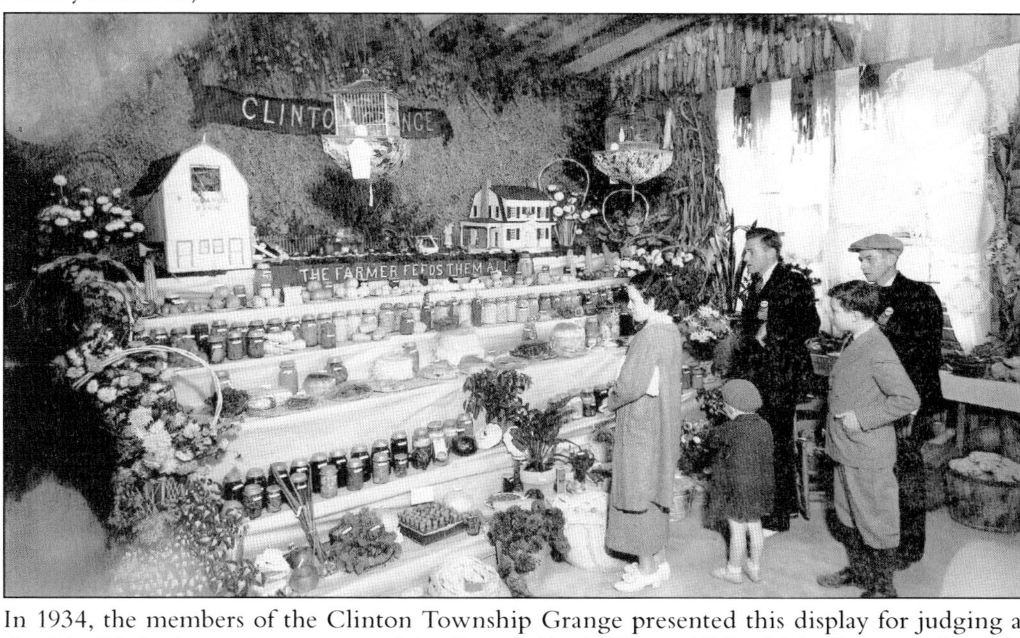

In 1934, the members of the Clinton Township Grange presented this display for judging at the fair. Their theme that year was "the Farmer Feeds Them All," which illustrated how the contribution of farmers affects everyone. The Grange organization in Pennsylvania was formed in 1873 and is dedicated to the betterment of rural America through community service, education, legislation, and fellowship. (Courtesy of the James V. Brown Library Archives.)

Four

Church Bells and School Bells

Early churches and one-room schools shared many similarities. Both were buildings with a bell on the roof that was rung to announce the beginning of the day, and both had seats positioned so that the audience could easily hear and see the speaker at the front of the room. Many of the earliest church societies actually worshipped in existing schoolhouses before their church buildings were constructed. And many schools, when they were built, were located near existing churches. Traveling long distances was not an option, so each neighborhood often established its own church and school.

Many of the one-room schools in and around Hughesville have been torn down, some are being used as private homes or community buildings, while a few stand empty as silent reminders of the past. Memories of the pot-bellied stove that overheated the tiny room and the long, lonely walks to and from school are fading as fast as the photographs that are seen on the following pages. A map and a list on pages 100 and 101 will help locate the 57 school buildings that once stood—with a bell on the roof and a teacher waiting at the front of the room.

There were about half as many churches as there were schools, but they were the centers of activity in the communities they served. While 5 churches formed in Hughesville, more than 20 churches in the surrounding townships held Sunday services, baptized their babies, and buried their dead. These microcommunities, each with at least one school and one church, covered the rural areas near Hughesville.

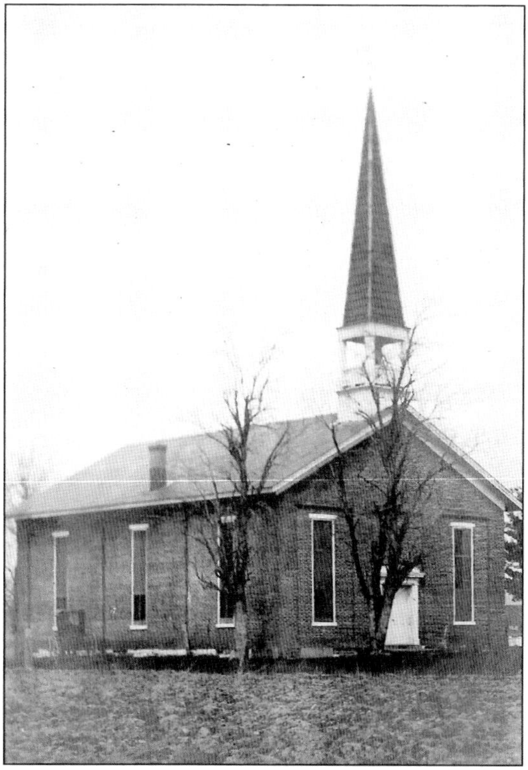

Built in 1791, the Immanuel Lutheran Church located south of Hughesville is considered the oldest church in Lycoming County. Originally known as the Emanuel Kirche, this structure was quite large in comparison to the simple log cabins in the area. It had a seating capacity of 600 arranged in a gallery on three sides of the building. It has been closed since 1920 except for special anniversary services. (Courtesy of Mary Fox Odell.)

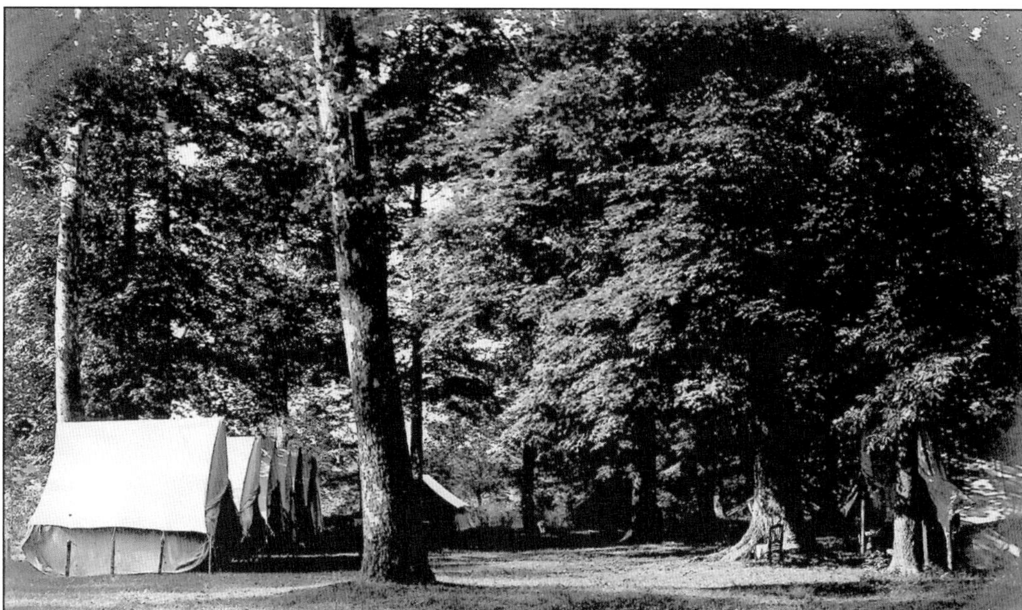

These meeting grounds were where the Society of Friends held their meetings between 1900 and 1905. Groups of over 60 people from Fribley, Opp, Montoursville, and other communities gathered on the island near the millrace. They camped in tents and rough dormitories and were known as the Holiness Camp Meeting Association. Other groups also used this remote area to hold revivals and rallies. (Courtesy of Mary Fox Odell.)

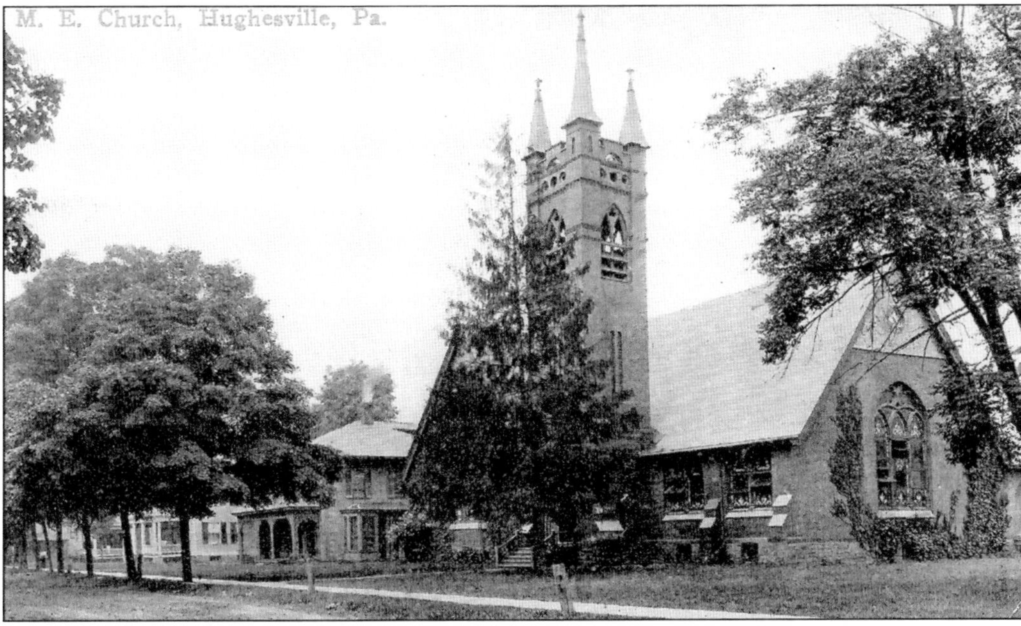

About 1833, the Methodist Society in Hughesville began meeting in the log schoolhouse at the corner of Main and Academy Streets. In 1844, the group built the first church building in Hughesville on Main Street between Academy and Cemetery Streets. In 1891, a new brick building was erected (above) that was Gothic in design. The new sanctuary (below), featuring large stained-glass windows, was dedicated to service in 1893. The total cost of the new Methodist Episcopal church building was $12,000. In 1925–1926, major renovations included the installation of a pipe organ in the church sanctuary, the addition of Sunday school rooms, and a social hall nearby. (Above, courtesy of Stewart Hill; below, courtesy of Mary Fox Odell.)

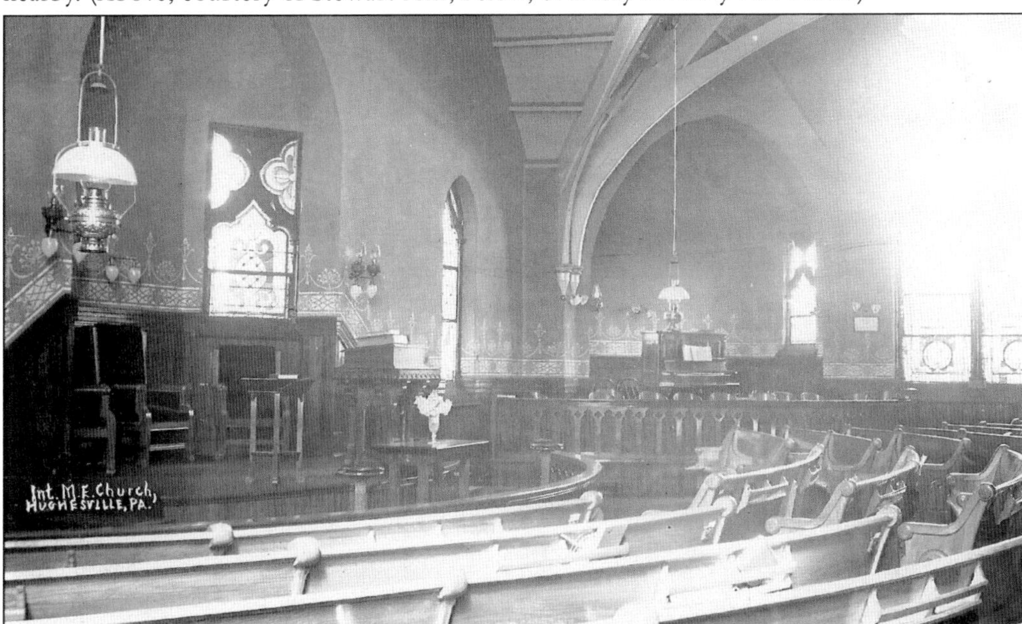

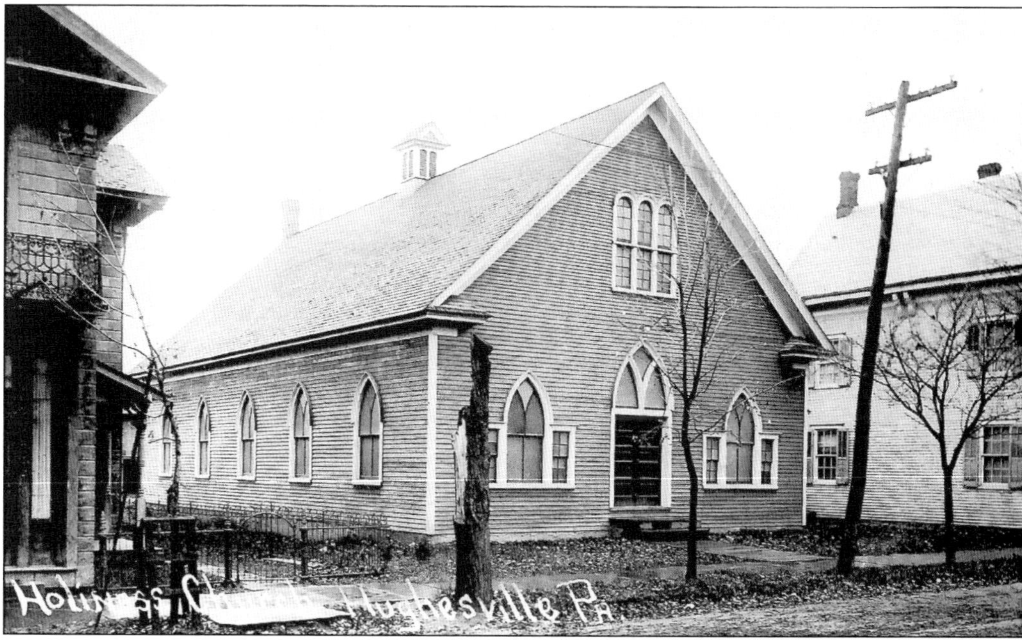

This Holiness Church building on East Water Street (above) was dedicated into service in April 1906 after followers of Sara P. Eckroyd held their meetings in a succession of locations including the Newman School, on the island in tent meetings, and an upstairs hall on North Main Street. By 1912, the Holiness congregation joined with the Meeting of Friends of Damascus, Ohio, to become the Friends Holiness Church. Note that the front steps of the church (below) were redesigned, and the unsightly tree stump in front had been cut. (Above, courtesy of Stewart Hill; below, courtesy of Mary Fox Odell.)

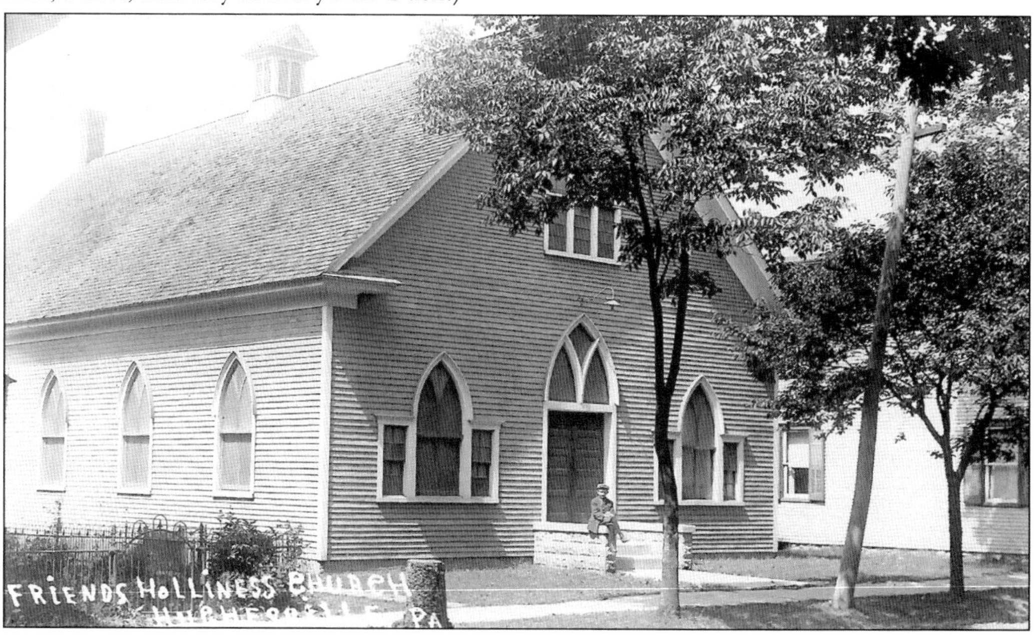

The first Baptist church (right) was built in Hughesville in 1891 on the corner of Water and Third Streets. Previously the Baptist congregation used the Wolf Township school building and commissioned Robert Lowry to preach for $1.50 per Sunday. Lowry was a composer and hymn writer who authored such pieces as "Shall We Gather at the River" and "Savior Thy Dying Love." (Courtesy of Kenneth D. Poust.)

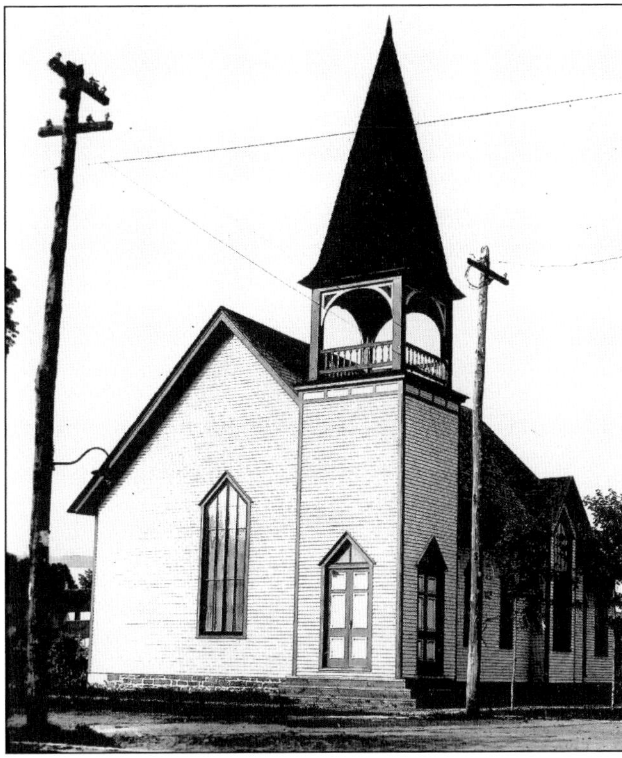

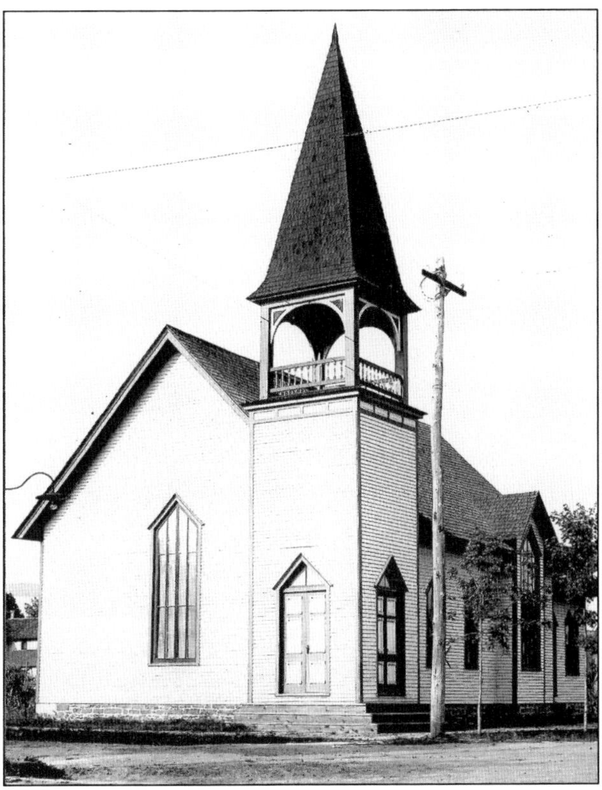

On this page are two identical images of the church with an amusing difference. To eliminate the offensive telephone pole seen on the left side of the top image, it was removed (left)—only to leave the wires suspended in the air, attached to an invisible pole. (Courtesy of Mary Fox Odell.).

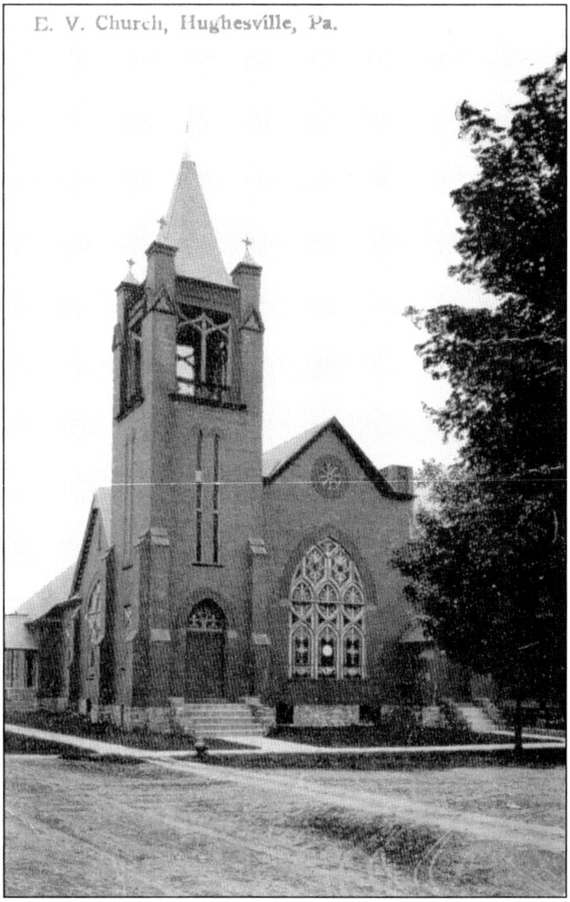

In 1866, the Bethany congregation in Hughesville was organized and joined the United Evangelicals in 1891. The redbrick church (left), at the corner of Second and Academy Streets, was built in 1897 at a cost of less than $6,000. Many pastors and their families enjoyed the convenience of living in the spacious parsonage next to the church on Second Street. Pictured below at the corner of the front porch are, from left to right, 10-year-old David Young and his 9-year-old brother, Reuben, sitting on the banister behind his father, Rev. David F. Young, who was pastor at the Evangelical church in 1912 when this photograph was taken. Sitting on the front steps are Reverend Young's wife, Jennie, and his 72-year-old mother, Dorothy, who lived with them. (Left, courtesy of Stewart Hill; below, courtesy of Mary Fox Odell.)

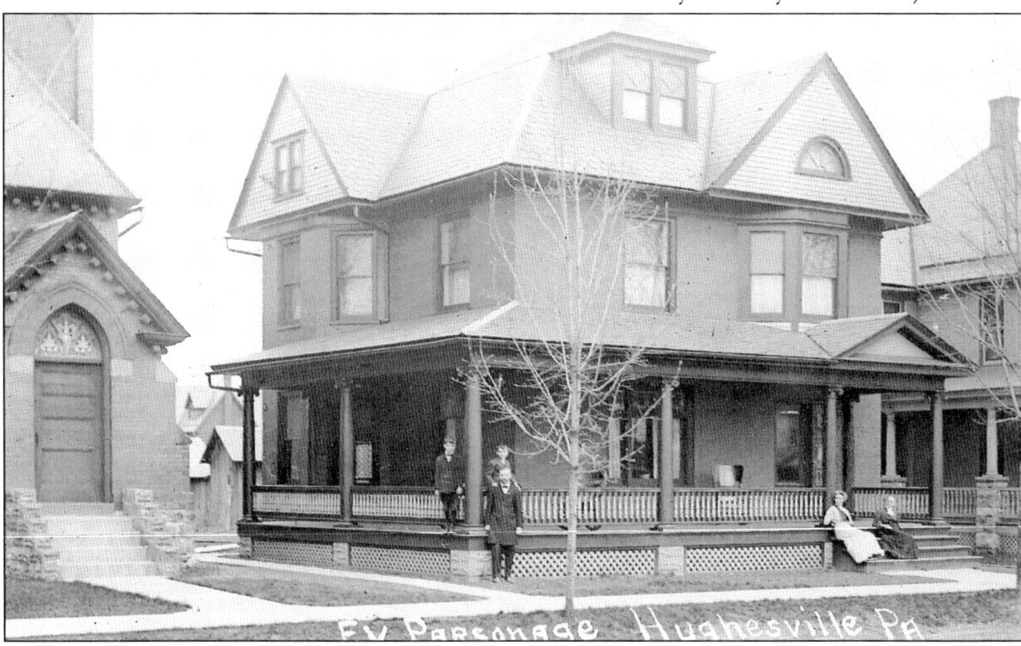

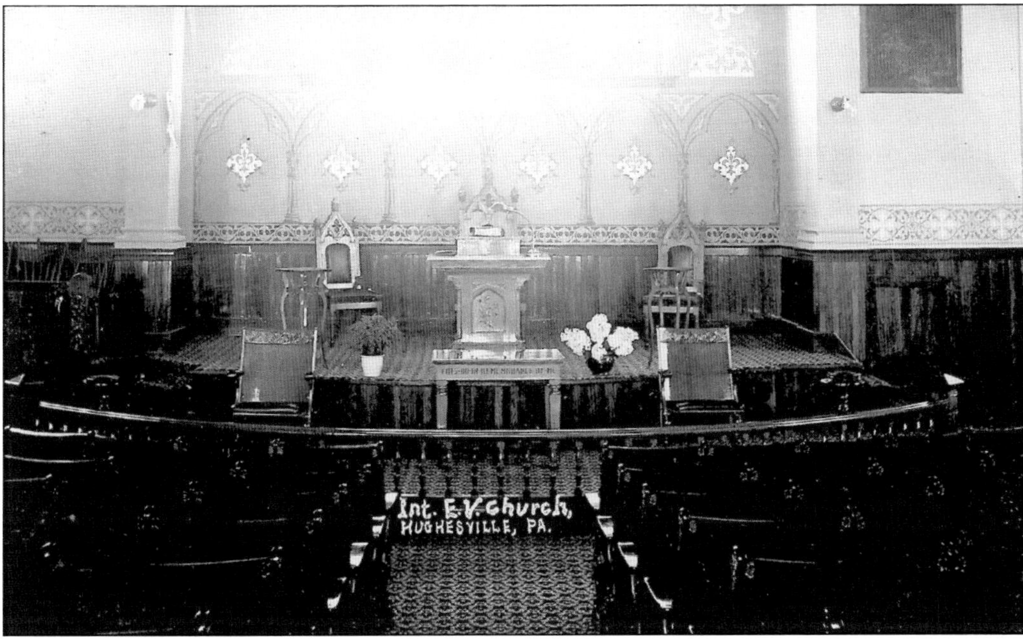

The original sanctuary of the Evangelical church measured 40 by 60 feet and featured hard wood chairs with flip-up seats situated on a gradually slanting floor (below). Large stained-glass windows were positioned to the right and rear of the seated congregation. Renovations in 1962 included the reorientation of the seating, moving the altar in the sanctuary, and the installations of a pipe organ, storm windows, insulation, and the ramp in the front of the building. During this reconstruction of the first floor areas, church services were held at the Wolf Elementary School Building at the corner of Academy and Main Streets. Rev. B. G. Hoffman officiated the rededication service in December of that year. (Courtesy of Mary Fox Odell.)

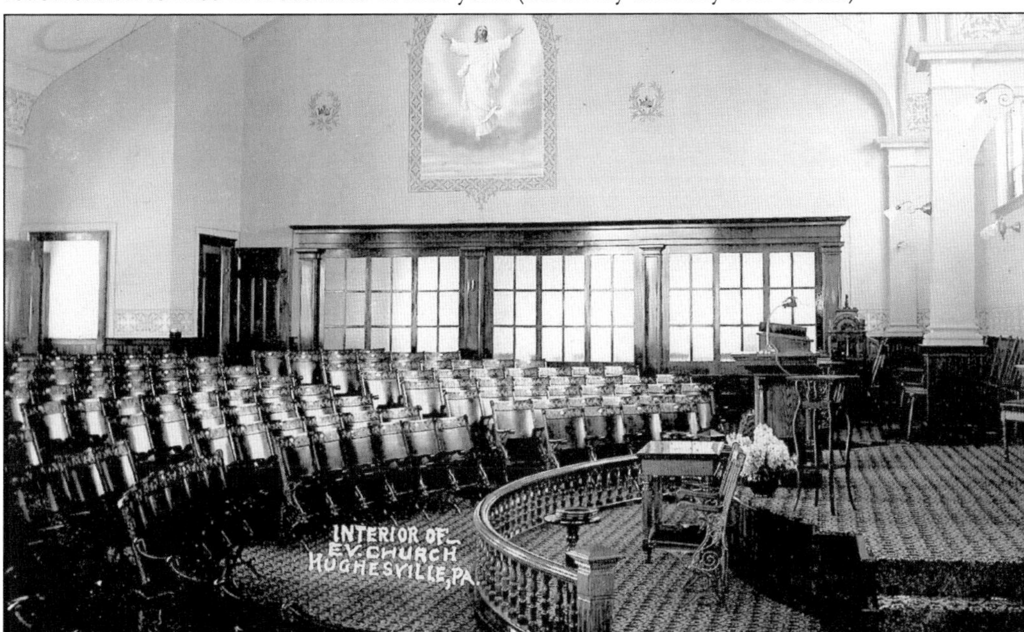

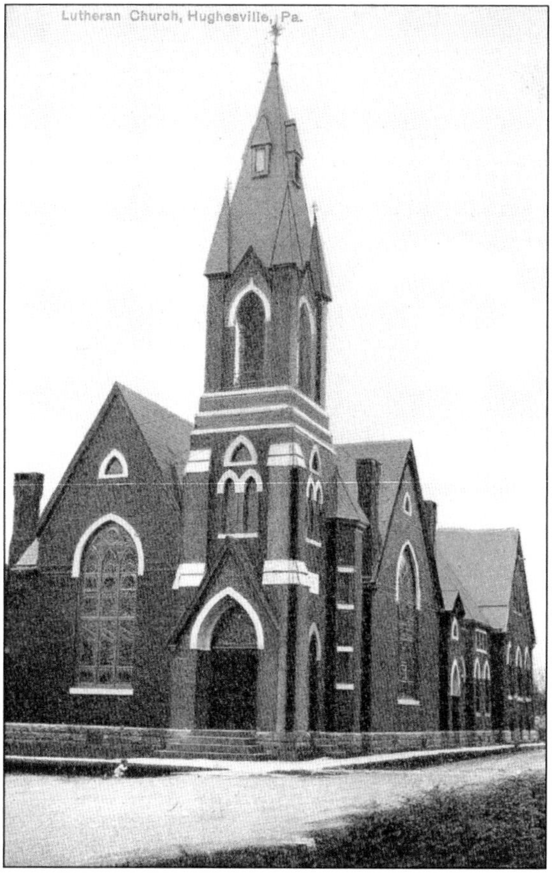

In 1850, about 300 members of the Lutheran congregation separated from the mother Immanuel Lutheran Church (see page 88). They built a church on Main Street near the public school building but within 25 years, a new brick church on the corner of Main and Academy Streets (left) was erected to accommodate the growing congregation and avoid repair of the old building. The cornerstone was laid in August 1884 and dedication services took place September 13, 1885. In 1915, a pipe organ (below, right) was installed in the church sanctuary. The organ was donated by Sen. Charles W. Sones in memory of his mother. (Left, courtesy of Joe Barlett; below, courtesy of the East Lycoming Historical Society.)

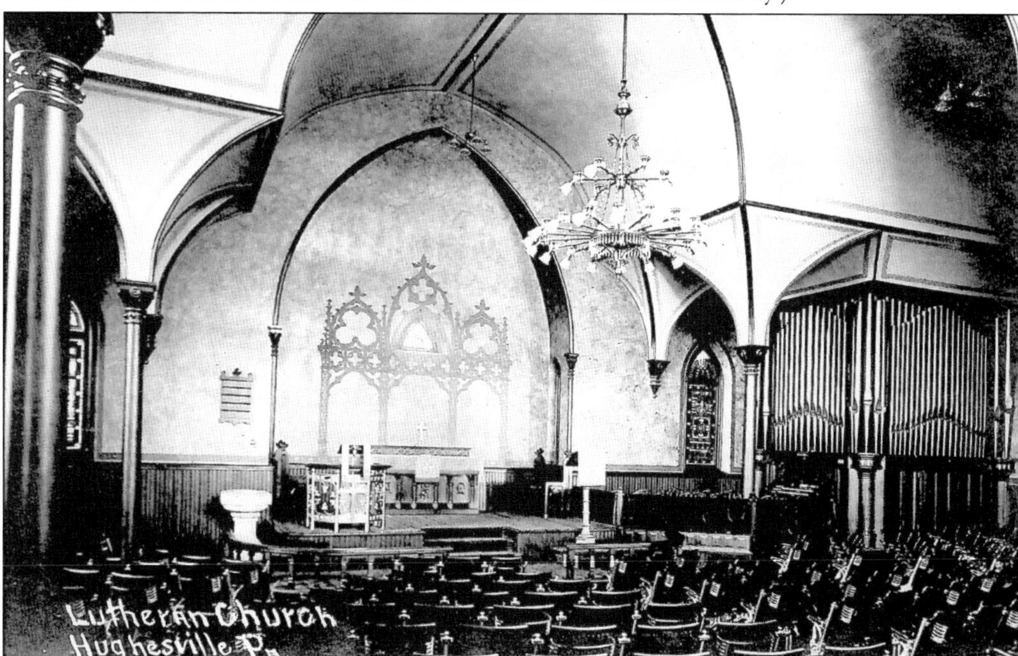

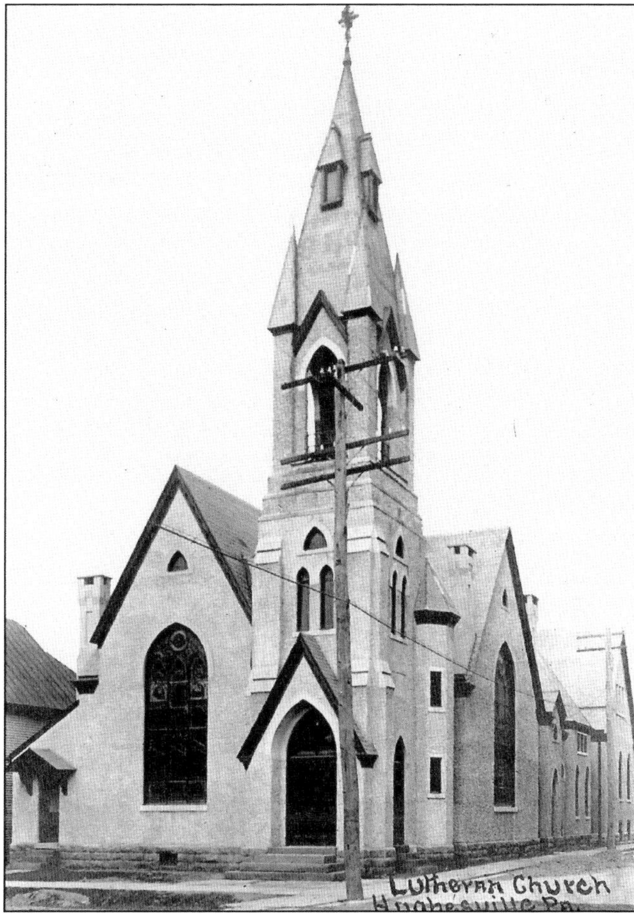

The exterior of the Lutheran church was transformed when it was stuccoed in 1915 (right) when other renovations were done. The stucco was applied by H. E. Shaffer of South Williamsport for $720 plus $65 to erect scaffolding. The church parsonage (below) was initially located on Water Street until property next to the church building was purchased in the 1930s. At that time, the present parsonage, located next door to the church, was built and completed in 1938. (Right, courtesy of Mary Fox Odell; below, courtesy of Edward Smits.)

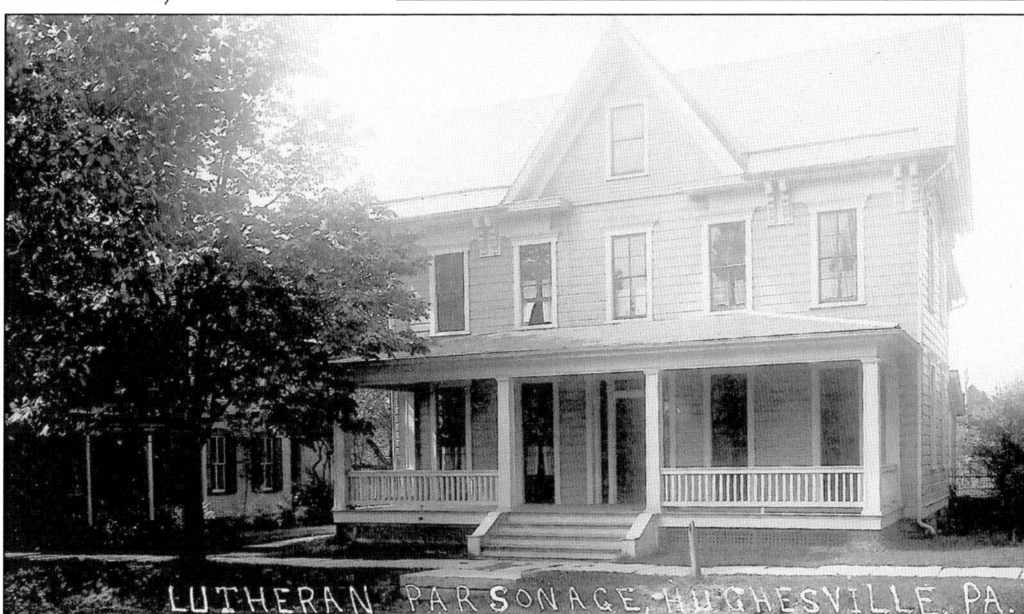

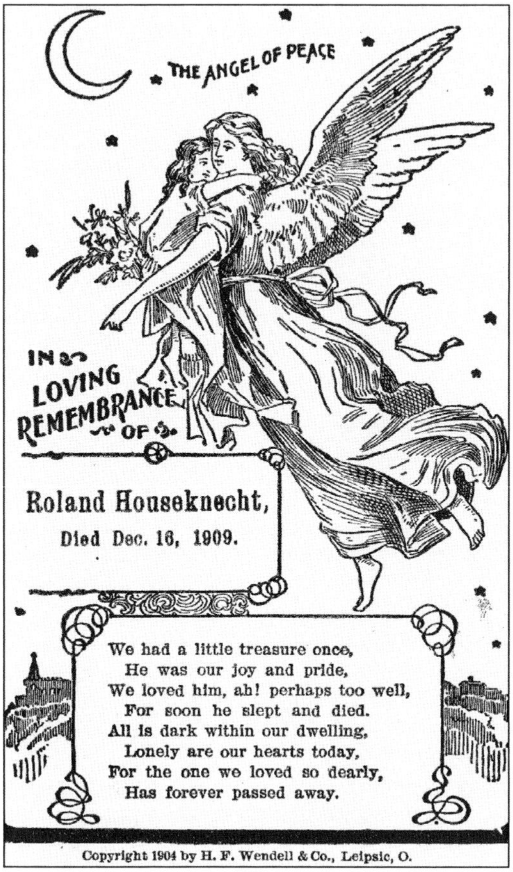

Death came early for many residents of Hughesville during the early 20th century. This funeral card (left) is in memory of young Roland Houseknecht, who was only seven years old when he died of an unrecorded cause. Inside the chapel (below) at Hughesville's Pleasant Hill Cemetery, the pump organ can be found that was contributed by Benjamin Welch, the manager of the Williamsport and North Branch Railroad. He had originally purchased it in 1894 for his daughter, 22-year-old Miriam, as a wedding gift. Tragically she was killed just weeks before her wedding in a train accident as she and her fiancé, Lewis McClenathen, were on their way to Williamsport to get their marriage license. He was also fatally injured. Miriam was buried in her bridal gown, beside her intended, at Pleasant Hill Cemetery, not far from the chapel. (Below, courtesy of Mary Fox Odell.)

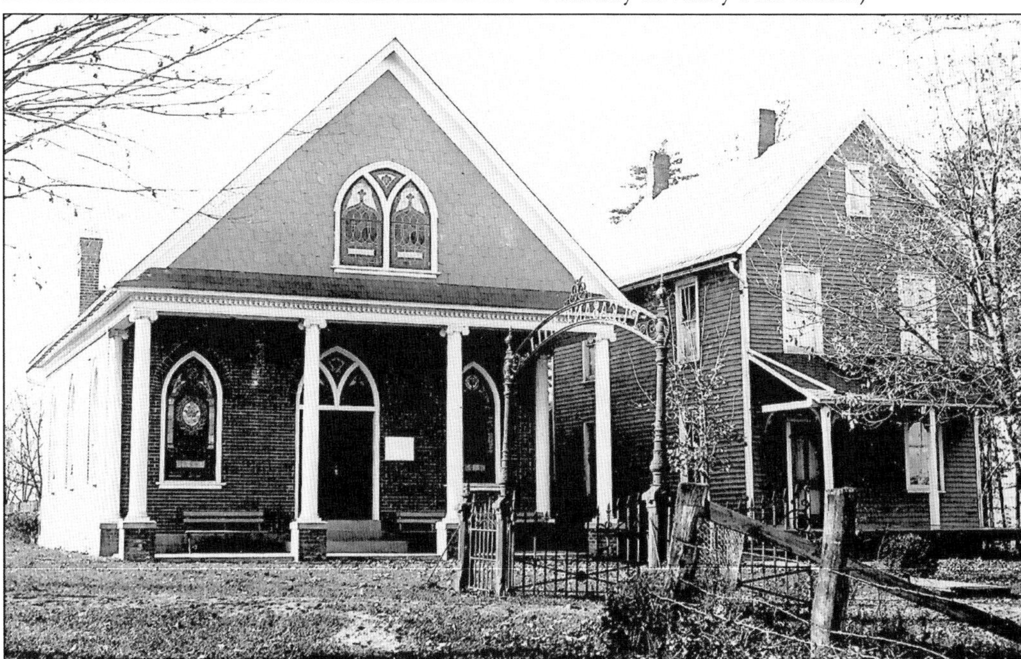

Lairdsville's Lutheran congregation built its first church around 1857 at the southern end of town. Early in 1890, a new building was erected (right), using stones found in nearby fields for the foundation and lumber cut at local sawmills. Materials from the old church building were sold to the school board to use in building a schoolhouse. (Courtesy of Nancy Hodge.)

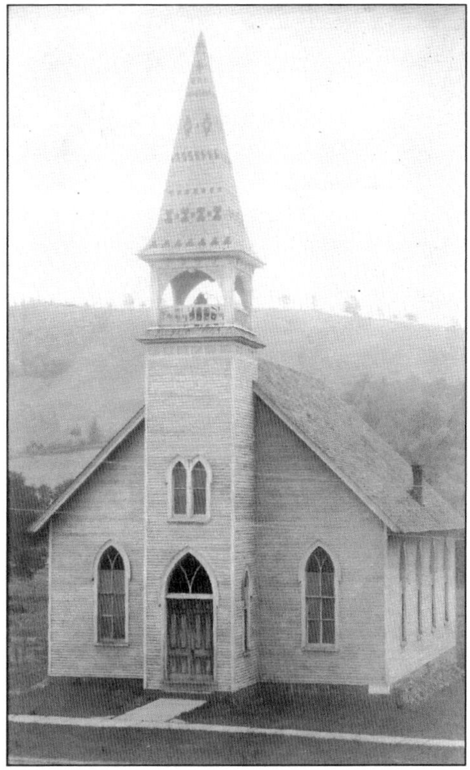

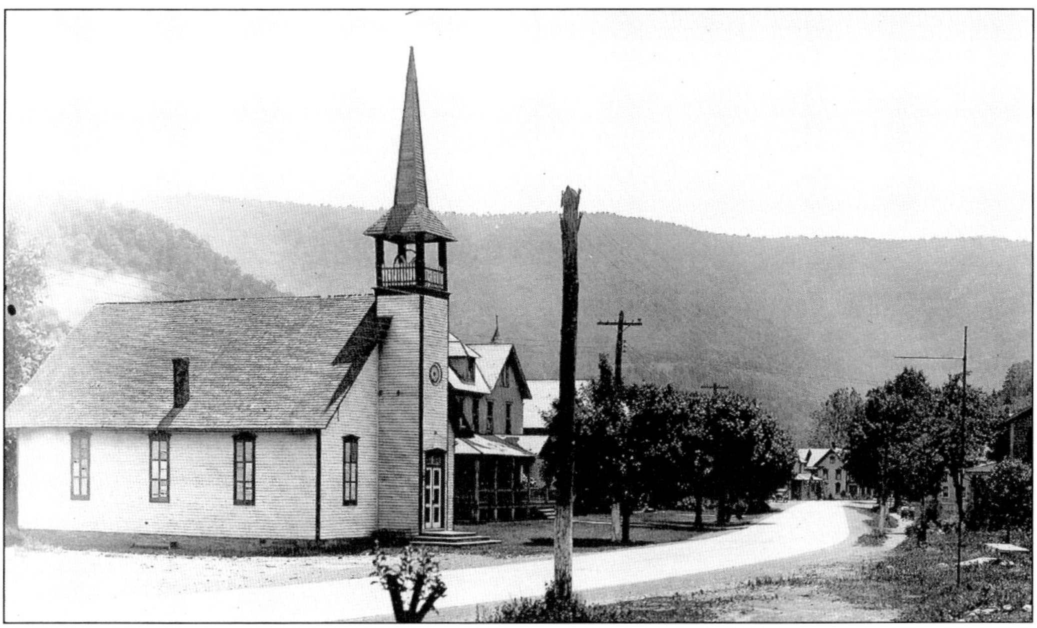

Originally built as a Baptist church, this building at the northern end of Lairdsville has led a very mysterious existence. When followers of the present Faith Church of Lairdsville assumed ownership of the building in 1985, no records of previous congregations were found. The building itself has been altered over the years, however. The entire front steeple has since been removed, as well as the front windows and steps. (Courtesy of the East Lycoming Historical Society.)

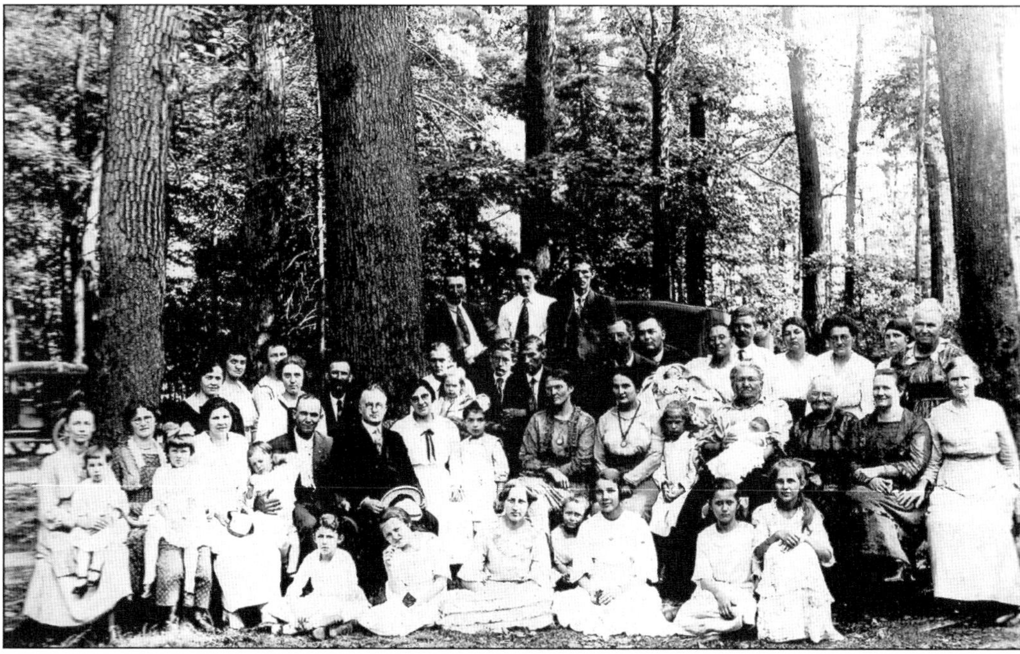

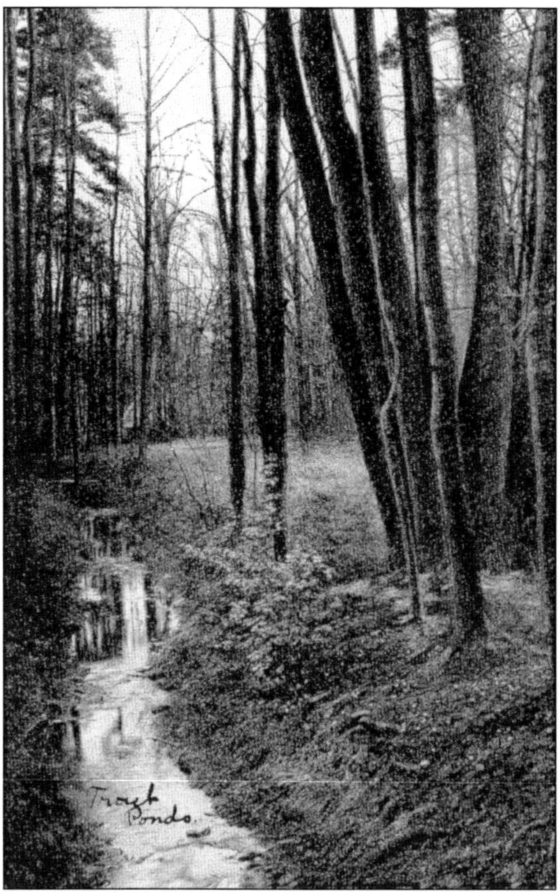

In 1922, members of Penn Township's Fribley Church Sunday school gathered for a picnic at Trout Pond Park (left). Seen above are, from left to right, (first row) Grace Miller, Helen Kepner, Lydia Pynearson, Eleanor Kepner, Bessie Carwley, Pauline Houseknecht, and Elva Holmes; (second row) Hazel Houseknecht, Clara Houseknecht, Naomi Miller, Annabell Miller, Edith Kepner, Paul Kepner, Valentine Kepner, Reverend and Mrs. M. W. Dayton, unidentified, Edith Poust, Laura Holmes, Laura Whitmoyer, Miriam Snyder, Viola Whitmoyer, Sarah Kepner, Leila Reed, and Ella Kepner; (third row) Viola Kepner, Lena Barto, Iva Kepner, Aola Parson, Russell Kepner, Sherman Crawley, Lena Dugan, Cleon Myers, Herman Poust, Thomas Alter Holmes, Irvin Holmes, ? Holmes, baby Irvin Holmes, Monroe Snyder, Alma Miller, Carrie Whitmoyer, Laura Rupert, and Melissa Snyder; (fourth row) Ernest Holmes, Alvin Holmes, and Harvey Whitmoyer. (Left, courtesy of Stewart Hill.)

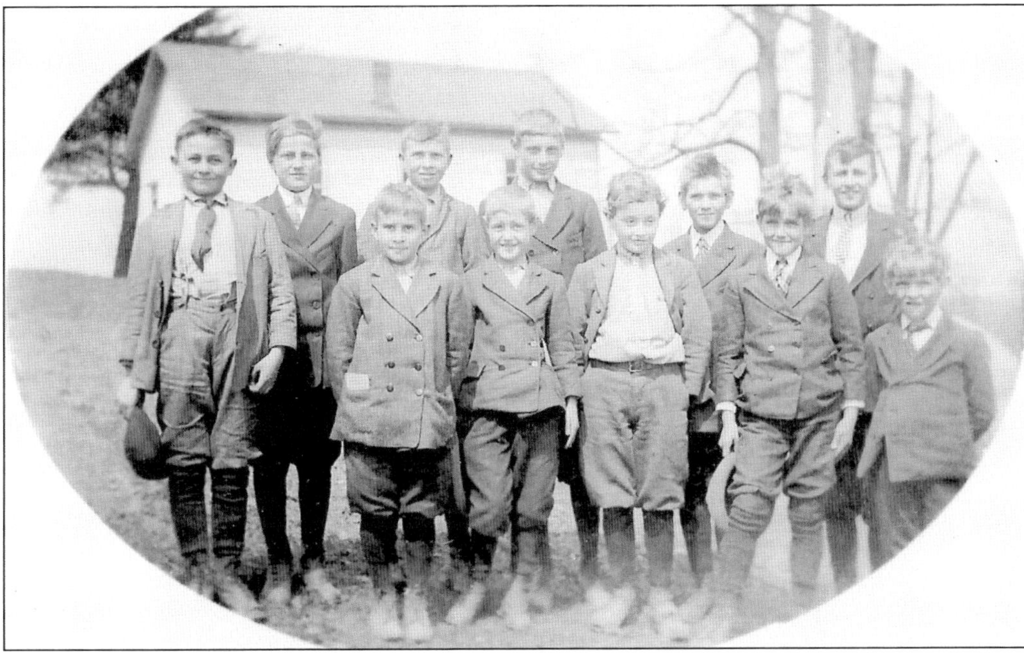

These boys (above) are members of a Sunday school class at Penn Township's Fribley Church. In 1914, they posed in their Sunday best and are, from left to right, (first row) Carl Figels, Cleo Green, Willis Snyder, unknown, and Clarence Crawley; (second row) Alvin Holmes, Jacob Poust, Howard Bogart, Burris Green, Joe Crawley, and Ernest Holmes. Below is the interior of the Methodist Episcopal church located at Point Bethel in Shrewsbury Township, near Glen Mawr. As was common around 1900, one pastor would minister at multiple churches. Services were often held at Point Bethel on Sunday evenings, after its pastor preached at neighboring Tivoli and Mapleton churches earlier in the day. (Below, courtesy of Elizabeth Rogers Knyrim.)

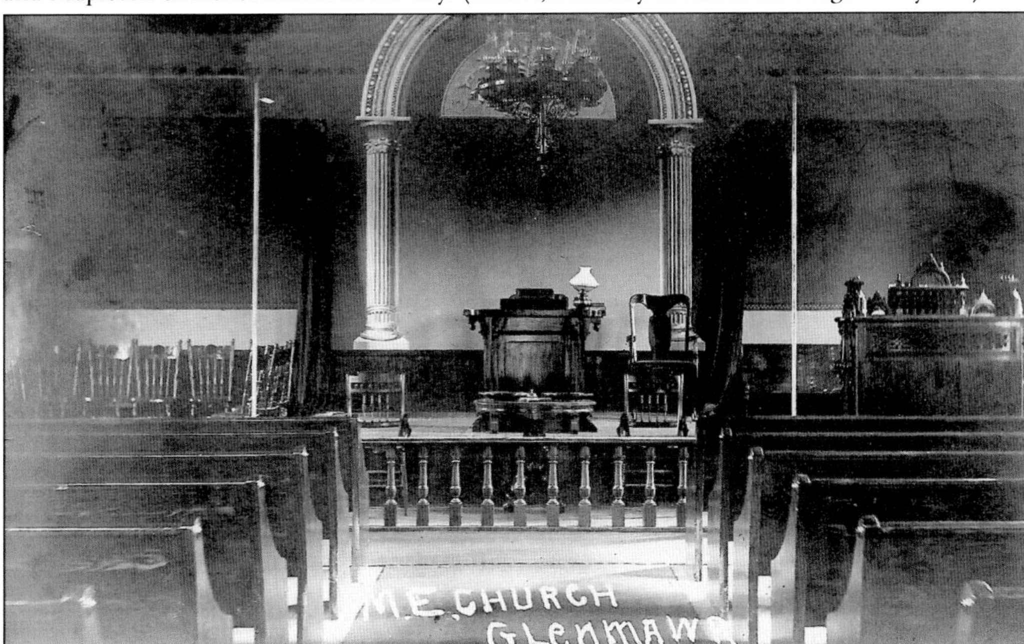

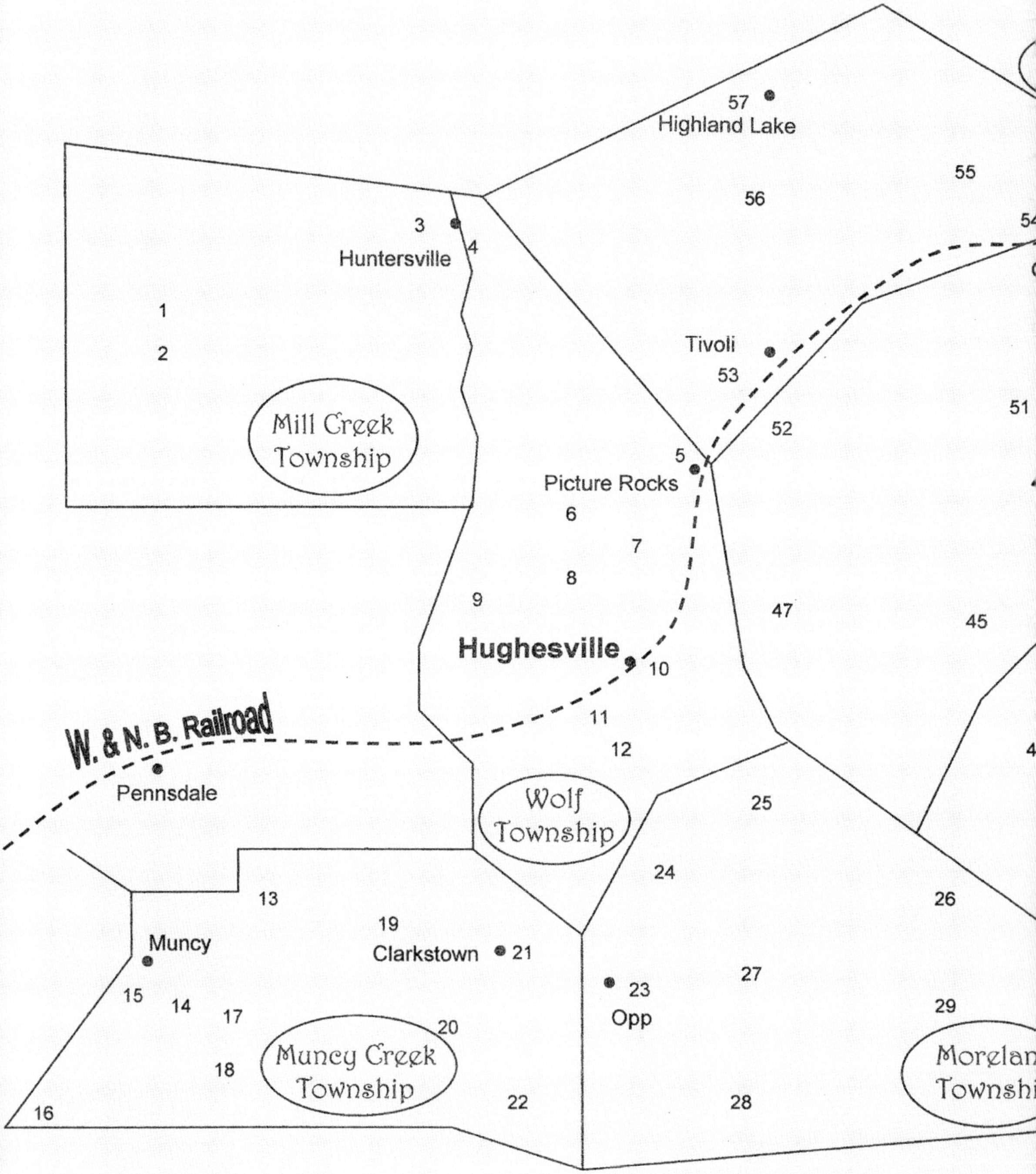
57
Highland Lake
55
56
3
4
Huntersville
1
2
Tivoli
53
51
52
Mill Creek Township
5
Picture Rocks
6
7
8
9
47
45
Hughesville
10
W. & N. B. Railroad
11
12
Pennsdale
25
Wolf Township
24
13
26
19
Muncy
Clarkstown
21
27
23
15
14
17
Opp
29
20
18
Muncy Creek Township
16
22
28

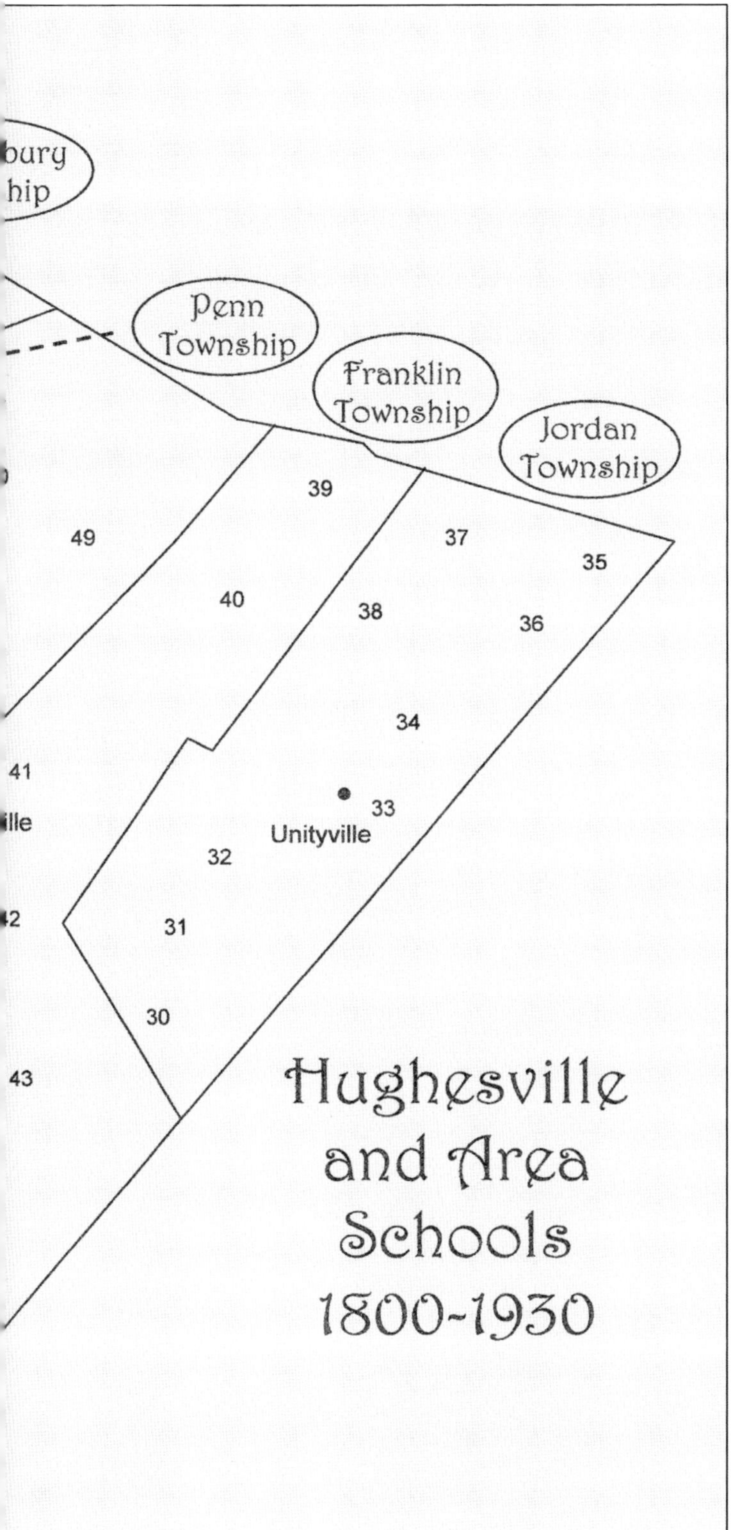

This map shows the locations for the 57 schools in the Hughesville area: Hites (1), Boyer (2), Gortner (3), Huntersville (4), Picture Rocks (5), Pine Run (6), Villa Grove (7), Newman (8), Keitly (9), Hughesville (10), Steck (11), Fairview (12), Buckley (13), Muncy Normal (14), Port Penn (15), Muncy Dam (16), Guide (17), Shane (18), Fairview (19), Glade Run (20), Clarkstown (21), Turkey Bottom (22), Opp (23), Hill (24), Green Valley (25), Frenchtown (26), Eight-Square (27), Pleasant Grove (28), Laurel Run (29), Gordner or Lore (Lohr) (30), Cleveland (31), Salem (32), Unityville (33), Grange (34), Peterman (35), Richard's Grove (36), Prairie (37), Biggertown (38), Pleasant Valley (39), Bald Eagle (40), Lairdsville (41), Germany (42), Chestnut Grove (43), Starr (44), Sugar Run (45), Derr (46), Frantz (47), Lyons (48), Marsh Run (49), Muncy Creek (50), McCarty (Fribley) (51), Neff (52), Tivoli (53), Point Bethel (54), Pine Grove (55), Mapleton (56), and Highland Lake (57).

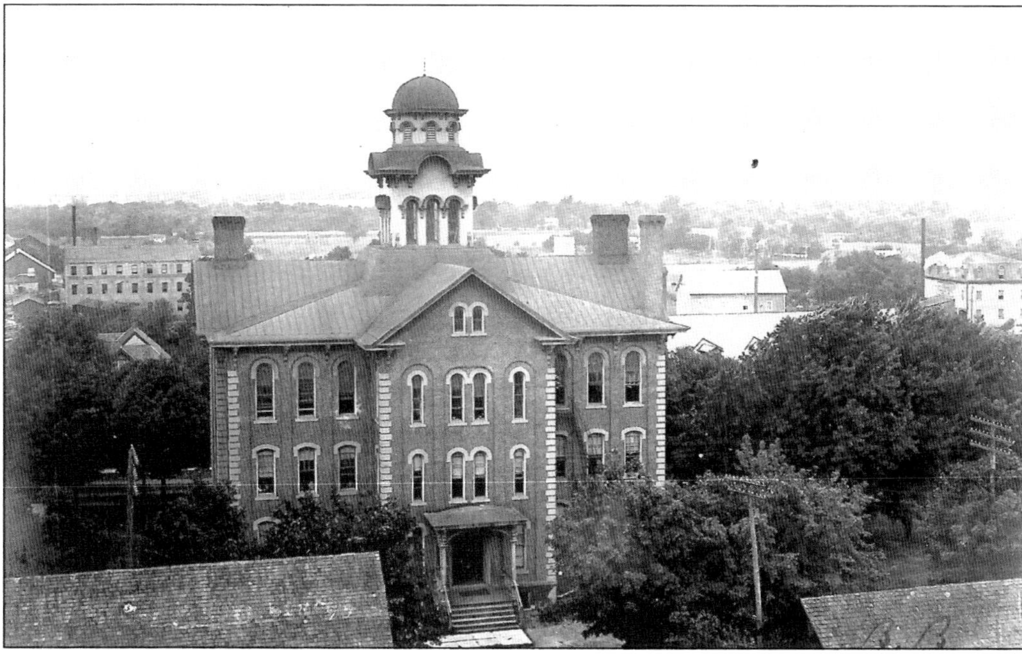

For years, only the children of parents who could pay tuition were offered the opportunity to attend school. The Free School Act of 1854, however, provided funding to offer education for all, which caused a demand for more trained teachers. The newly elected county school superintendent T. F. Gahan organized the first county teacher training school in Montoursville in 1870. It was moved to Muncy in 1875 where it operated as the Muncy Normal School (above)—the term *normal* refers to teaching standards or norms—until the 1920s. Below is a group of potential teachers in 1916 enjoying an outdoor exercise session. (Courtesy of Harold Hill.)

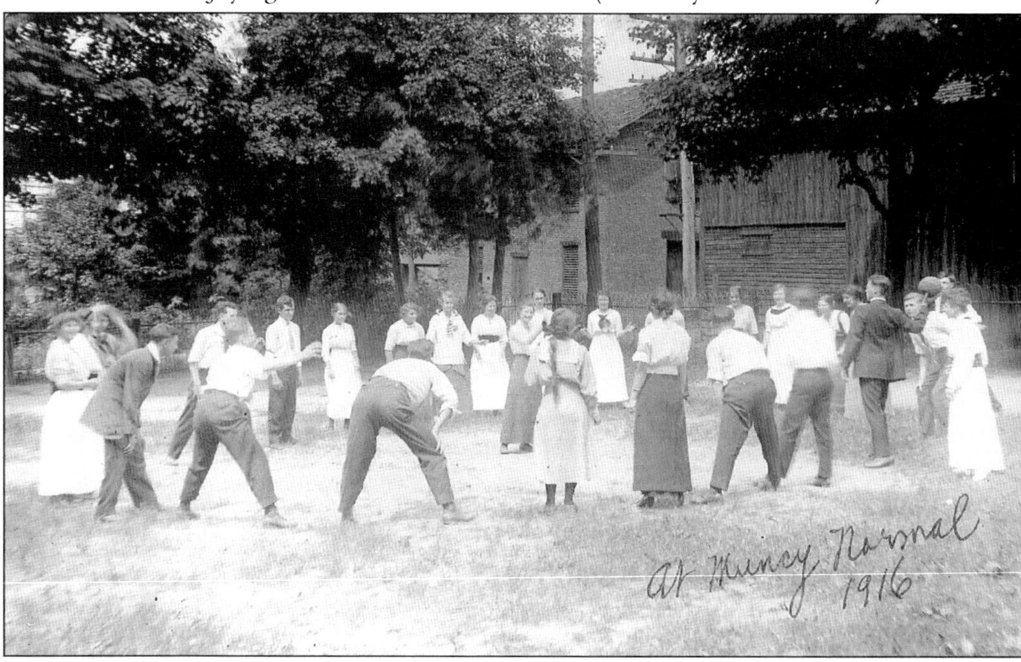

The first school in Hughesville was built in 1818 of crude logs and was heated during the winter by a large 10-plate stove made of 10 cast iron plates fitted together to make a tall, rectangular box stove. Originally built in 1875, this school building (right and below) was remodeled in 1889 when rooms were added to house the 265 students who were enrolled that year. While this was the only school within the town boundaries, over 50 other schools also held classes in surrounding townships. The corner of Main and Academy Streets was the location of every school building built in Hughesville until 1972, when the Wolf School was demolished and an apartment building was erected at the site. (Right, courtesy of the East Lycoming Historical Society; below, courtesy of Edward Smits.)

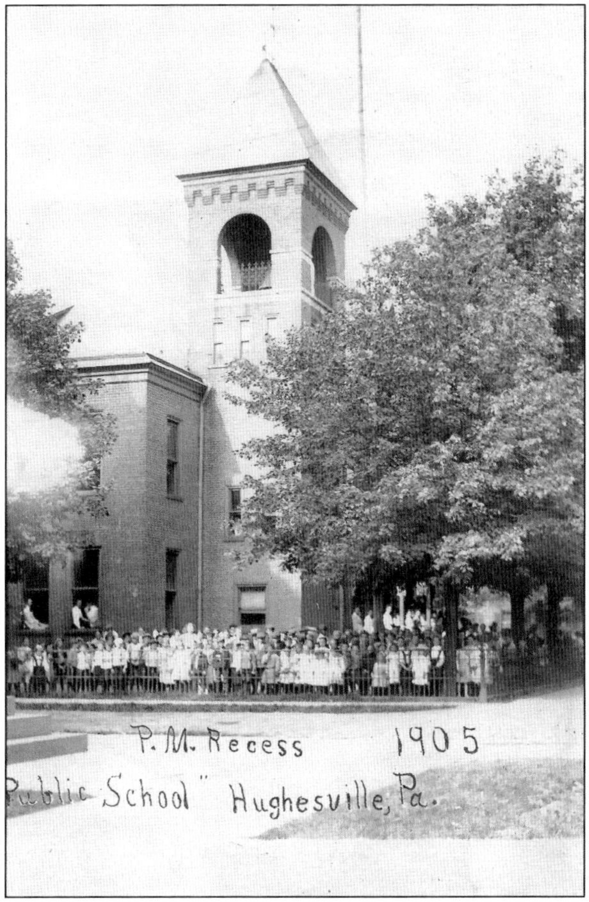

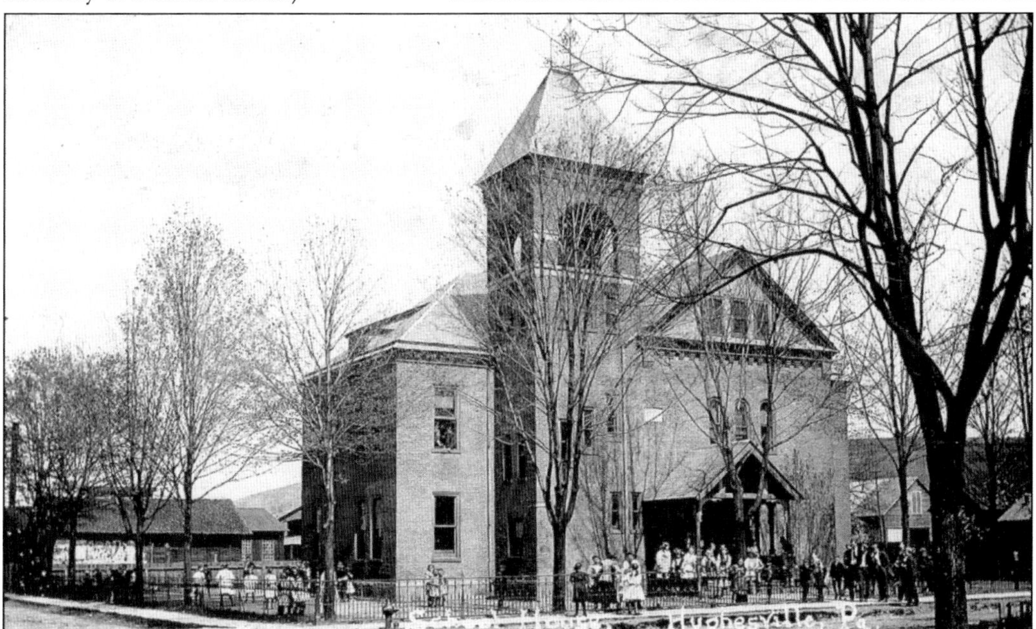

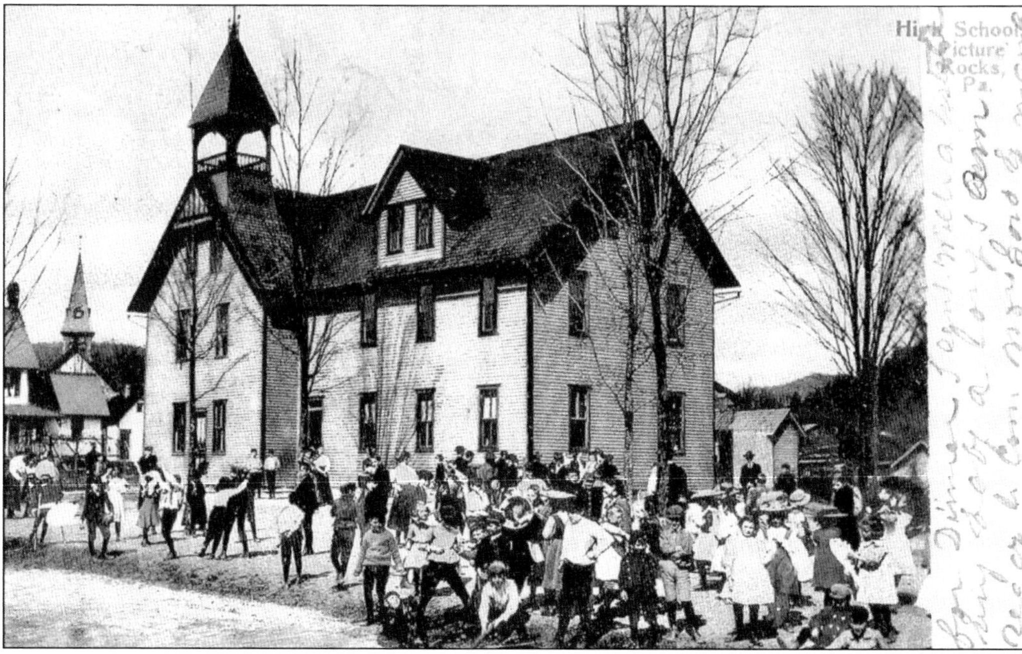

Seen above, this school at Picture Rocks offered classes for children of all ages. In 1896, the first high school class graduated, and in 1921, the school became one of the first vocational high schools in the state. The group of children seen below attended the Tivoli School during 1910–1911 and are identified as, from left to right, (first row) Howard O'Connor, Otis Mills Sr., Earl Taylor, Gay Taylor, Ernest Montgomery, Herbert Leonard, and Brady George; (second row) Ernest Croman, Dorsey Stroup, Viola Newman, Frances Fraley, Mabel Smith, Dorothy Mills, Lulu O'Connor, Pauline Montgomery, Pearl Mills, Russell Brooks, Horace Croman, Delbert Croman, and Glen Mills; (third row) Thomas Montgomery, Harry Houseknecht, Florence Croman, Mary Eschenback, Harry Sauders (teacher), Celia Mills, Bertha Clark, and John Taylor. (Above, courtesy of Stewart Hill; below, courtesy of Aaron Houseknecht.)

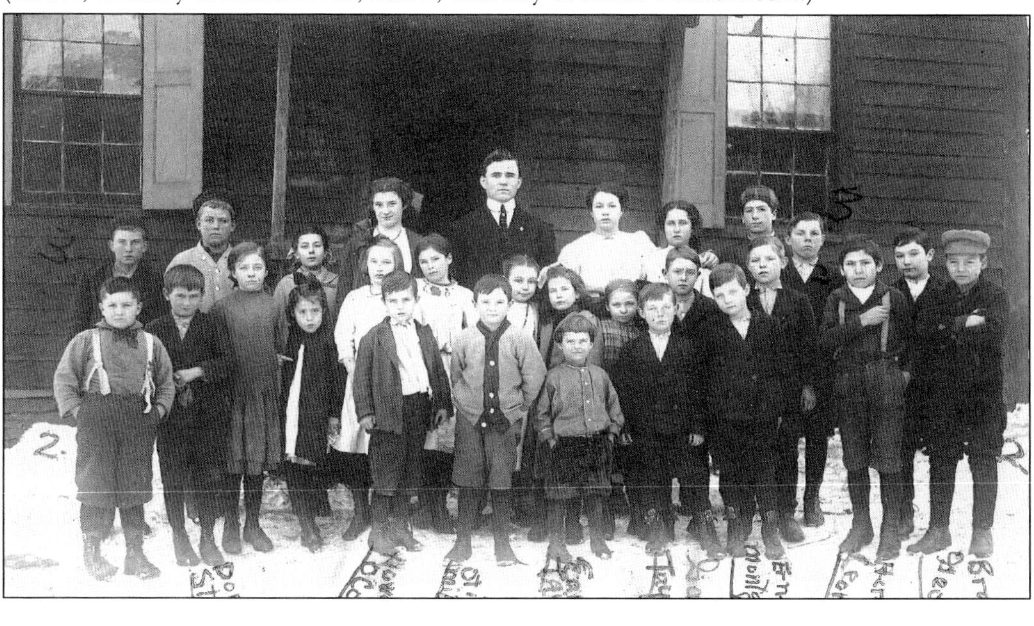

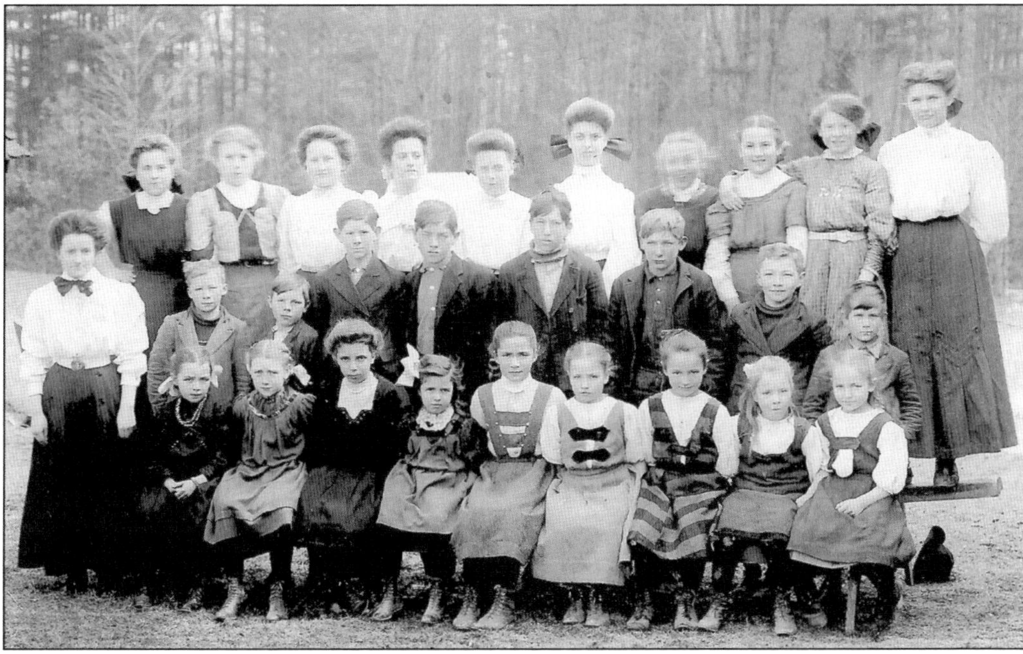

Pictured above is the class of 1908–1909 at the Mapleton School in Shrewsbury Township. The students are, from left to right, (first row) Kathryn Fox, Aola Parson, May Clark, Marie Clark, Elsie Van Horn, Jennie Weaver, Leana Weaver, May Minnier, and Mary Weaver; (second row) unidentified, Harvey Fox, Debert Croman, Lester Goldy, Otto Croman, Raymond Taylor, Ira Van Horn, Larue Fox, and Thomas Winders; (third row) Effie Weaver, Laura Hall, Margaret Weaver, Clara Weaver, Cora Parson, Cora Clark, Florence Fox, Laura Weaver, Oral Goldy, and Ocie Van Horn. Below is a group of children from the Villa Grove School in 1928. All children are unidentified except for (first row, second from left) Peggy Koch Glidewell. The teacher (third row, right) was Clayton Houseknecht. (Above, courtesy of Sue Shaner; below, courtesy of the East Lycoming Historical Society.)

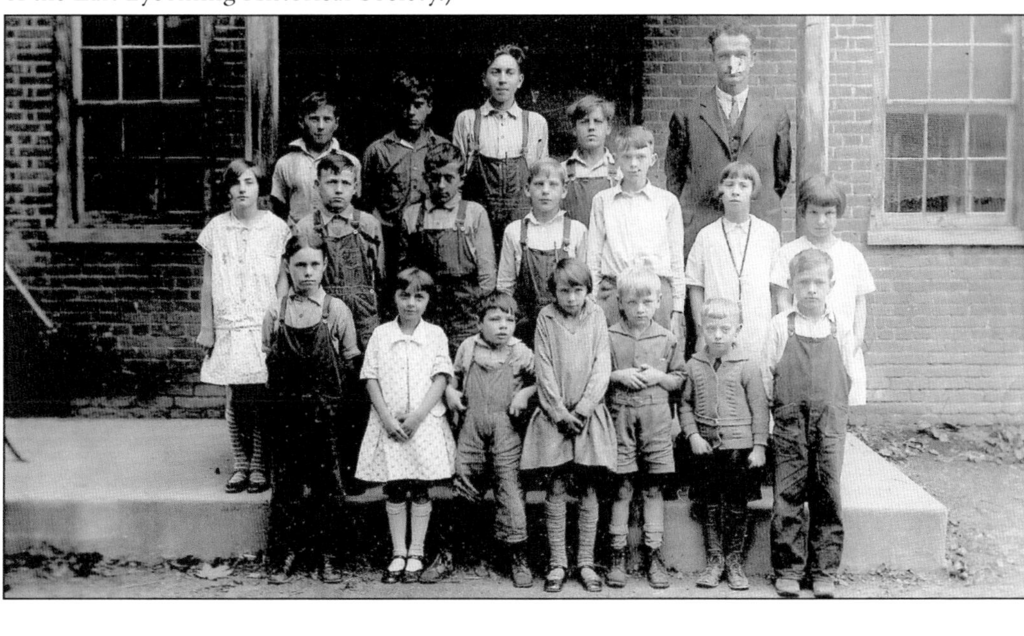

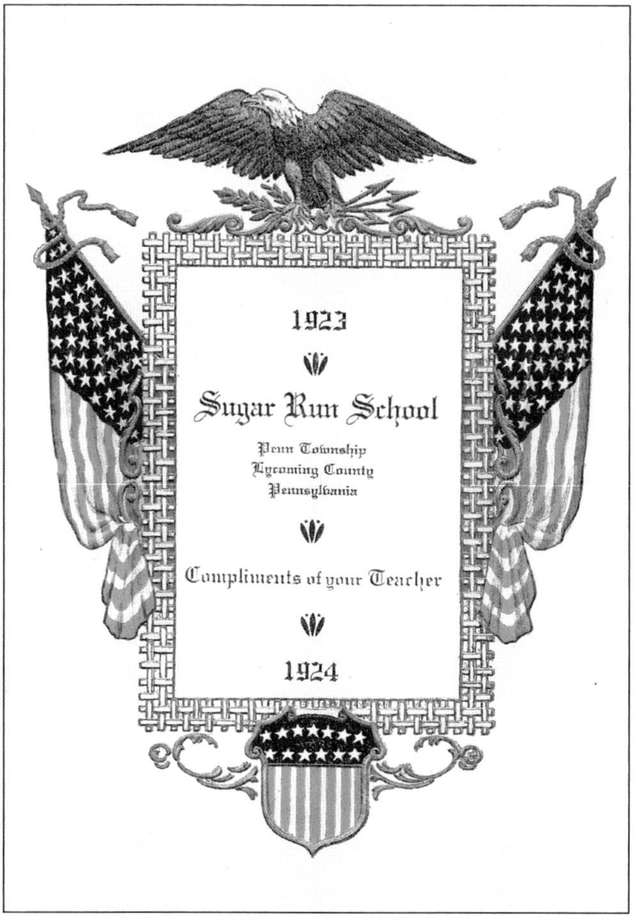

At left is the school souvenir that was given to each student who attended Penn Township's Sugar Run School in 1923–1924. During that school year, J. Heilman Hill was the teacher. Below is the class attending the Lores (Lohrs) School in 1914. Their teacher was F. Del Roy Kessler with the following students in (first grade) Laura Vandine, Mary Whitmoyer, Mary Gower, Ruth Craig, and Thomas Bartlow; (second grade) Howard Bartlow, Pearl Vandine, and Margaret Whitmoyer; (third grade) Fannie Gordner, Pearl Gower, Meryl Gower, and Judson Gordner; (fourth grade) William Lohr, Alberta Vandine, and Mable Bartlow; (fifth grade) Clifton Cole; (sixth grade) Roy Gardner, Linis Bartlow, Oscar Bartlow, and Sarah Gordner; (seventh grade) Rollie Steinruck, Thomas Steinruck, Blanche Gardner, Frank Gordner, Leroy Bartlow, Pauline Gordner, and Frank Bartlow; (eighth grade) Rollie Bartlow. (Below, courtesy of Aaron Houseknecht.)

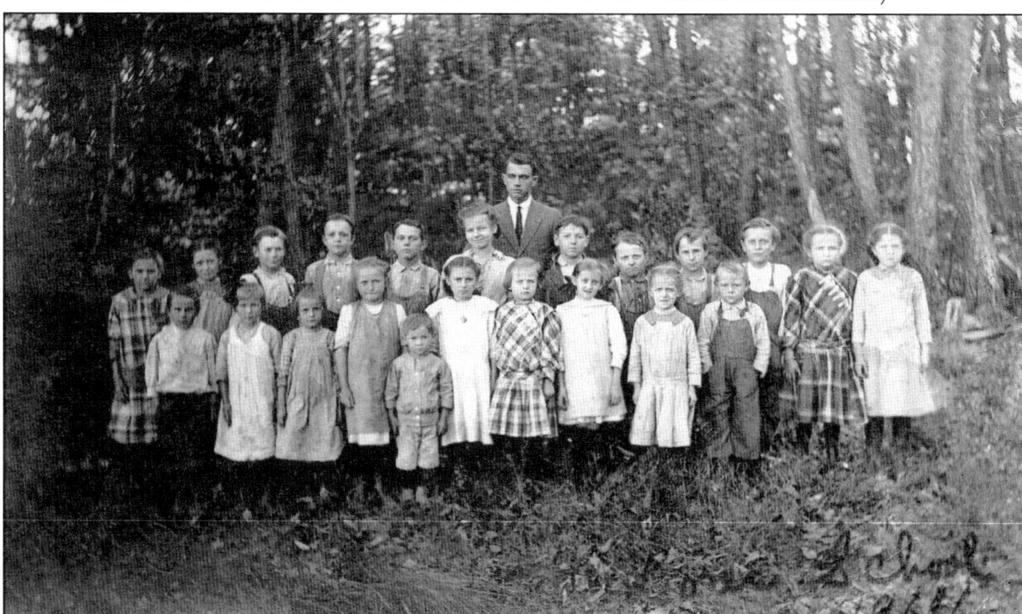

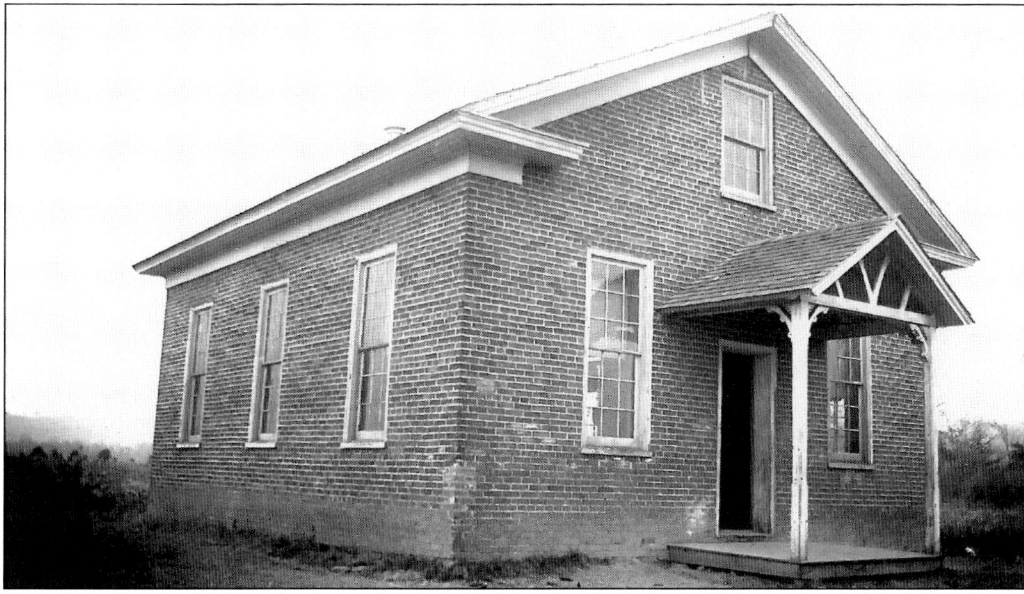

The Steck School (above) was located southwest of Hughesville and operated until 1932 when it was closed. The land it was built on was returned to its original owner to be used as farmland. Torrence Houseknecht, the teacher at the school in 1914, would later own a 100-acre farm in Penn Township. Other men and women who taught at Steck include Fannie Hess, Russell Smith, Ralph Ritter, Ambrose Steck, Blanche Smith, Bill Reed, Glenna Reese, Charles Frey, and Grace Myers Kohler. Below is a nice example of the school souvenirs that are now collectibles and family treasures. (Above, courtesy of Stewart Hill.)

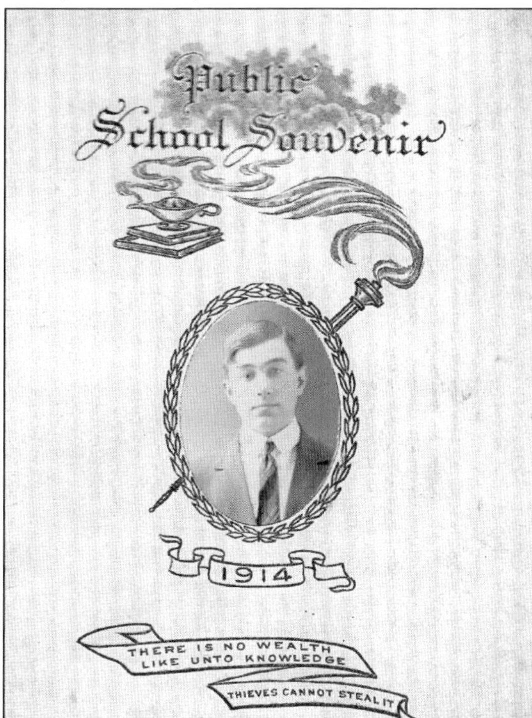

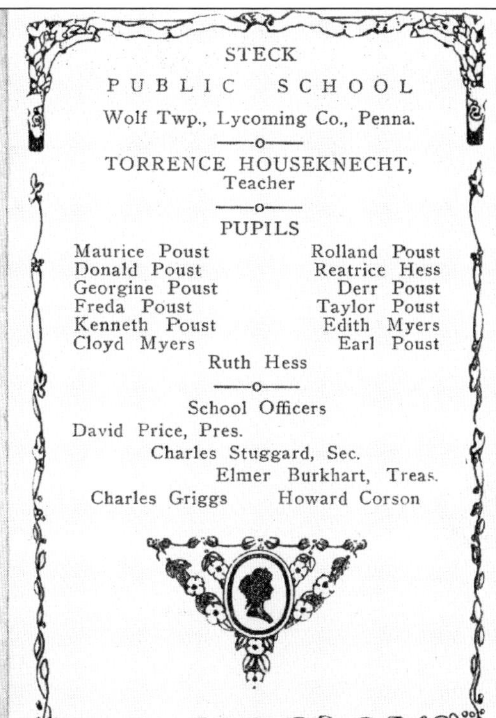

STECK

PUBLIC SCHOOL

Wolf Twp., Lycoming Co., Penna.

TORRENCE HOUSEKNECHT,
Teacher

PUPILS

Maurice Poust	Rolland Poust
Donald Poust	Reatrice Hess
Georgine Poust	Derr Poust
Freda Poust	Taylor Poust
Kenneth Poust	Edith Myers
Cloyd Myers	Earl Poust

Ruth Hess

School Officers

David Price, Pres.
Charles Stuggard, Sec.
Elmer Burkhart, Treas.
Charles Griggs Howard Corson

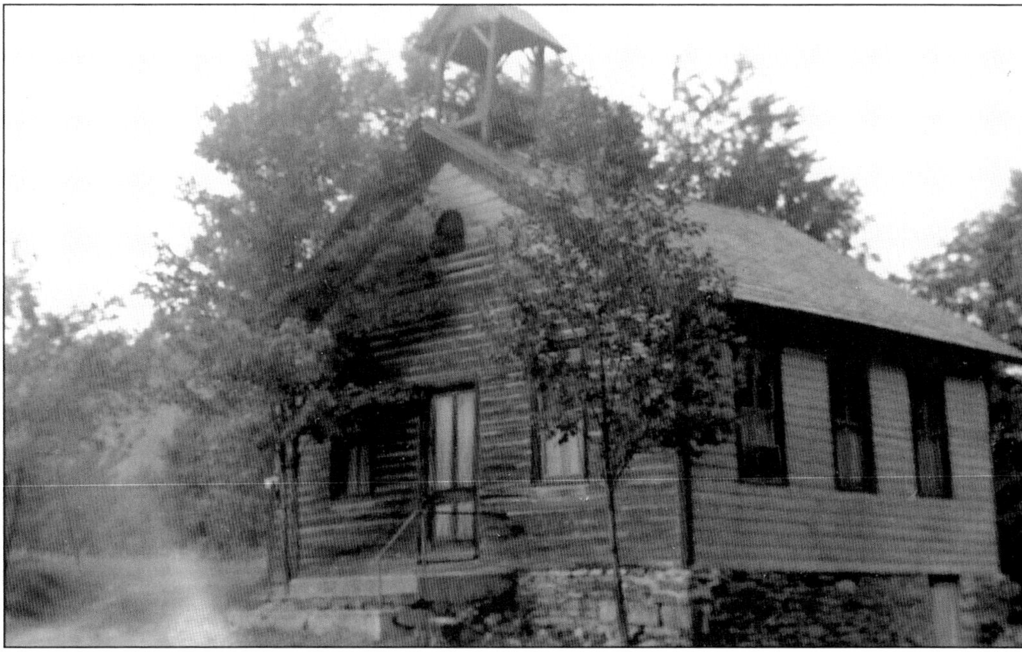

The Derr School (above) was one of five one-room schools in Penn Township that was operating during the latter half of the 19th century. Schools were open four months and the estimated cost of teaching a student at that time was 48¢ per month. Derr School was closed in 1937 but is one of only two that remain standing in the township. Pictured below is the Derr School class from 1902 and 1903 that includes, from left to right, (first row) Torrence B. Houseknecht, Delay Poust Sr., Grover Poust, Mertie Houseknecht, and Mertie Bartlow Berger; (second row) Jasper Derr (teacher), Ward Bartlow, Harry Bartlow, Bertha Spring, Ada Houseknecht, Maggie Spring Smith, and Mae Poust.

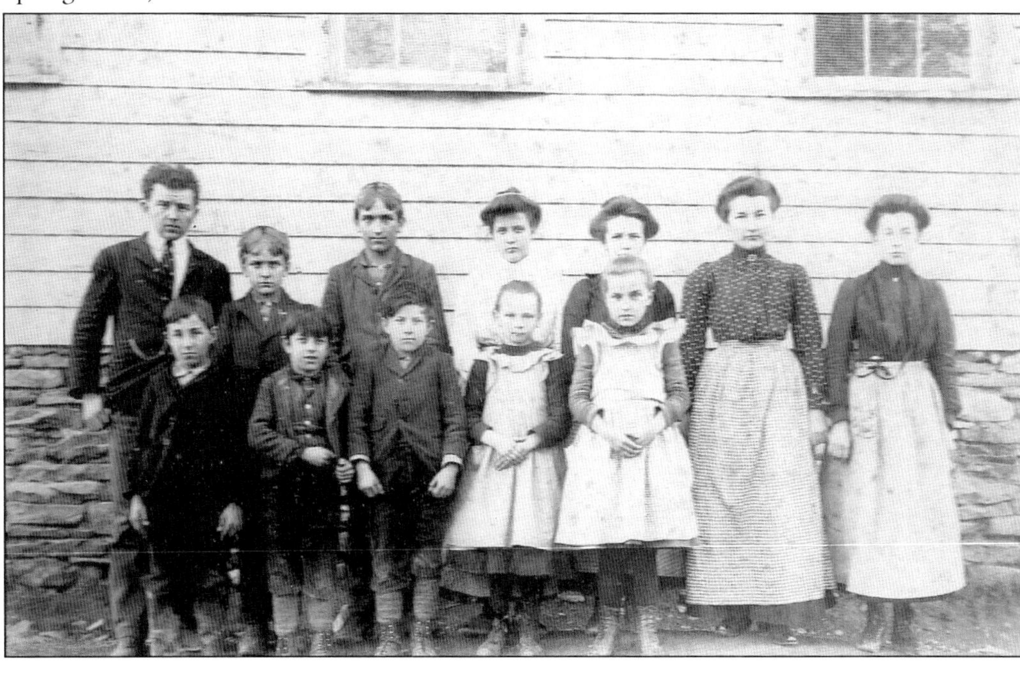

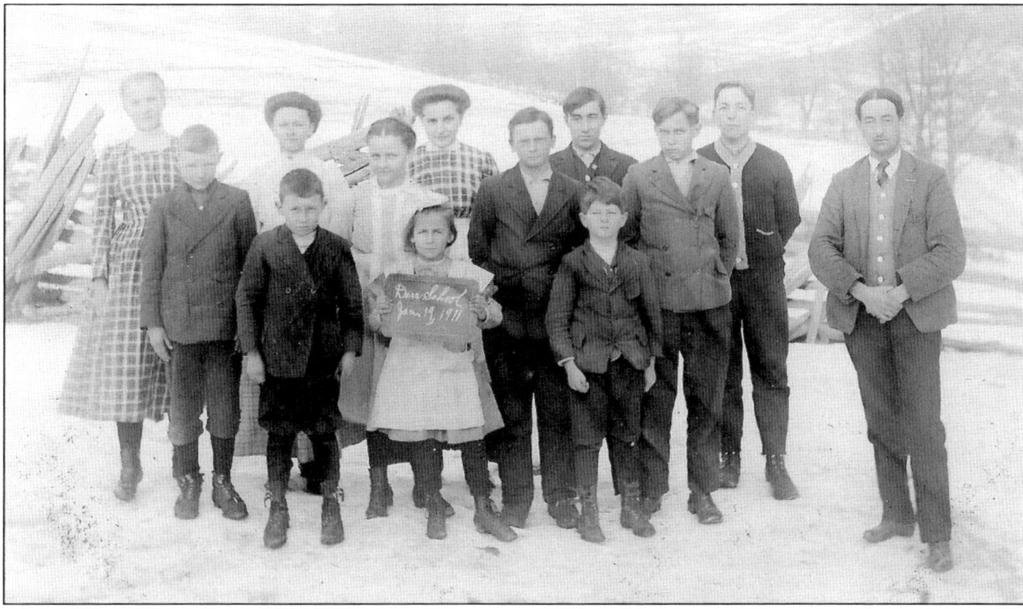

During 1910 and 1911, these students (pictured above) attended Derr School. They are, from left to right, (first row) Donald Milheim, Lois Milheim (holding chalkboard), and Harry Confer; (second row) Edgar Smith, Florence Houseknecht, Walter Houseknecht, and Edward Houseknecht; (third row) Grace Spring, Mertie Reed, Mertie Bartlow, Torrence Houseknecht, Bruce Bartlow, and Ralph Ritter (teacher). The teachers were paid between $15 to $21.25 per month (with the men receiving the higher salary than the women did). Pictured below is the class of 1925 from the Derr School. The students are (first row) Evelyn Spring McClemon and Harley Rupert; (second row) Vera Rupert Nichols, Marian Poust West, Leona Rupert Ritter, Clara Houseknecht Wheal, Harry Houseknecht, Lewis Hill, Howard Houseknecht, Paul Poust, Alberta Houseknecht Shaner Myers, and Chalmer Houseknecht; (third row) Floyd Rupert.

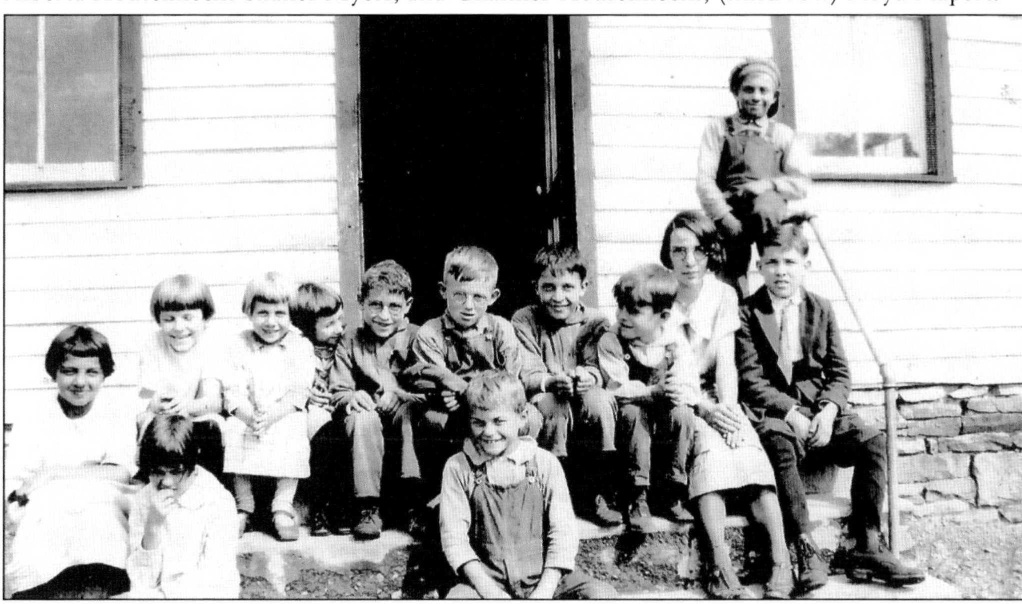

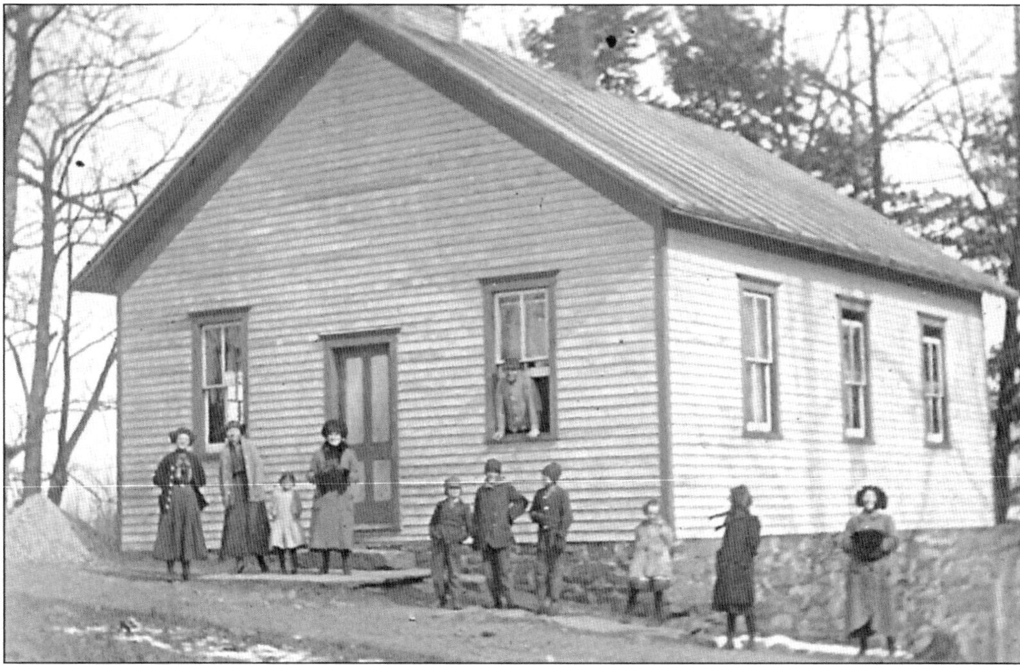

Located in Penn Township, the McCarty School (above, around 1902) was often referred to as the "Fribley" School because of its close association with the nearby Fribley Church. A class from the Fribley School (1904–1905) is pictured below. They are, from left to right, (first row) Iva Kepner Houseknecht, Dennis Holmes, Liza Wilson, and Edna Green Fry; (second row) Ellis B. Houseknecht Sr., Jasper Holmes, Charles Houseknecht, Jane Holmes Myers, Hazel Holmes Houseknecht, Martha Snyder Kepner, Della Holmes Temple, Ruth Rogers, and Cloyd Snyder; (third row) Arthur Rogers, John Rogers, Valentine Kepner, Brady Craig, Jesse Gordner (teacher), Leila Kepner Reed, Lavina Poust Montgomery, and Clarence Green.

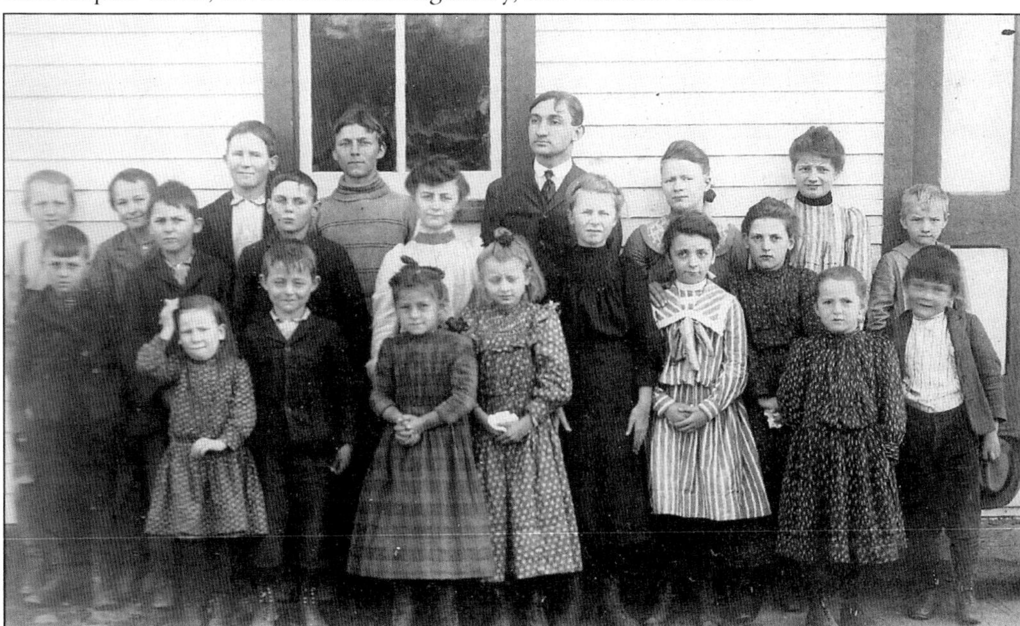

Five

Water, Wheels, Roads, and Rails

During the late 1700s, the pioneers settling the lands of central Pennsylvania were hardy men and women who were determined to find a piece of land to call their own. Most came from the Philadelphia or Harrisburg area and traveled north and east along the west branch of the Susquehanna River. Their adventurous spirit brought them even further east, up Muncy Creek and its tributaries. They used Native American trails and eventually traveled on the horse and cart paths worn down between forts and settlements. They made their own trails and traveled inland.

Before Hughesville was connected to other areas by the railroad, which was built in 1872, transportation to and from anywhere was only as fast as a horse could travel, and anything that needed to be shipped into the area was floated in on canal boats. Life around Hughesville was slow-paced. Roads in and out of town were either a dusty path or a muddy, rut-filled quagmire, where wagon wheels could sink up to the axle.

The 1880s was a decade that experienced great advances in transportation with the introduction of cheap and fast train excursions in and out of town. Then in the 1920s, the automobile offered families a way to travel that was not dictated by the schedule set by the railroad. Roads were improved, railroad stations were abandoned, and tracks were removed by the end of the 1930s. Here is a brief look at how the natural resources have been used and the different ways that have been found to transport possessions and people.

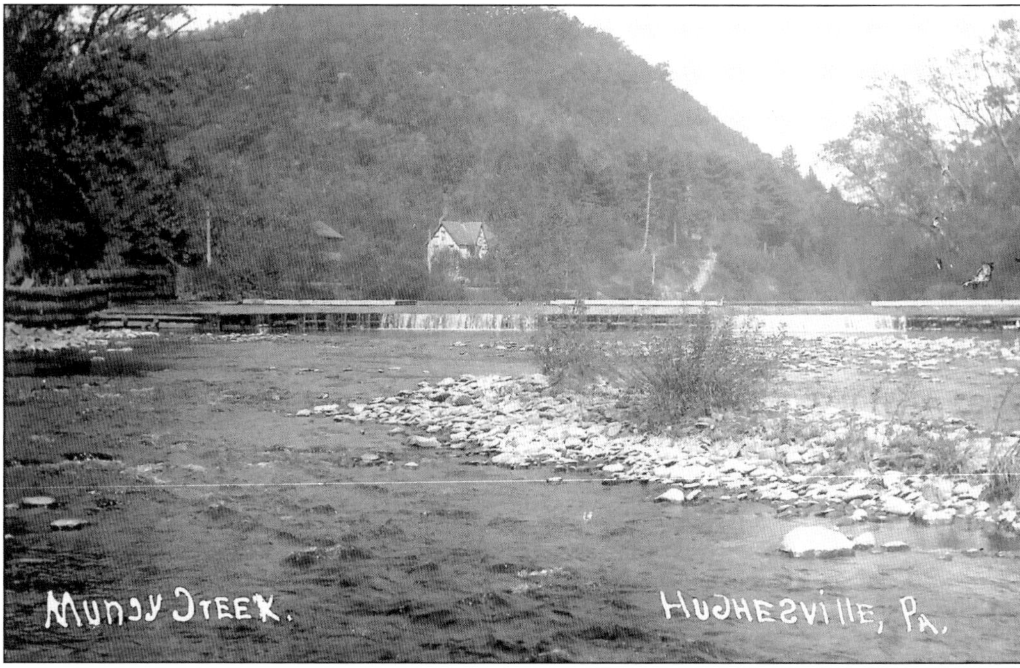

For local kids, Muncy Creek has always been the source of limitless amusement and the place to go to pass time on a summer day. Just sitting on its shore and listening to the gurgling water can lull children to sleep while others can be found with fishing poles in hand and a bucket at their feet, waiting for a tug on their line. Centuries ago, pioneers understood the importance of running water and built their mills nearby to access its power. In Hughesville, Jacob Clayton built the first gristmill along Muncy Creek in 1816. (Courtesy of Mary Fox Odell.)

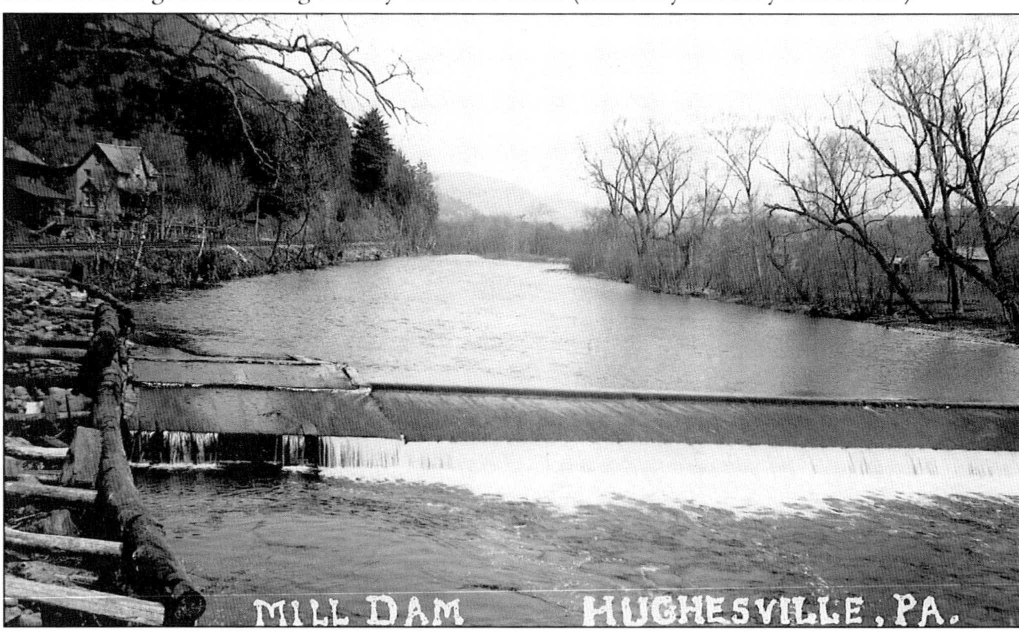

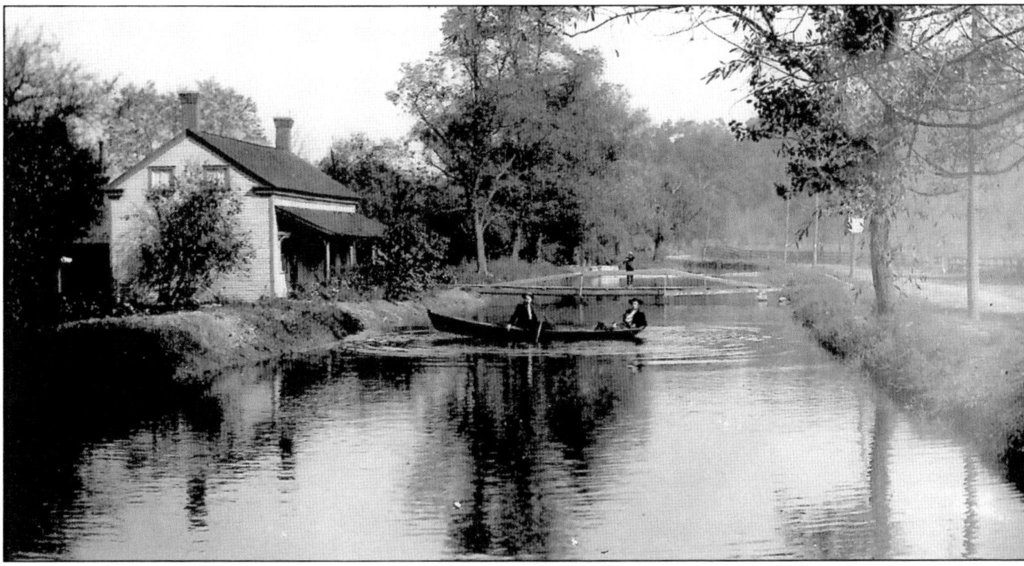

Frank Schug, farmer and lumberman, began a lumber business at Beaver Dam in 1880, and in 1889, he purchased what is known as the Lyon farm. He was able to arrange for the erection of the water and electric substation on his farm near Hughesville. The race of water running nearby came to be referred to as "Schug's Race." The real-photo postcard above captures two men taking a canoe ride on the race. The same view is artistically reproduced below, which is one of the most common postcards that can be found in collections that feature scenes from Hughesville. (Above, courtesy of Mary Fox Odell; below, courtesy of the East Lycoming Historical Society.)

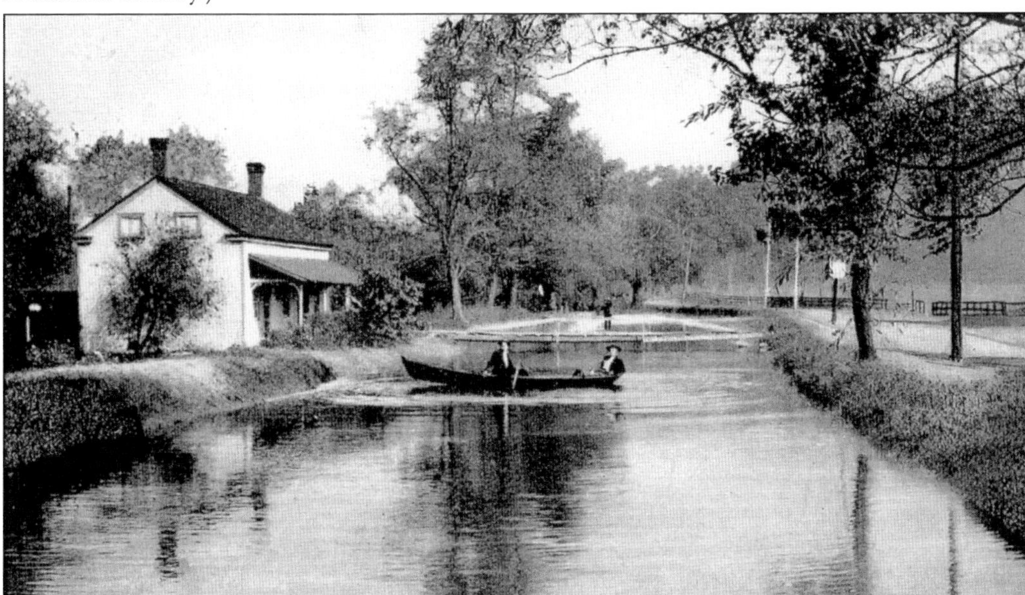

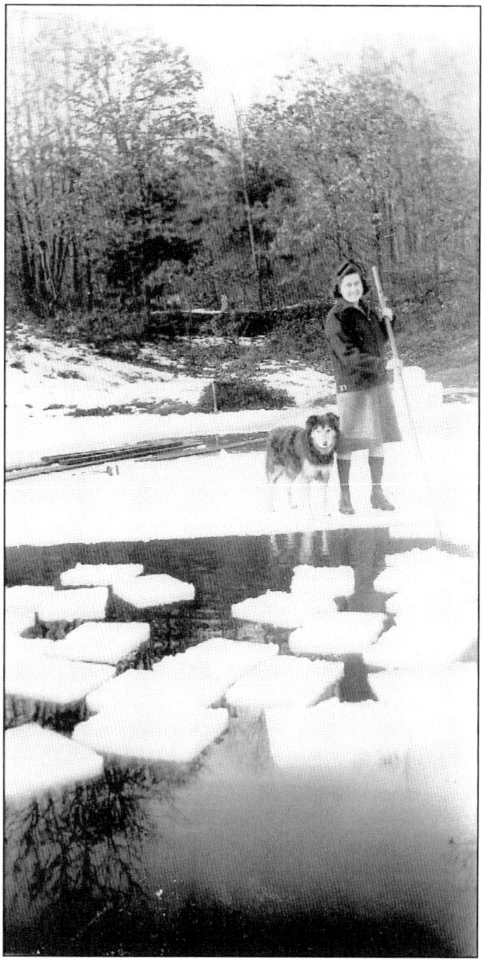

During the winter, ice cut from lakes and dammed areas of the creek provided food refrigeration for private homes, local hotels, and restaurants. In Hughesville, a large icehouse was run by Francis Smith. Before power equipment, the 8- to 10-inch blocks of ice were cut with hand saws and then sold or stored for use in the summer. Pictured here is the ice-cutting operation that took place on Highland Lake during the 1930s. At left are, from left to right, Towser the dog and Rhoda Taylor Campbell; below are Rhoda Taylor Campbell, Jean Taylor Morgan and two men identified as "the Garner men." (Courtesy of Sue Shaner.)

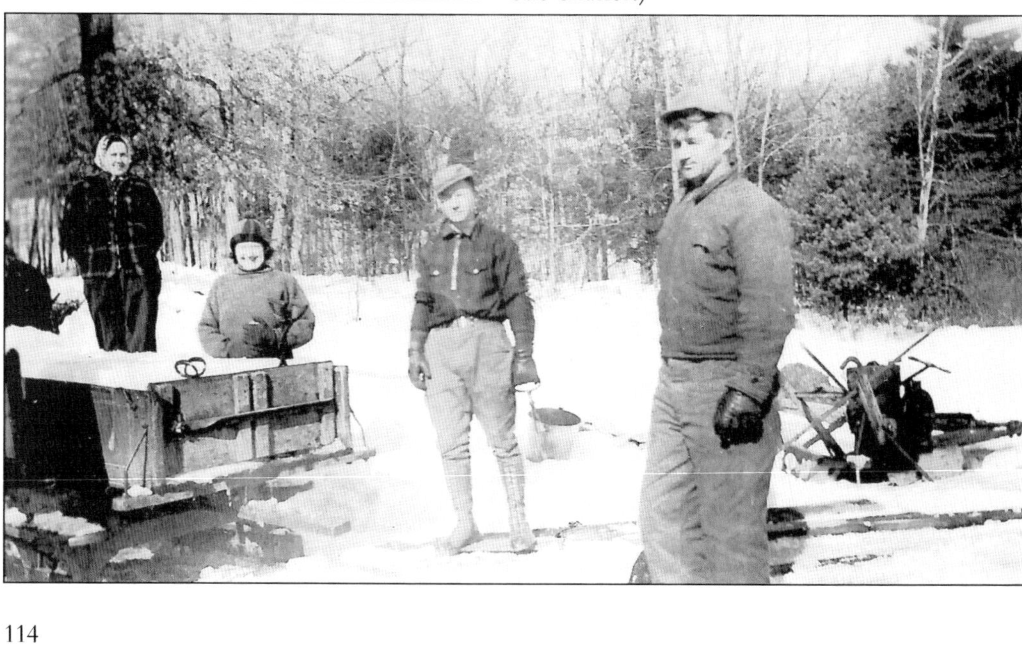

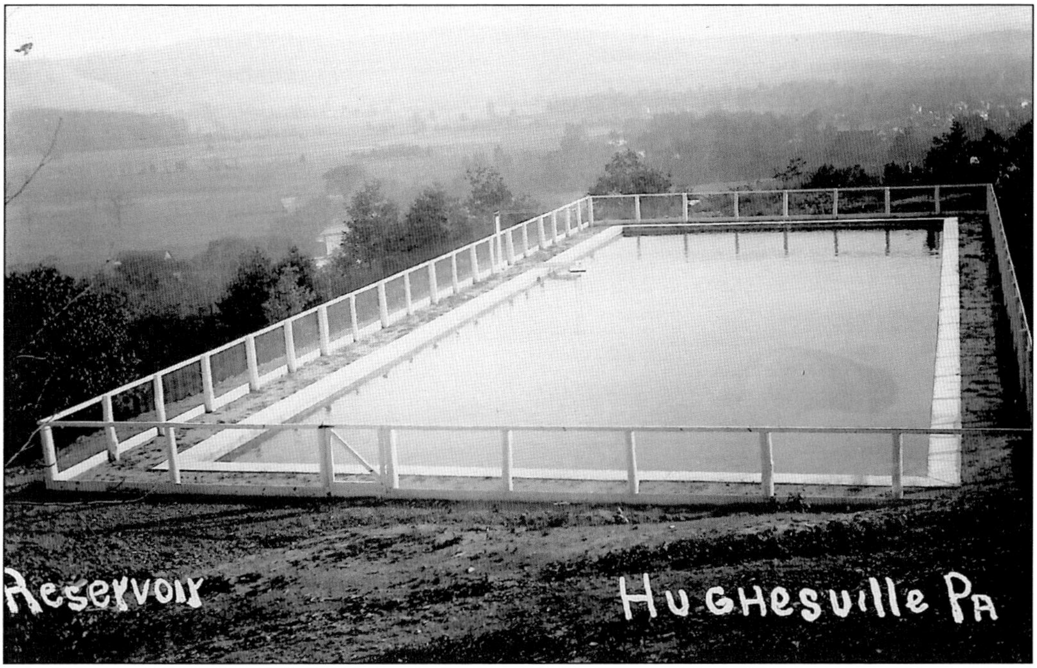

Before 1900, this half-million gallon capacity reservoir constructed north of town was built 170 feet above ground level. Steam was used to pump the water out of four 100-foot wells that provided Hughesville with an unending supply of fresh well water. Pipelines that stretched for more than seven miles were installed beneath the streets of town. Historians reported that while a team of horses pulled the plow that broke the ground's surface, a crew of men finished the ditch digging and were paid 12.5¢ per hour. (Above, courtesy of Mary Fox Odell; below, courtesy of Elizabeth Rogers Knyrim.)

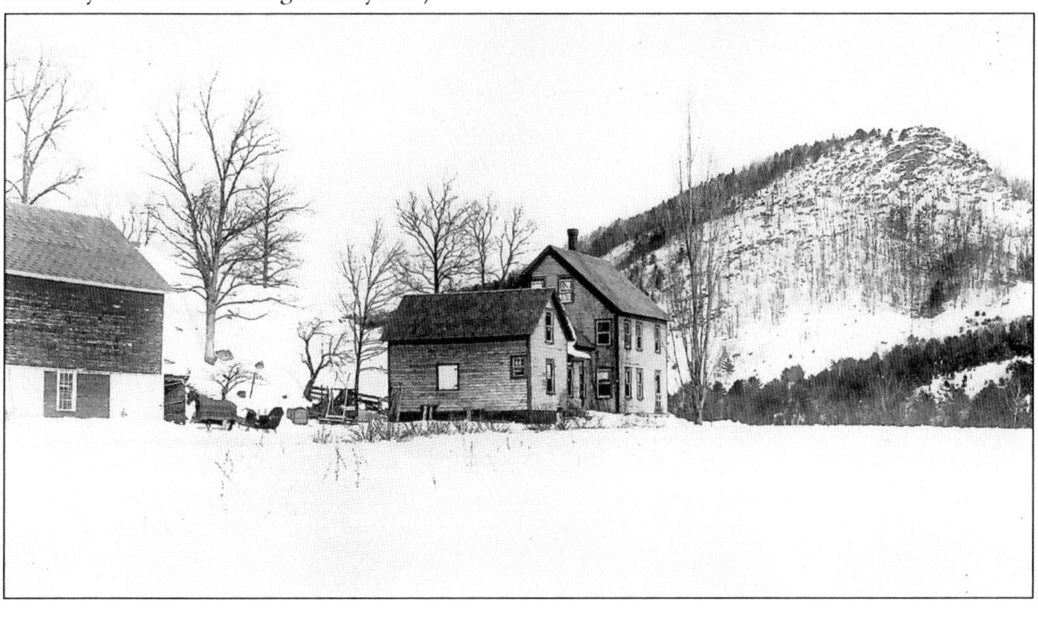

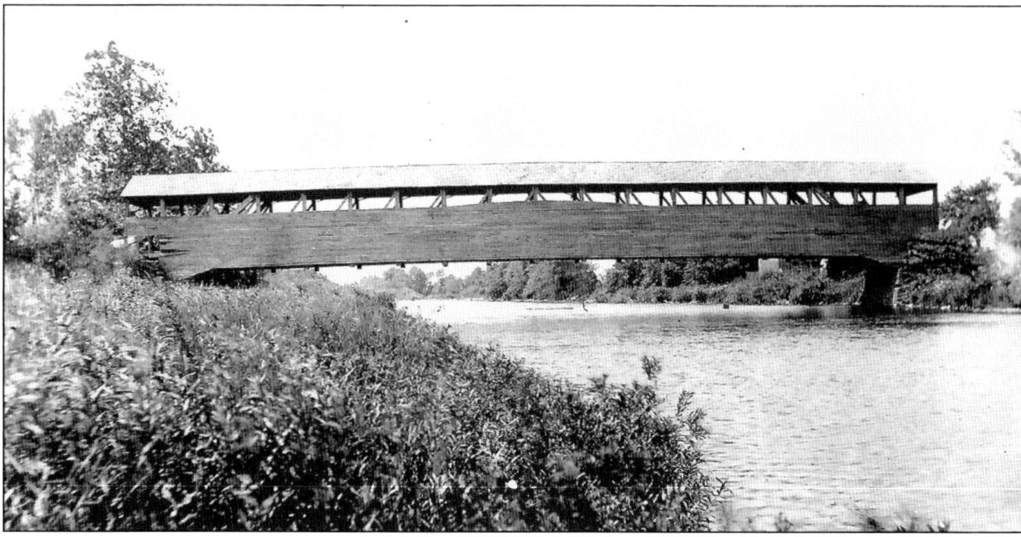

Also known as the Biddle Bridge (no doubt named for early town councilman Gersham Biddle), this covered bridge on Water Street at the east end of town was replaced in the early 1920s with a cement bridge during a road paving project. (Courtesy of Kenneth D. Poust.)

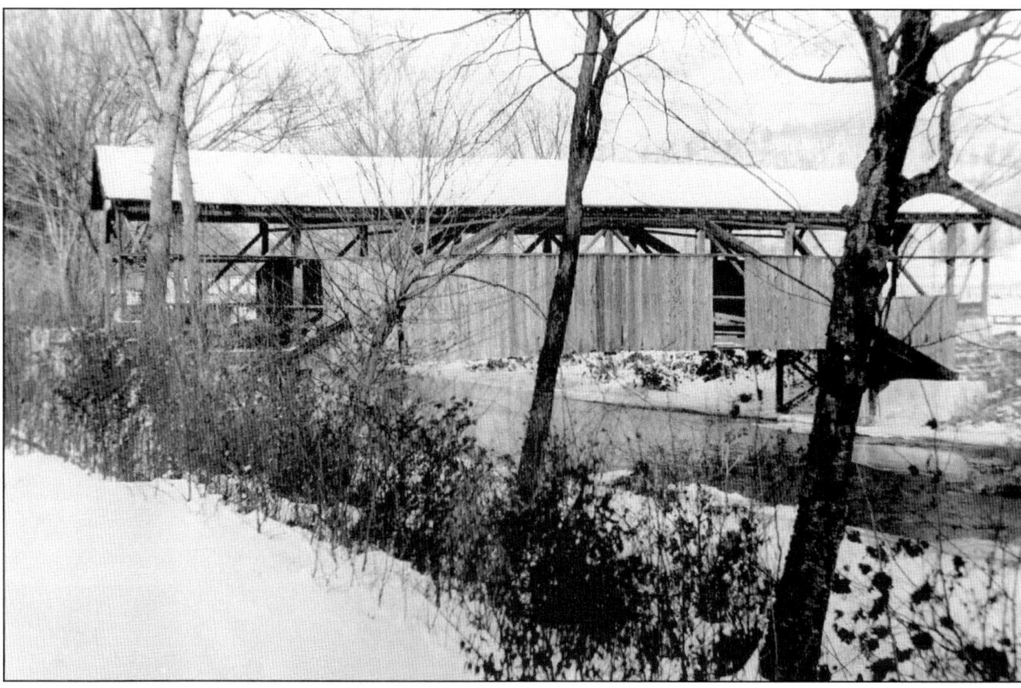

This smaller covered bridge spanning Muncy Creek shows one in the beginning stages of decay. A bridge built entirely out of wood, without any protective covering, may last 10 to 15 years. But early bridge builders discovered that if the bridge was protected with a roof, the bridge could stand for many more years. (Courtesy of the James V. Brown Library Archives.)

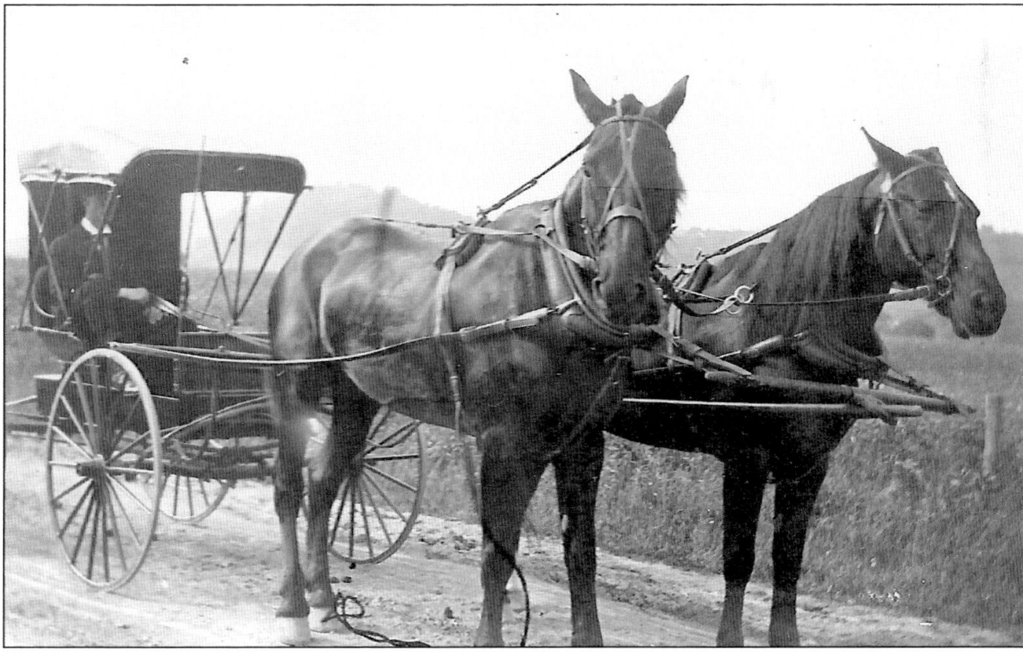

Undertaker Judson O. Coleman is seen here in his horse-pulled buggy, the typical mode of transportation used around 1900. Before Coleman brought his business to Hughesville in 1906, John Houghton provided undertaking services and also had a "first-class livery stable" near the American House Hotel. (Courtesy of the Sullivan County Historical Society and Museum.)

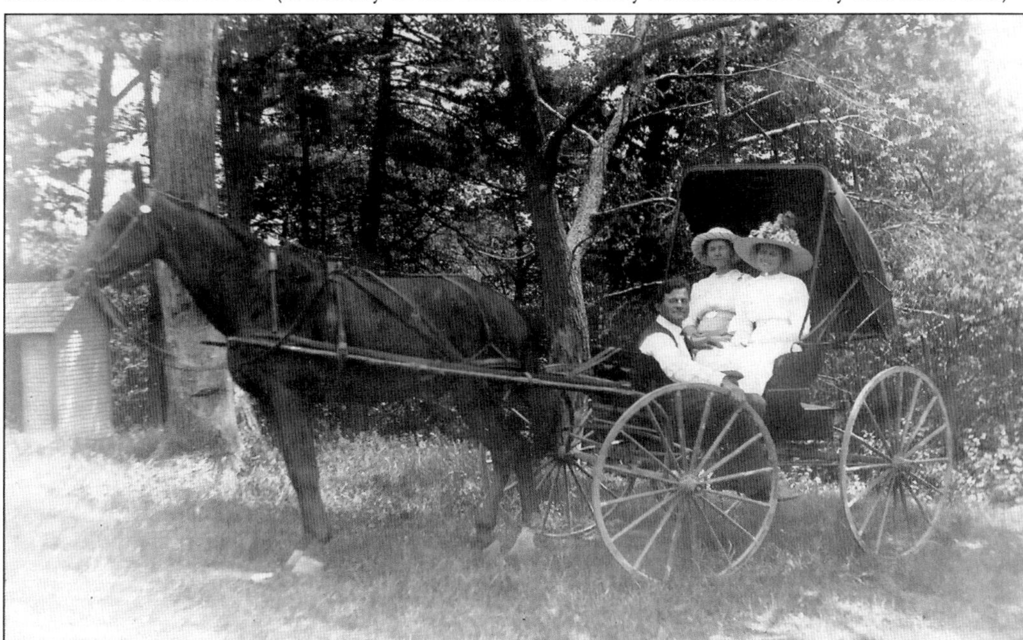

These three friends, Hazel Holmes Houseknecht (left), Mame Poust McClain, and Clyde Poust, are enjoying one another's companionship under a shade tree near the Fribley Church in Penn Township. After services on Sunday morning, members of the congregation would linger and spend some time catching up with neighbors before returning home.

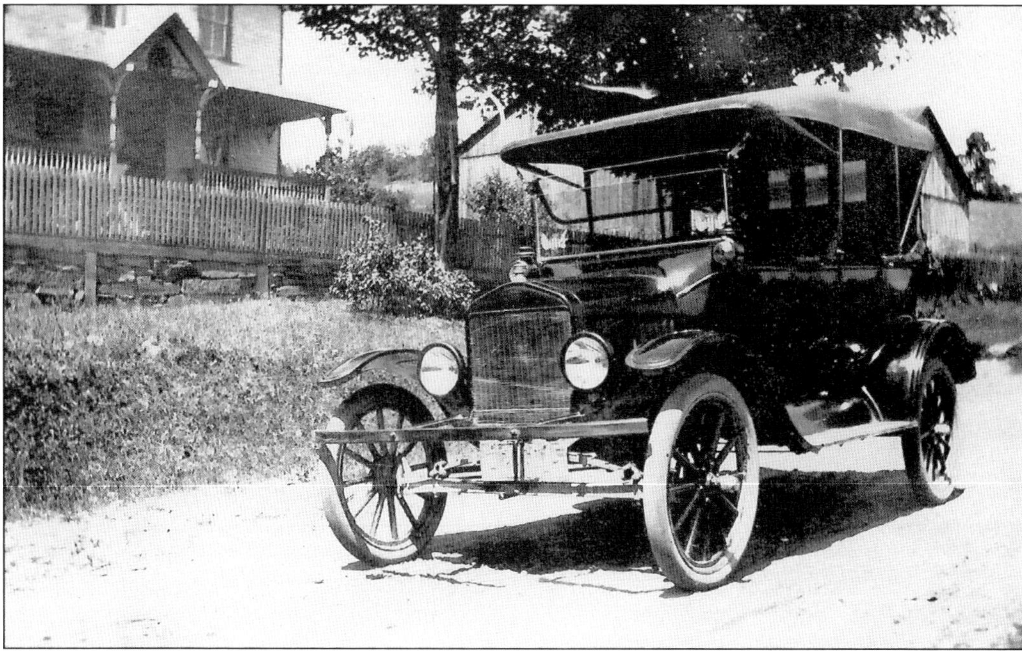

Living in the Highland Lake area of northeastern Lycoming County offered quiet solitude that many farmers yearned for. But this often resulted in isolation before the introduction of an affordable and easily obtainable form of transportation that was faster than a horse and buggy. By 1915, however, Highland Lake resident Raymond Taylor purchased his first car, pictured here. (Courtesy of Sue Shaner.)

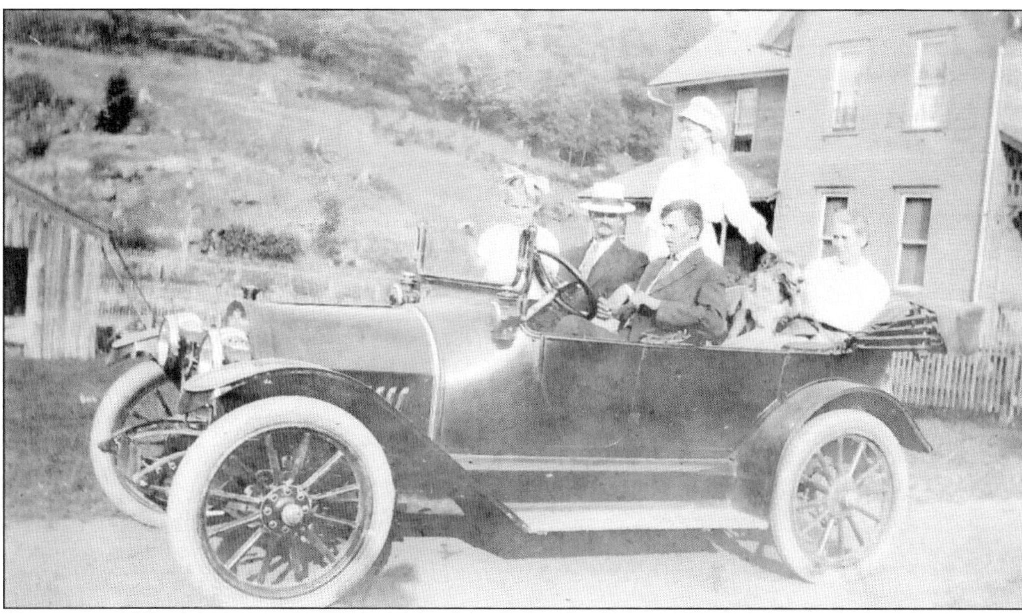

"Finish up them chores, git yer Sunday-go-ta-meetin' clothes on, put the top down and let's git going!" Pictured here is the Holmes family from the Glen Mawr area getting ready to take a drive in their 1922 Buick touring sedan. Above are, from left to right, Elva, Cyrus, Ernest, Isabella (with dog), and Hazel (standing).

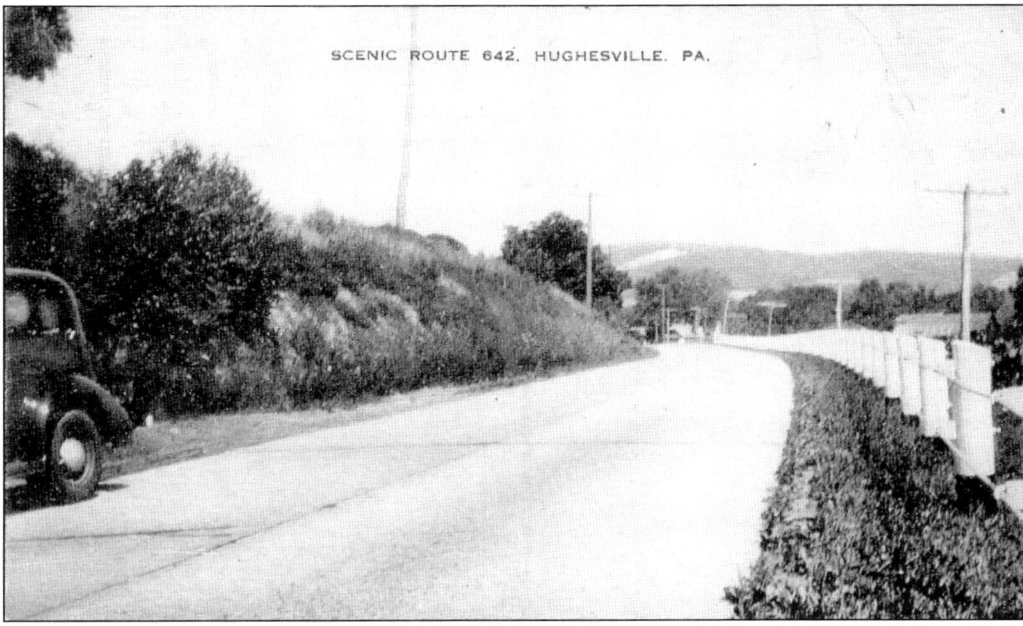

When roads were paved, travel became safer, smoother, cleaner, and faster. Main Street and Water Street in Hughesville were paved around 1920, as well as the road from Hughesville to Picture Rocks. Pictured on this page, Route 642 was the stretch of road between Hughesville and Lairdsville. Known as the "pike" from the 1920s through the 1950s, it was paved in stages. In 1930, the span between Hughesville and Green Valley Road was paved, and then the section between Green Valley Road and Lairdsville was surfaced in 1932. And finally, in 1939, the section between Lairdsville and Holmes Hollow Road was paved. (Above, courtesy of Elizabeth Rogers Knyrim; below, courtesy of the East Lycoming Historical Society.)

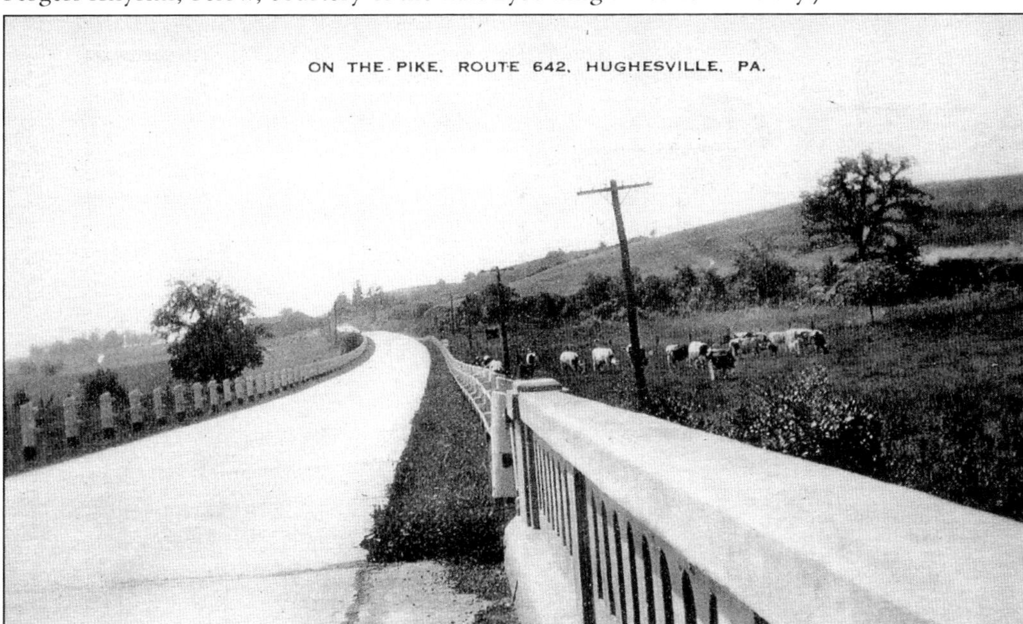

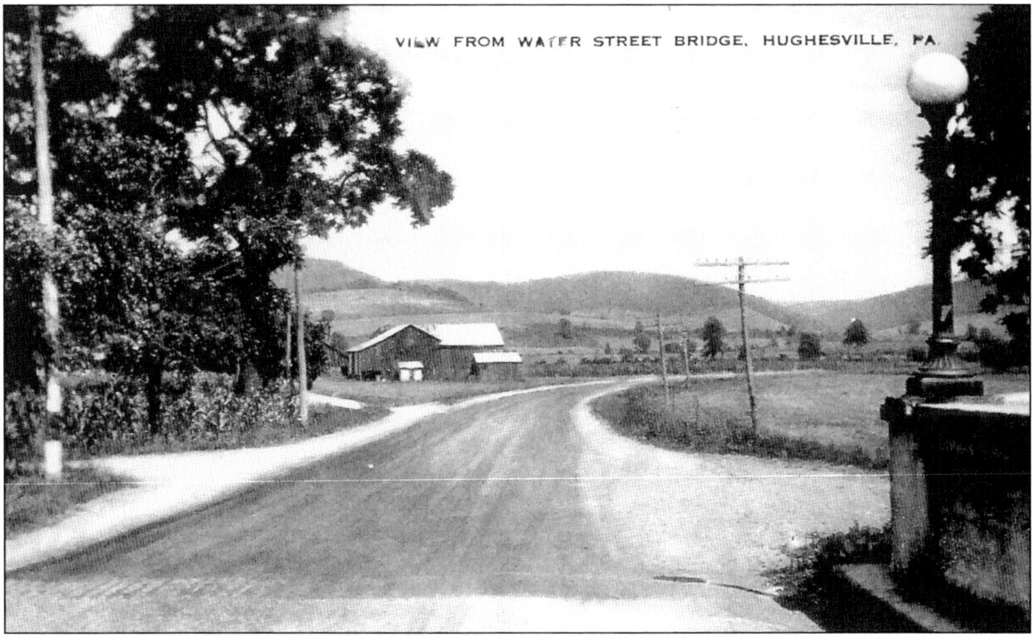

This is a view from the eastern end of Water Street on the cement bridge that spans Muncy Creek, looking east toward the farmland of Penn, Franklin, and Jordan Townships. The communities of Lairdsville and Unityville can be found directly east from this point on what was then known as Route 642 (see previous page). (Courtesy of Stewart Hill.)

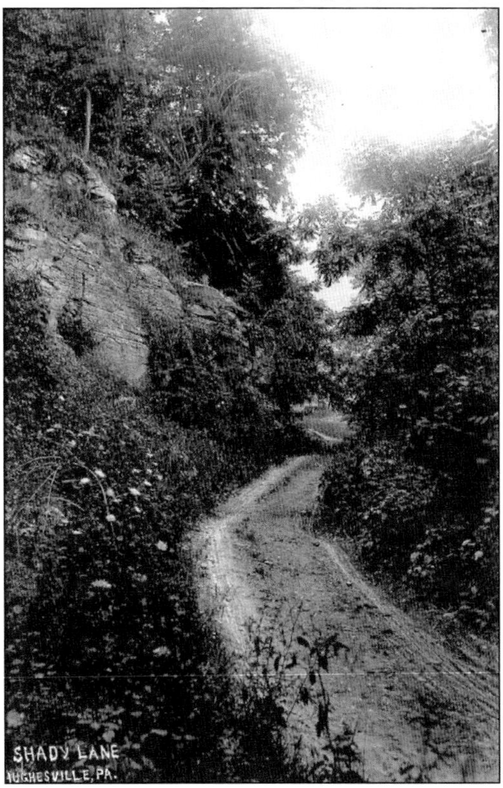

The sender of this picture postcard (postmarked August 28, 1907) writes, "This is the road up at the stone quarry. I am sending the opening chapters of 'The Plum Tree' from the *Gazette and Bulletin*. You said you would like to read it." *The Plum Tree* was a novel exploring contemporary social issues written by David Graham Phillips in 1905. (Courtesy of Stewart Hill.)

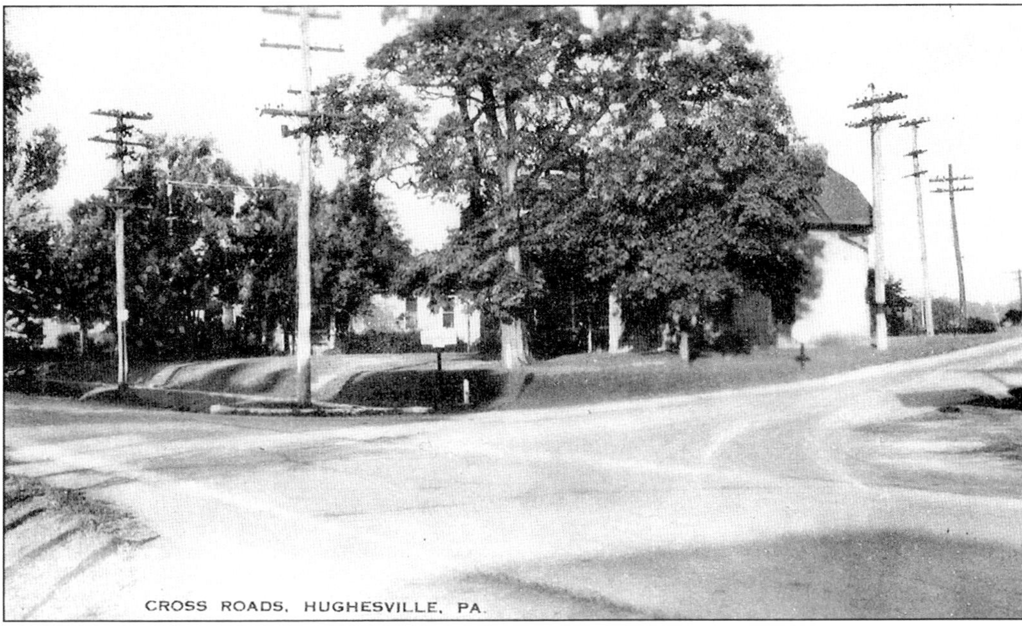

The crossroads at the north end of Hughesville show the beginning of Main Street going south on the left side of the picture and the road heading west (now Route 220) toward Pennsdale and Montoursville on the right side. This is also the site of a Pennsylvania Power and Light (PPL) substation. (Courtesy of H. Scott Knyrim.)

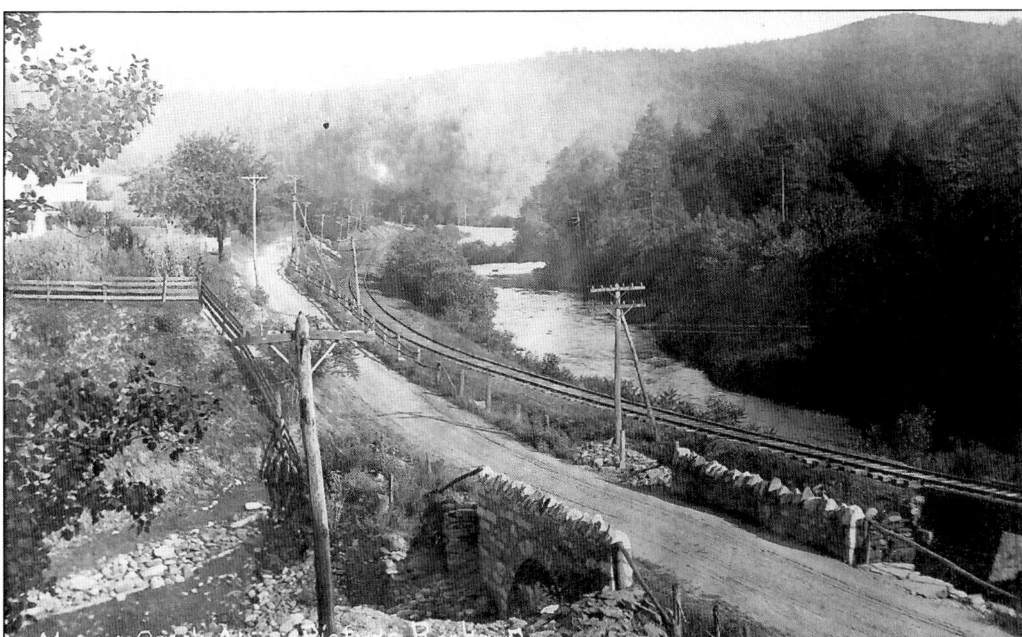

Various modes of transportation possibilities, including travel by water, rail, and country road, are shown side-by-side in this idyllic scene found between Picture Rocks and Tivoli. The owner of the neighboring farm undoubtedly found this a prime location to settle, build a home, and raise his family. (Courtesy of Stewart Hill.)

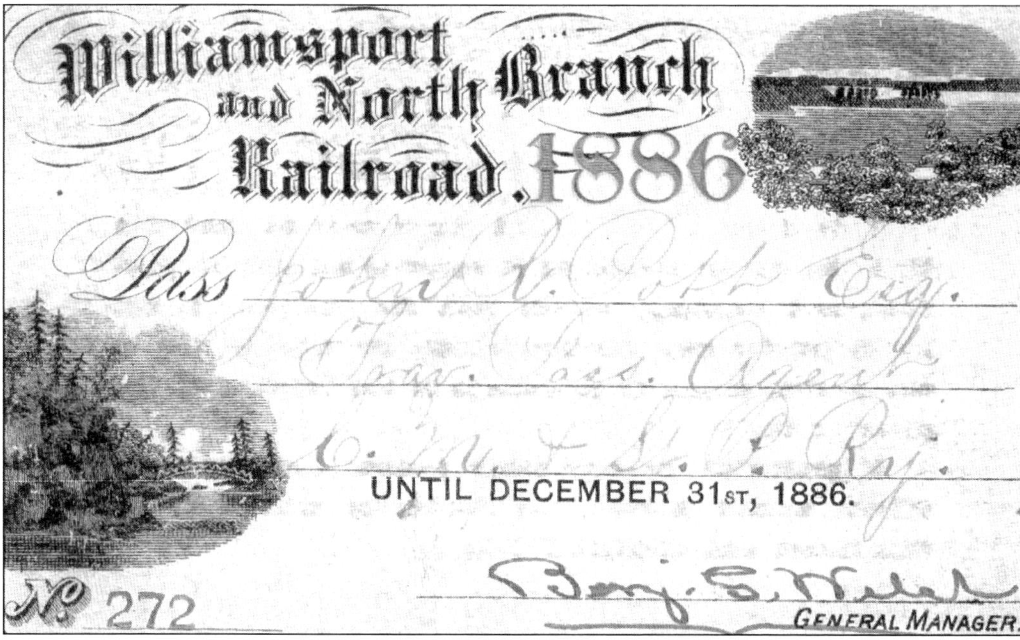
Williamsport and North Branch Railroad. 1886

Pass

UNTIL DECEMBER 31ST, 1886.

№ 272

GENERAL MANAGER.

This railroad pass was signed by Benjamin G. Welch of Hughesville, one of several bondholders who bought the foreclosed Muncy Creek Railroad and Coal Company in 1882. The new company was named the Williamsport and North Branch Railroad, although the train itself never reached either point—the city of Williamsport to the west and the North Branch of the Susquehanna River to the east. (Courtesy of David L. Richards.)

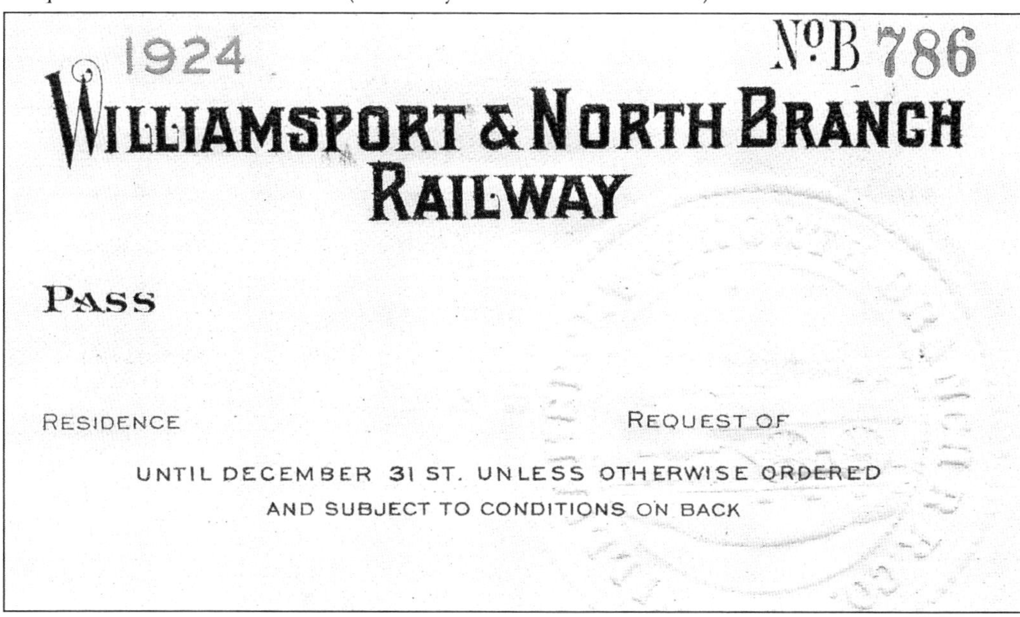
1924 №B 786

WILLIAMSPORT & NORTH BRANCH RAILWAY

PASS

RESIDENCE REQUEST OF

UNTIL DECEMBER 31 ST. UNLESS OTHERWISE ORDERED AND SUBJECT TO CONDITIONS ON BACK

While earlier passes featured hand-drawn scenes of the towns that the railroad serviced, images of a steaming engine, or other artwork, this unused pass from 1924 has only an embossed stamp of a doomed company. Within a year of the date this pass was issued, passenger services were discontinued as well as mail transport. Freight service was continued for only another 10 years. (Courtesy of Joe Barlett.)

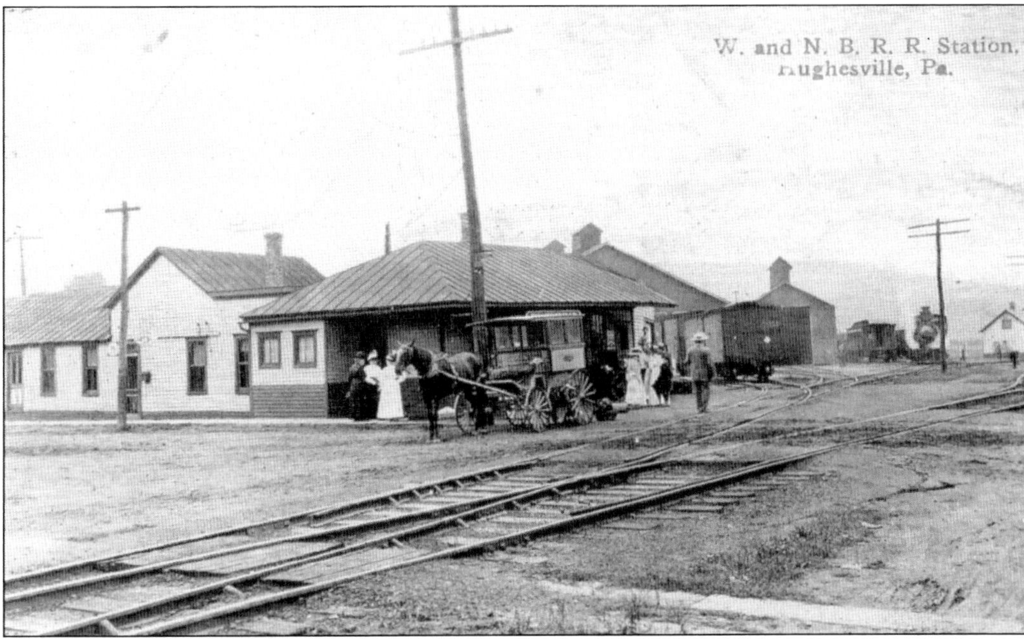

The Williamsport and North Branch Railroad train depot at Hughesville was located a block behind Main Street, with the railroad tracks running perpendicular to it. Augustus Deininger (center) was the owner of the horse-drawn bus and from that hauled mail, passengers, and luggage to the depot. (Courtesy of the East Lycoming Historical Society.)

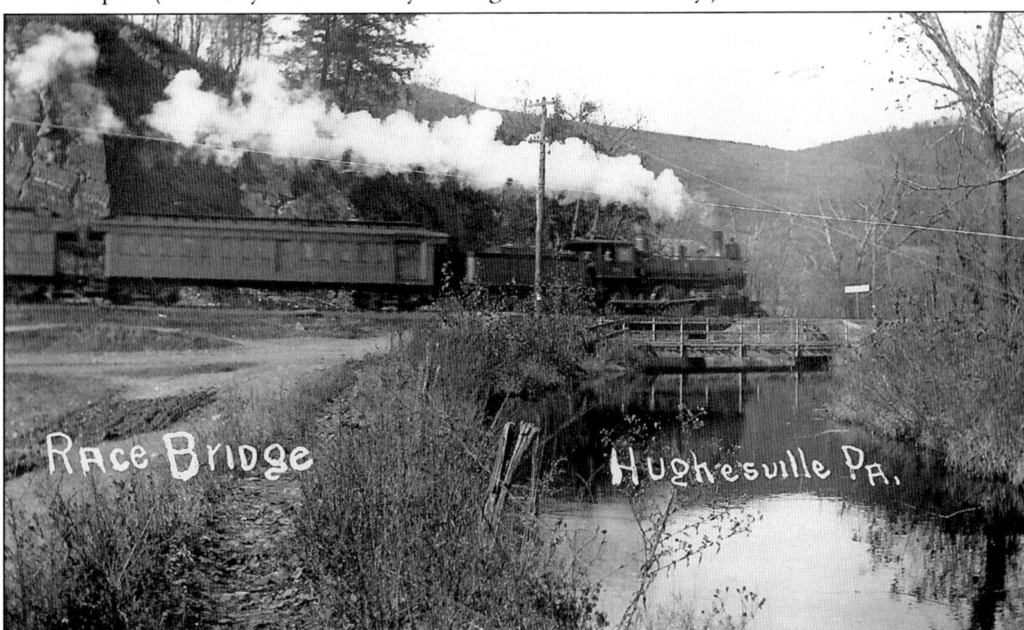

A Williamsport and North Branch Railroad engine pulls a trainload of passengers out of Hughesville and passes the quarry on the left. It rumbles over the small bridge that spans the race of water that flowed toward the gristmill at the edge of town. Two miles north, the train steams by a small post office and the woolen mill at Bryan Mill (or Bryantown). (Courtesy of the East Lycoming Historical Society.)

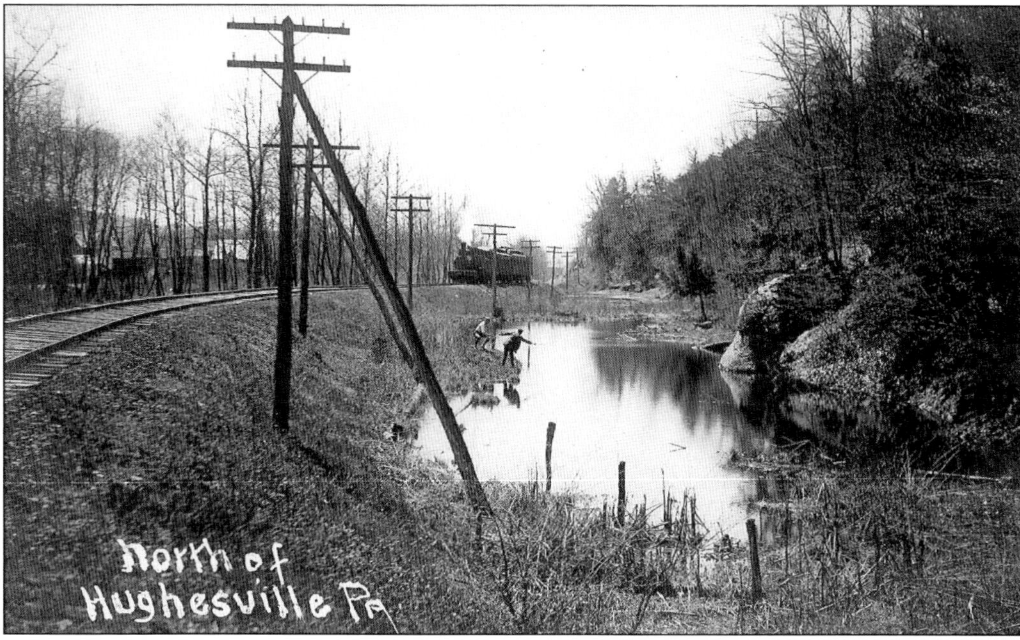

In the summer of 1875, when the tracks were laid north of Hughesville, lack of funds prevented the railroad owners from laying traditional tracks. Instead, they used wooden rails. By 1883, the newly formed Williamsport and North Branch Railroad Company reportedly spent $30,000 per mile rerouting and replacing the eight miles of track from Hughesville north toward the Sullivan County line. To avoid building and replacing costly bridges that were often washed away with springtime flooding of Muncy Creek, the rail company routed the tracks along the west side of the creek all the way to Glen Mawr. (Courtesy of Mary Fox Odell.)

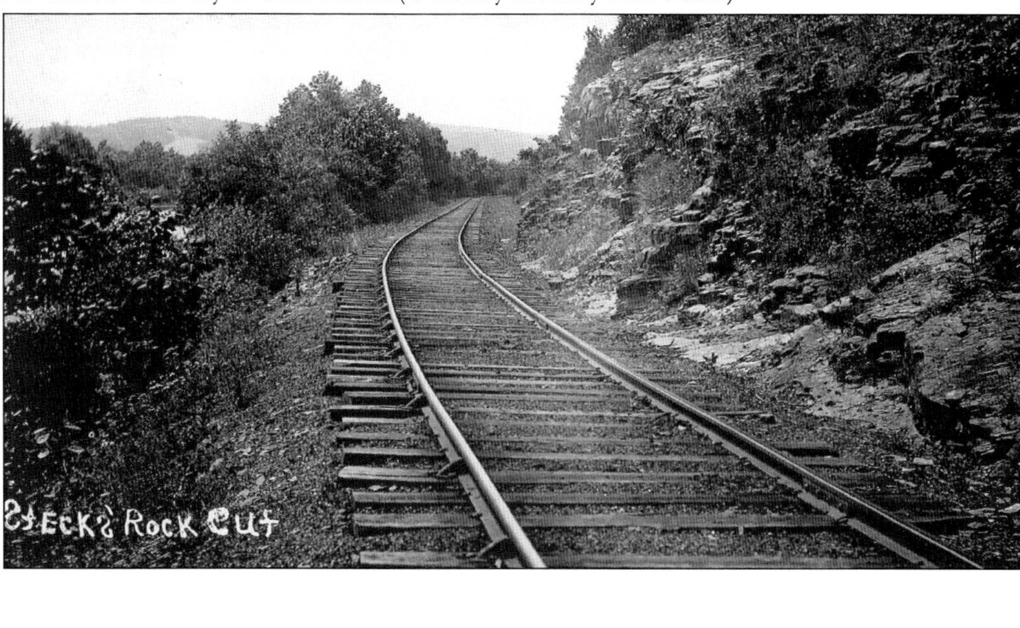

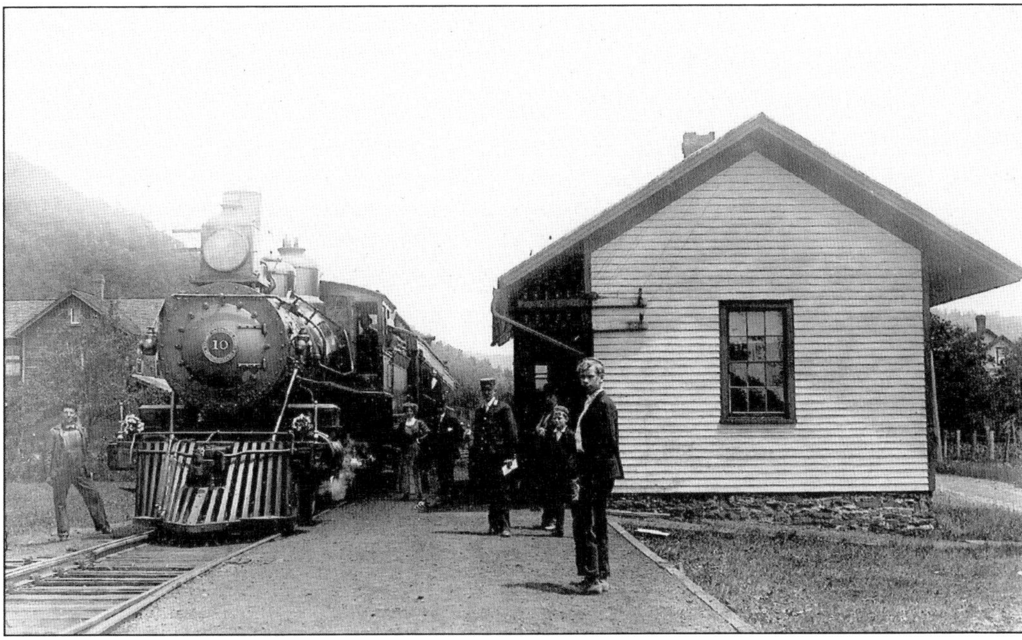

About three miles north of Hughesville, the next scheduled stop for the train was at Picture Rocks, the home of the Burrows Brothers and Company furniture factory. Lumber would be delivered by freight train and processed into fine furniture at the factory. Here uniformed station agent John D. Musgrave awaits the arrival of the train pulled by engine No. 10. (Courtesy of the East Lycoming Historical Society.)

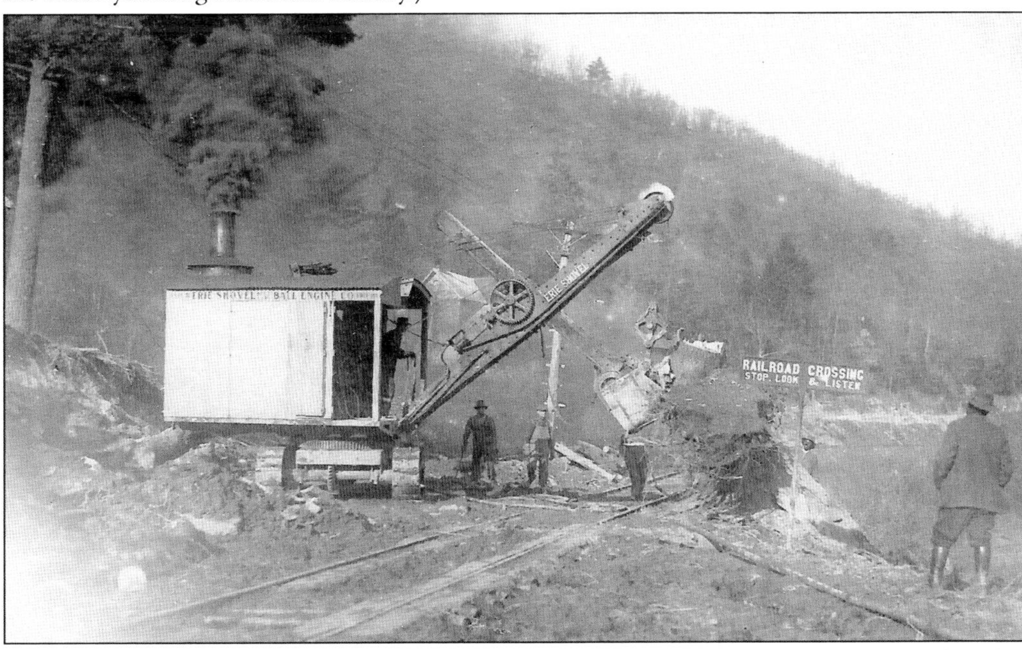

Working at the tracks above Picture Rocks, Charlie Long operates an Erie steam shovel to extract a tree stump. This kind of heavy equipment was also used to excavate fill material used in road paving, which took place around Hughesville and surrounding towns during the 1920s. (Courtesy of the East Lycoming Historical Society.)

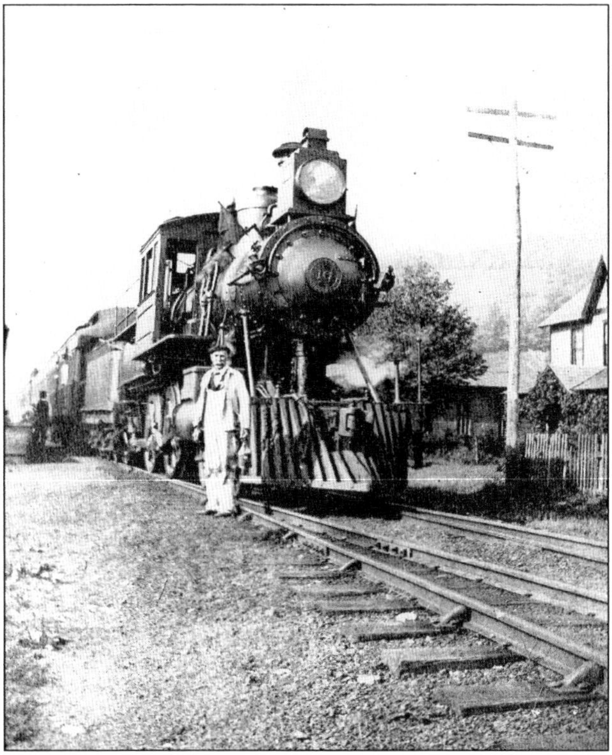

Engine No. 16 is shown here at the Tivoli depot (also known as Chamouni or Essick) with train conductor G. B. Edkin during the summer of 1905. The following year, on October 6, 1906, this engine's boiler exploded, killing engineer David (Davy) Davis instantly and injuring fireman Cleon Karshner, who died within hours. (Courtesy of the Sullivan County Historical Society and Museum.)

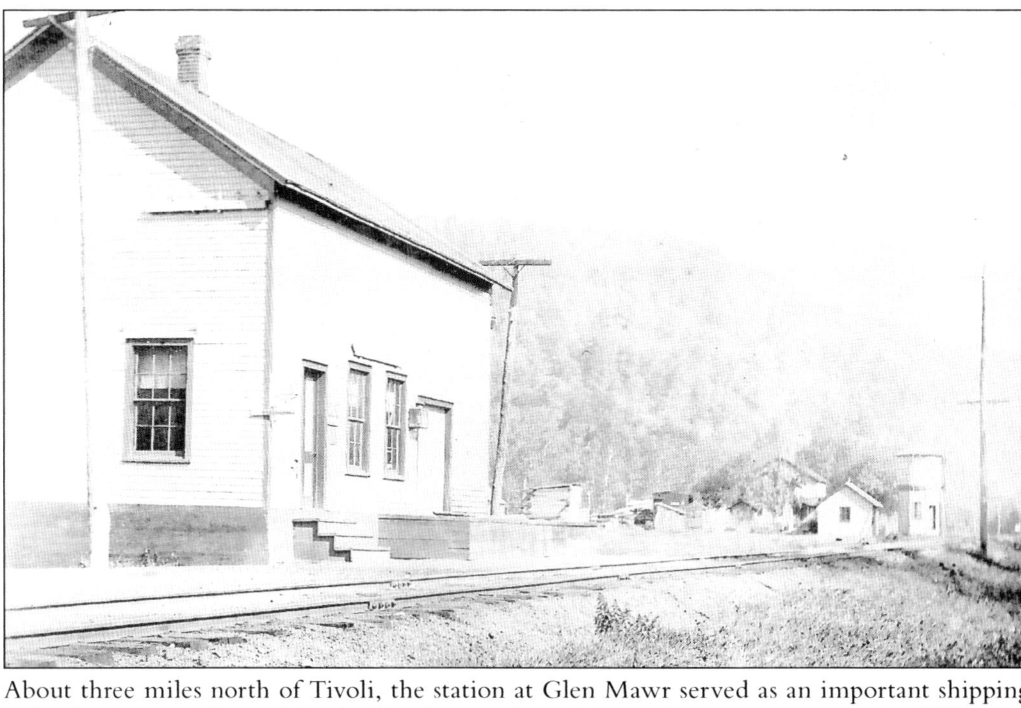

About three miles north of Tivoli, the station at Glen Mawr served as an important shipping point for the raw hides and finished leather products shipped from the tannery in the Hillsgrove area. The station closed in 1905 after a logging railroad was built from Eagles Mere to service the tannery. (Courtesy of Elizabeth Rogers Knyrim.)

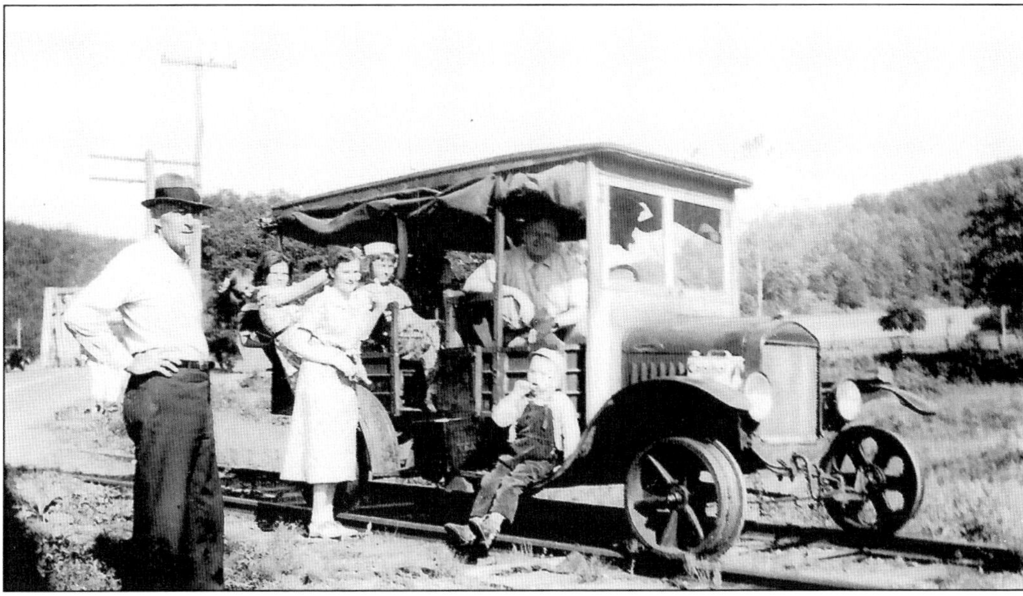

By late 1937, the end of the line had come for the Williamsport and North Branch Railroad. But here in Glen Mawr, before all the rails were removed, Clarence "Stubby" Stoltz (behind the wheel) offers a last ride to (from left to right) Curtis Springer, Janet Kohler, Helen Kohler, Patty Bubb, and Jimmy Springer in the customized station wagon that had been used as an inspection car since 1924. (Courtesy of Janet Kohler.)

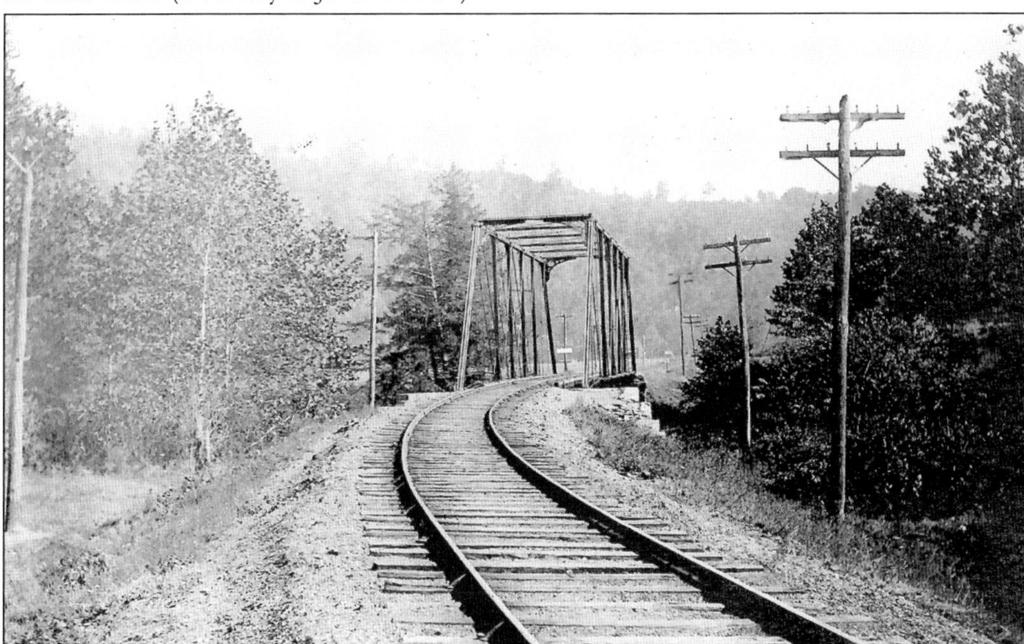

As this tour of the Hughesville area ends, one is reminded of a logger known only as Joe who was working more than 150 years ago on a cliff near this bridge at Glen Mawr. Joe somehow made a misstep and he, along with his team of horses, made a fatal plunge into the creek below. The "Joe Hole," a favorite swimming spot for locals, was named to honor this unfortunate woodsman. (Courtesy of Stewart Hill.)